Leading High-Performance Teams

for dummies®

A Wiley Brand

Leading High-Performance Teams

by Shirley Davis, PhD

Leading High-Performance Teams For Dummies®

Published by: **John Wiley & Sons, Inc.,** 111 River Street, Hoboken, NJ 07030-5774, www.wiley.com

For general information on our other products and services, please contact our Customer Care Department within the U.S. at 877-762-2974, outside the U.S. at 317-572-3993, or fax 317-572-4002. For technical support, please visit https://hub.wiley.com/community/support/dummies.

Wiley publishes in a variety of print and electronic formats and by print-on-demand. Some material included with standard print versions of this book may not be included in e-books or in print-on-demand. If this book refers to media that is not included in the version you purchased, you may download this material at http://booksupport.wiley.com. For more information about Wiley products, visit www.wiley.com.

Library of Congress Control Number is available from the publisher.

ISBN 978-1-394-35662-1 (pbk); ISBN 978-1-394-35663-8 (ebk); ISBN 978-1-394-35664-5 (ebk)

Printed and bound by CPI Group (UK) Ltd, Croydon, CR0 4YY

C9781394356621_161225

Contents at a Glance

Table of Contents

Introduction

L eading a team in today's workplace is one of the most rewarding and challenging responsibilities a leader can have. The success of organizations depends less on individual brilliance and more on how well teams come together to innovate, collaborate, and deliver results. High performance is a business imperative and a competitive advantage, especially in an age of constant disruption, rapid technological advances, shifting demographics, and heightened customer expectations. Moreover, the ability to build and sustain high-performance teams can be the key differentiator between organizations that thrive and those that simply survive.

As I often remind leaders, teams are not simply collections of talent. They become high performing when the right conditions are created, such as building trust, setting clear goals, and making every individual feel both valued and included.

High performance is not about busyness or checking more boxes. It's about focus, alignment, and harnessing the collective energy of diverse individuals. The most effective teams know how to balance urgency with excellence, and they consistently deliver results that exceed expectations.

Creating such teams requires leadership at its best. That is the real work of leadership today; not just directing tasks, but cultivating environments where people bring their whole selves, feel motivated to contribute, and see their work as meaningful.

About This Book

This book is designed to be your practical playbook for building and leading high-performance teams in a rapidly changing world. It goes beyond theory to show you how to create the conditions that allow teams to consistently excel. You'll find proven strategies grounded in neuroscience, psychology, and organizational behavior combined with lessons I've learned from decades of working with leaders and teams across industries and around the globe.

Throughout these pages, I explain what drives motivation, resilience, and accountability at the team level and how leaders can use that knowledge to elevate performance. You'll explore models of team effectiveness that help diagnose and improve dynamics, find out how to strengthen your own leadership competencies, discover how to move from a risk-averse to a risk-ready leader, and understand what it takes to recruit and onboard the right talent. You'll also discover ways to create thriving cultures that reduce burnout, build trust, and foster well-being while navigating conflict and change with confidence.

Importantly, this book is forward-looking. It prepares you not only to tackle today's challenges but also to anticipate the future of teamwork, from managing hybrid environments to leading multigenerational groups and harnessing technology and AI to amplify results. My goal is to give you a resource that you can return to often when you need clarity, direction, best practices, or inspiration for how to get the best from your team.

To help you navigate the content, I've divided the book into five parts:

>> **Part 1** lays the groundwork by explaining the science, models, business benefits, and attributes that define high-performing teams.

>> **Part 2** focuses on developing your leadership skills and behaviors so you can unlock the full potential of your team.

>> **Part 3** addresses recruiting, selecting, and onboarding the right talent to build a strong team foundation.

>> **Part 4** highlights how to create and sustain a world-class culture where people thrive, including strategies for well-being, psychological safety, and accountability.

>> **Part 5** provides quick, high-impact best practices, tools, and forward-looking insights to accelerate your journey toward high performance.

Foolish Assumptions

After decades of working with leaders at every level (from first-time supervisors to CEOs of global organizations to C-suite executives), I've seen the common challenges, questions, and aspirations that so many of them share. I've listened in boardrooms, facilitated workshops, coached executives, and partnered with organizations across industries. From these experiences, I know the realities leaders face today. With that knowledge in mind, I made a few assumptions about you as I wrote this book:

>> **You're the team leader of at least one other person.** Although this group of people may each work alone occasionally, it's necessary for them to work together some of the time.

>> **You want more than average results.** You're committed to leading in a way that brings out the best in people and creates an environment where they can thrive. Whether you are stepping into leadership for the first time or have been leading for years, you recognize that yesterday's skills are not enough for today's demands or tomorrow's uncertainties.

>> **You've seen the difference between a group and a team.** You know that having talent isn't enough. It takes clarity, trust, discipline, and a leader who can inspire and empower. You may also feel the pressure of faster change cycles, shifting employee expectations, and customers who demand more, and you're seeking strategies that will help your team rise to the occasion.

>> **You're committed to your own growth.** You may be curious, cautious, or even skeptical about what it really takes to build and sustain a high performance team — but you're open enough to explore, learn, and apply. That tells me you're serious about becoming the kind of leader who doesn't just manage people but unlocks their full potential.

>> **You recognize that the workforce of the future will look dramatically different.** You understand that demographic shifts, advancing technologies, and new workplace models will continue to reshape how teams are built and how they operate. Preparing now to adapt, stay agile, and lead effectively in this evolving landscape is essential.

Icons Used in This Book

Throughout this book, icons in the margins highlight certain types of valuable information that call for your attention. This section explains the icons you'll encounter:

TIP

This icon alerts you to helpful hints that may save time, effort, stress, embarrassment, and money while developing and implementing some of the practices.

REMEMBER

This icon marks information that's especially important to know. If you're in a hurry, you can siphon off the most important information from each chapter by reading through these icons and skimming the rest of the text for useful tidbits.

WARNING

The Warning icon tells you to watch out! It marks important information that may save you headaches, time and money.

Beyond the Book

The lessons and strategies you'll find in these pages provide a solid foundation for leading high-performance teams. But leadership is a journey, not a destination. The best leaders are lifelong learners who keep stretching, adapting, and growing. That means your learning doesn't stop when you close this book — it's only the beginning.

To continue your development and keep sharpening your leadership edge, consider these resources and opportunities:

>> **Dummies resources:** Visit www.dummies.com to find bonus content, updates, and the downloadable Cheat Sheet that accompanies this book for quick reference. You can find the Cheat Sheet by typing **High-Performance Leadership For Dummies Cheat Sheet** in the Search field on the home page.

>> **My other books:** Expand your toolkit with my earlier works, *Diversity, Equity & Inclusion For Dummies* and *Inclusive Leadership For Dummies*, which complement this book and deepen your understanding of how inclusion fuels high performance.

>> **Online learning:** Explore my LinkedIn Learning courses, especially "Leadership Foundations" and "Inclusive Leadership" in which I bring these concepts to life with video lessons, real-world examples, and AI-powered practical exercises you can apply immediately.

>> **Coaching and consulting:** If you or your organization need tailored support, training, leadership coaching or strategic guidance, connect with me through www.drshirleydavis.com.

>> **Professional networks:** Join leadership communities, attend conferences, and engage in peer learning to exchange insights and best practices with others who are committed to building strong, thriving teams.

REMEMBER

High performance is not a one-time achievement; it's a sustained commitment. By continuing to seek out new insights, applying what you learn, and investing in yourself and your team, you position yourself as the kind of leader who doesn't just manage performance but inspires it at every level.

Where to Go from Here

This book is designed for flexibility. Some readers will want to start at the very beginning and read it cover to cover. Others may want to flip directly to the chapters that address their most pressing needs right now. Either way works. Think of this book as both a reference manual and a toolkit that you can return to whenever a challenge or opportunity arises with your team.

If you're brand new to leading teams, begin with Chapter 1 to understand the science of high performance and Chapter 3 to learn the essential attributes of successful teams. If you're dealing with change or uncertainty, go to Chapter 8 for practical strategies on leading your team through transitions. If conflict is undermining your progress, head to Chapter 15 for proven conflict resolution models and techniques.

When you're focused on building the right team, you'll want to spend time in Chapters 9 through 11, which guide you through understanding changing workforce demographics, sourcing and selecting top talent, and onboarding new members effectively. If culture and well-being are your priorities, Chapter 12 explains how culture is formed, Chapter 13 helps you diagnose challenges, and Chapter 14 shares strategies for promoting positivity, resilience, and mental health on your team.

For leaders who want to elevate their skills, Chapters 5 through 7 explore the core and advanced competencies that distinguish high-performance leaders, including accountability, empathy, risk-readiness, and the ability to coach and mentor others.

Finally, if you're looking for quick wins and easy-to-apply ideas, turn to Chapters 19 through 22, where you'll find best practices for multigenerational teams, productive meetings, trust-building activities, and insights on how high-performing teams will evolve by 2035.

No matter where you begin, my goal is that you'll come away with practical strategies you can apply immediately and the confidence to lead with greater clarity, purpose, and impact. Use this book as a resource whenever you need inspiration, guidance, or reassurance, because leading a high-performance team is an ongoing journey, and each step you take makes a difference.

1

Getting Started with High Performance Teams

Chapter **1**

Understanding the Science of High Performance

'veworked with organizations around the globe, and I'll let you in on a secret: Your team's greatest competitive advantage isn't just their skills; it's their brains. Yep, that three-pound miracle between our ears is the engine of innovation, resilience, and extraordinary results. Yet, too often, we try to drive performance with outdated tactics such as key performance indicators, more meetings, and tighter deadlines without ever tapping into what truly moves people: the science of motivation, mindset, and belonging.

High-performing teams are not accidents. They're intentionally designed. They're the result of thoughtful leadership, deliberate strategies, and an understanding of how our brains and bodies function under pressure, purpose, and pursuit. In my decades of experience coaching leaders and organizations around the world, I've learned that excellence isn't just about willpower; it's about wiring. The more we understand the neuroscience, psychology, and behavioral science of performance, the better equipped we are to lead ourselves and others toward sustainable success.

This chapter will take you on a journey through the performance trifecta — dopamine, cortisol, and serotonin — and show you how, by harnessing these neurochemicals, you can transform your team from good to unstoppable. We'll dig into the role of sleep, diet, exercise, mindset, and emotional intelligence, and I'll share real-life examples, practical strategies, and reflection questions to help you activate high performance that lasts.

Explaining the Unique Impact of Dopamine, Cortisol, and Serotonin on the Brain

To understand what drives human behavior at work, it helps to look inside the brain. This section breaks down how dopamine, cortisol, and serotonin influence your team's motivation, stress levels, and sense of belonging.

Dopamine: The motivation molecule

Dopamine is your team's rocket fuel. It's the brain chemical that gets people excited about their goals, keeps them coming back for more, and rewards them for making progress, not just for crossing the finish line. When you set clear, attainable goals and recognize small wins, dopamine surges. That's why checking off a task feels so good. It's not magic; it's biology.

At a Fortune 500 technology company that I consulted with, the CEO implemented daily "win celebrations." At the conclusion of each team meeting, employees highlighted their microwins, such as resolving technical issues or receiving positive customer feedback. Additional programs allowed for sharing of risks and rewards (or lessons learned) without penalty and permitted staff to publicly acknowledge a "staff hero/shero" who stepped up or went out of their way. Those were huge hits. Employee engagement increased by 28 percent over nine months in the category of Rewards and Worker Recognition. Workers stated how much they appreciated the opportunity to share their successes and to see the CEO take the lead.

TIP

Break large projects into microgoals. Celebrate every milestone, no matter how small. Use visible progress trackers (think dashboards, leaderboards, or kudos boards) to keep dopamine flowing.

Cortisol: The stress regulator

Cortisol is the body's main stress hormone. In the right dose, it's a lifesaver. It sharpens your awareness, helps you meet deadlines, and pushes you to innovate under pressure. But when cortisol sticks around too long, trouble starts (for example, absenteeism, disengagement, and even conflict).

When stress becomes chronic, when people feel unsafe, marginalized, or unsupported, cortisol floods the system, which leads to burnout, poor decisions, and a breakdown of trust. In fact, according to Gallup, unregulated stress leads to $190 billion in annual healthcare costs and is a leading cause of employee turnover. In Chapters 9 and 14, I cover more on workplace stress.

In inclusive teams, leaders are "stress aware." They model healthy boundaries, encourage self-care, check in on workload, and make it safe to speak up about what's overwhelming. They also watch for patterns: Who's always the one "taking one for the team"? Who's not raising their hand but clearly feeling the burn?

TIP

Create performance rituals that blend motivation, recovery, and connection. It's not about avoiding stress but about orchestrating energy.

Let me share two quick stories from my own consulting work: I once coached a manager who realized, after a team meeting, that only certain team members ever felt comfortable voicing deadlines that felt unreasonable. Others, especially those from underrepresented groups, kept quiet and were afraid of being labeled as complainers or not being "team players." Changing that norm, and actively inviting all voices to the table, cut team stress in half and boosted engagement.

In another instance, I was consulting with a health services company during a major merger. My role was to advise on the culture integration and to assess the significant differences as well as the risk levels of merging the cultures. The workers' stress levels spiked during that time, but leaders got proactive. They began introducing "recharge rooms" for brief meditation, scheduling "no meeting" afternoons, and equipping managers with burnout recognition training. Ultimately, it resulted in a decrease in turnover by 11 percent over the next year.

TIP

Normalize stress conversations. Build in regular "pulse checks," encourage mindfulness breaks, and make recovery part of every workweek, just like you'd schedule a critical team meeting.

Serotonin: Building trust, well-being, and belonging

I can't talk about thriving teams without mentioning serotonin, also called the "well-being" neurochemical. When serotonin flows, people feel calm, valued, and connected. They trust their leader and each other. Serotonin is what makes people feel seen, heard, and safe. It's the secret ingredient of trust, collaboration, and emotional intelligence. When serotonin flows, teams communicate better, innovate more, and bounce back from setbacks. Refer to Chapter 3 for a more detailed description of these team competencies.

How do you boost serotonin on your team?

Start with rituals of appreciation, acts of kindness, and a relentless commitment to equity. When team members see that everyone (regardless of background, role, or identity) is treated with respect and given equal opportunity, trust grows, and serotonin follows.

Here are some practical inclusion strategies that have worked for me:

>> Schedule regular check-ins. Not just about work, but about well-being and growth.

>> Rotate meeting roles and responsibilities to give everyone a chance to shine and contribute.

>> Invite team members to share their goals, passions, and strengths; then connect those to team projects and initiatives.

>> Be transparent about decision-making. When people know the "why," trust deepens.

>> Celebrate diverse holidays, backgrounds, and life experiences. Make room for everyone at the table.

Understanding What Motivates High Achievers and Builds Resilience

High achievers aren't superhuman; they're just really good at structuring their environments and routines to work with, rather than against, their brains. Motivation isn't just a feeling; it's a process that can be engineered.

Motivation is about purpose, meaning, and momentum. It's often sparked by dopamine and sustained through discipline. But when the going gets tough, resilience takes over. That's when serotonin and a regulated cortisol system help people stay emotionally centered. (See the preceding section for more information about dopamine, cortisol, and serotonin.)

I've coached leaders who were on the verge of burnout, yet they found a way to reset through reframing challenges, recommitting to purpose, and leaning into community. These aren't just psychological tricks; they're neurobiological strategies that tap into the brain's resilience network.

Dopamine drives action, cortisol signals danger, and serotonin stabilizes mood. High performers master all three, fueling momentum, managing stress, and building resilience to weather storms.

Resilience is less about gritting your teeth and more about knowing how to recover and reframe. The most resilient teams aren't immune to adversity; they've just built the habits and relationships that help them "bounce forward." Refer to Chapter 3 where I cover more on resilience.

Optimizing Team Output through These Key Drivers

High achievers don't just work hard. They live in ways that support brain optimization. Every high-performing team I've coached shares one thing: a relentless commitment to the foundational drivers such as sleep, diet, exercise, mindset, motivation, discipline, emotional intelligence, and commitment.

In the discussion about leading high-performing teams, it's easy to focus on systems, strategies, and skill sets. But the real foundation of sustainable success isn't just what's happening around the team; it's what's happening within each individual. The science of high performance reminds us that human beings are wired for rhythm, restoration, and regulation. If we ignore the biological and psychological drivers that fuel performance, we may get results, but they'll be short-lived and unsustainable.

In the following sections I explore three essential lifestyle factors (sleep, nutrition, and movement) that directly influence cognitive performance, emotional balance, and overall team effectiveness.

Sleep

One of the most powerful, yet underestimated, drivers of high performance is sleep. Yes, sleep. Not hustle. Not willpower. Not caffeine. Sleep. It's the ultimate recharger, and when it's prioritized, it restores memory, focus, and emotional regulation. During deep sleep, our brains reset dopamine, regulate cortisol, and produce serotonin. All of these are critical neurochemicals for motivation, stress resilience, and social cohesion. But when we neglect sleep, those systems fall out of balance, and performance suffers. Research from the National Institutes of Health found that even one week of sleeping less than six hours a night can lead to a 30 percent drop in cognitive performance.

One client I worked with implemented a "no email after 7:00 p.m." policy and saw an immediate shift in team morale, productivity, and overall well-being. When leaders model rest and recovery, teams learn to value it too.

Diet

Diet is another key factor that directly shapes how we think and feel. The connection between the gut and the brain is now well documented in neuroscience and nutrition science. The foods we eat influence our mental clarity, our moods, and our ability to regulate emotions. Omega-3 fatty acids and nutrient-rich foods such as leafy greens and lean proteins support healthy brain function, while sugar crashes and caffeine spikes undermine performance.

I've worked with organizations that made simple changes like swapping sugary vending machine snacks for nuts, fruit, and whole grains, and employees reported feeling more alert, energized, and focused throughout the day. It's a reminder that performance starts in the kitchen as much as in the boardroom or the cubicle.

Exercise/movement

Movement is another form of medicine. Exercise presses the brain's reset button. It boosts the three performance chemicals I mention earlier in this chapter (dopamine, serotonin, and cortisol) and improves focus, energy, and emotional control. Studies by the American Psychological Association show that even just 20 minutes of moderate aerobic activity can improve memory and cognitive flexibility.

One tech firm I coached launched a simple "movement matters" campaign. Twice a day, teams took a 15-minute walking break. Not only did productivity increase, but collaboration and communication improved as well. When I worked at the Society for Human Resource Management, the staff enjoyed our yoga sessions on

Thursdays, the fitness center on the first floor, and the subsidized onsite massages every other week. It increased worker engagement, creativity, and overall well-being according to our employee surveys.

REMEMBER

The important point to take from these examples is that when leaders create space for movement and exercise, it demonstrates that physical health is a performance strategy, not a luxury. And when it is a priority, teams follow suit.

Mindset

If there's one thing I've taught again and again in my LinkedIn Learning courses and coaching sessions, it's that your attitude determines your altitude. This is now known as a *growth mindset*. The term was coined by Dr. Carol Dweck, and it's referring to the belief that talent and intelligence can be developed through effort, feedback, and learning. This mental flexibility fuels curiosity, risk-taking, and innovation, all of which are vital ingredients for high-performing teams. I once worked with a nonprofit that created a "fail forward" wall where teams documented experiments that didn't go as planned, alongside the lessons learned. The result? Risk-taking increased, and so did the number of creative breakthroughs. When we normalize effort over perfection and celebrate progress as much as results, we invite high performance in through the front door.

Mindset alone isn't enough. People need motivation to sustain effort, especially when outcomes are delayed or challenges arise. Intrinsic motivation, which comes from curiosity, passion, and purpose, burns longer and cleaner than the temporary thrill of external rewards. Daniel Pink's book *Drive* (Riverhead Books, 2011) lays out the pillars of lasting motivation: mastery, autonomy, and purpose (also referred to as MAP).

REIGNITING PURPOSE IN EVERYDAY WORK

One hospital system I consulted with in a large metropolitan area and serving a diverse community had been experiencing alarming turnover rates among its nursing staff. Burnout was high, morale was low, and exit interviews consistently revealed that nurses felt disconnected from their purpose. They loved patient care, but the daily grind of charting, shift coverage, and administrative tasks had begun to overshadow the impact of their work.

The leadership team knew they needed to reignite a sense of meaning and purpose among their frontline caregivers. So, they launched a storytelling initiative that

(continued)

(continued)

highlighted how nurses were directly changing lives. They began sharing real patient testimonials, heartfelt videos, handwritten letters from families, and in-person thanks during staff huddles that spoke to the difference individual nurses had made. These stories were tied back to specific actions, connecting the nurses' daily work to real human outcomes.

They also created a "Purpose Board" in the breakroom where team members could write why they chose this profession and what still fuels their passion today. Nurse managers regularly asked in check-ins, "What part of your work this week reminded you why you're here?" It was a simple, yet powerful question that grounded staff in mission and meaning.

Within six months, the hospital reported a double digit increase in nurse retention and a notable rise in employee engagement scores. Nurses weren't working fewer hours or encountering fewer challenges, but they were reconnected to the *why* behind their work. And that made all the difference.

I give an example of the power of purpose as a motivator in the nearby sidebar. But another factor that affects motivation is structure, which helps people to stay consistent. That's where discipline comes in. High performers don't rely on inspiration; they rely on habits. They create systems and routines that make high performance automatic.

Research published in the *European Journal of Social Psychology* found it takes an average of 66 days to form a habit that sticks. One marketing team I worked with adopted a "Power Hour" (60 minutes of uninterrupted, focused work time every Friday). They turned off notifications, shut down email, and dialed into deep work. It quickly became their most productive time of the week, and the habit spread across the department. The lesson from this example shows that discipline is the multiplier of talent — it takes what you have and makes it repeatable.

Emotional intelligence

The other drivers I've mentioned won't work without emotional intelligence (EQ), which is the ability to manage your own emotions and navigate others'. I also cover this in detail in Chapter 5. Teams with high EQ are more adaptable, more collaborative, and more innovative. In fact, TalentSmart research shows that 90 percent of top performers have high EQ, and it's no surprise. Emotionally intelligent leaders stay calm under pressure, listen actively, resolve conflict with empathy, and foster psychological safety.

I've seen the power of EQ firsthand. One startup I supported began each team meeting with a two-minute "emotional weather report." Everyone had a chance to share how they were feeling with no judgment, just acknowledgment. That simple shift built trust, reduced misunderstandings, and opened the door for more honest feedback and deeper collaboration. I actually began to implement this great practice in my own team meetings and with clients, and I can attest that this simple shift contributed to greater team inclusion, offers of support where applicable, and overall greater team spirit.

REMEMBER

The drivers of sleep, nutrition, exercise, mindset, motivation, discipline, and emotional intelligence are not isolated habits. They're interconnected pillars that build the foundation of high performance. They're inextricably linked and build on each other. They influence how people show up, connect, lead, and recover. They aren't just individual practices; they are cultural values. And when they're embedded into the DNA of a team, performance becomes not just a goal, but a way of life. I speak more about workplace culture in Chapter 12.

Commitment

Another vital driver that often goes unspoken but is felt in every high-performing team is commitment. While motivation gets people excited to start something, commitment is what keeps them going long after the excitement fades. It's the difference between showing up because you have to and showing up because you're invested. In today's workplace, where change is constant and attention is scattered, commitment is the glue that holds performance together.

Commitment is what transforms talent into traction. It's what keeps a team aligned and focused when priorities shift, deadlines loom, and setbacks arise. Committed team members don't just do their job, they own outcomes. They see the work through, they care about the impact, and they hold themselves and others accountable. This isn't about blind loyalty or toxic hustle, it's about a deep sense of responsibility to the mission, to the team, and to doing the work with excellence.

When I worked with a global financial services company that was undergoing a major digital transformation, I experienced this first hand. The senior leaders were all in on the new changes, but many workers were hesitant, unsure about the changes and feeling overwhelmed by the pace of implementation. One team, however, stood out. They consistently met project milestones, stayed optimistic through the transition, and adapted quickly to the new systems. When I interviewed the manager to understand what was different, she said, "We committed early, not just to the outcomes, but to each other. We agreed that we weren't going to let fear or fatigue fracture our progress." That kind of team-based commitment created psychological safety, accountability, and resilience (see Chapter 3 for more on this). Their team not only met its goals ahead of schedule but also became a model for others across the organization.

Commitment also shows up in the small things: staying late to help a colleague prepare for a big pitch, giving honest feedback when it's uncomfortable, or continuing to improve a process even when no one is watching. It's about consistency, not perfection. And it's about being invested not only in what you do but in *how* you do it.

WARNING

Commitment must be rooted in purpose, not pressure. When commitment is confused with overwork or martyrdom, it turns into burnout. I've seen too many high achievers push themselves to the brink in the name of being a "team player," only to end up exhausted, resentful, or disengaged. That's not sustainable. Real commitment includes healthy boundaries. It includes saying yes with intention and saying no when capacity is exceeded. Leaders must model that balance and encourage teams to commit with clarity, not compulsion.

TIP

One of the best ways to foster commitment on your team is to co-create expectations. Don't just assign responsibilities. Instead, invite your team to align on what success looks like and what behaviors will get you there. When people help shape the plan, they feel more responsible for its execution. Invite conversations about what everyone is committing to, what they need to stay accountable for, and how the team will support one another when motivation inevitably dips. That shared commitment becomes a contract of trust, not just a checklist of tasks. In Chapter 11, I detail what a team contract (or charter) can look like.

Remember, commitment, when practiced well, becomes a culture. It's felt in how people talk about their work, how they show up for one another, and how they bounce back when things don't go according to plan.

REMEMBER

Commitment anchors purpose, fuels consistency, and reinforces the idea that success is not just about the work, it's about the *willingness* to stay the course together.

In my decades of coaching and consulting, I've seen countless teams with brilliant ideas, impressive skills, and big visions. But the ones who consistently rise above are those whose commitment is unwavering. They don't just start strong, they finish well. And that, more than anything, is what high performance is all about.

REMEMBER

High-performing teams don't emerge by accident. They're the result of intentional design. When workplace cultures prioritize well-being as a business strategy, develop leaders who model the behaviors they want to see, and implement systems that reinforce what science already confirms they experience optimized human performance.

REFLECTION QUESTIONS

As I close out this chapter, I want to leave you with a few questions to reflect on.

- Which of the three neurochemicals (dopamine, cortisol, serotonin) most influence your team right now?

- What are two ways you could intentionally boost dopamine in your daily operations?

- How does your organization handle stress and burnout, and what needs to change?

- Which habits — sleep, movement, nutrition — could you champion to support sustainable performance?

- How can you build more emotional intelligence into your leadership and team culture?

Chapter **2**

Exploring Common Models of Teams

A leader of a high-performing team needs not only to understand the physiology and neuroscience that drives people to be motivated but also needs to have a fundamental understanding of what a team actually is.

"What is a team?" may sound like an obvious or easy question, but there are many considerations to how you define a team. Why does a team exist? When is a team necessary? How is a team different from a family unit or a group of friends?

Luckily, many prominent thinkers have tackled the question of what a team is. They 'haven't necessarily agreed on every point, but by looking at all their work together, you can start to piece together what works for you and the team you lead.

'I want to start by establishing a working definition of "team." I like the way the American Society for Quality (or ASQ) defines team on its website (https://asq.org/quality-resources/teams): "a group of people who perform interdependent tasks to work toward accomplishing a common mission or specific objective." Note that this definition could describe anything from a volleyball team to a group of professionals who work together in an office setting.

Breaking the definition down into its parts, a team is first and foremost a group of people. I suppose a group of dogs pulling a sled through the snow could be defined as a team, but for the purposes of this book, we're going to assume that a team is made up of a group of human beings. You may often hear people describe themselves as a "team of one," but that's more of a figure of speech than an accurate descriptor. My assumption as I write this book is that you're the team leader of at least one other person.

Next, this group of people perform interdependent tasks, meaning that while team members may work alone occasionally, it's necessary, at least some of the time, for them to work together.

Finally, this group of people performing interdependent tasks have a common mission or specific objective they are working toward.

REMEMBER

Teams come in many forms. Some work together for a short time and then end. Others continue as long as needed. A team might be large or just two people. It could be made up of employees, partners from other groups, or even volunteers. Each type of team looks to its leaders for what it specifically needs, and those needs can be very different.

Now that you have a basic understanding of what a team is, 'read on to explore some models of team leadership.

Richard Beckhard's GRPI Model

One useful framework for understanding what teams need is Beckhard's GRPI model, first introduced in 1972. GRPI stands for goals, roles, processes, and interpersonal relationships, and it helps leaders design teams, set clear expectations, and diagnose challenges when they arise.

According to Beckhard, a team leader should be able to account for the major questions associated with each of these areas. Once a team has been established and problems invariably arise, the model can also be used to diagnose the root cause of these issues and correct them.

Figure 2-1 illustrates the four core components of the GRPI model and how they relate to one another in supporting overall team effectiveness. For a more detailed explanation of this model, visit www.aihr.com/blog/grpi-model/?utm_source=chatgpt.com.

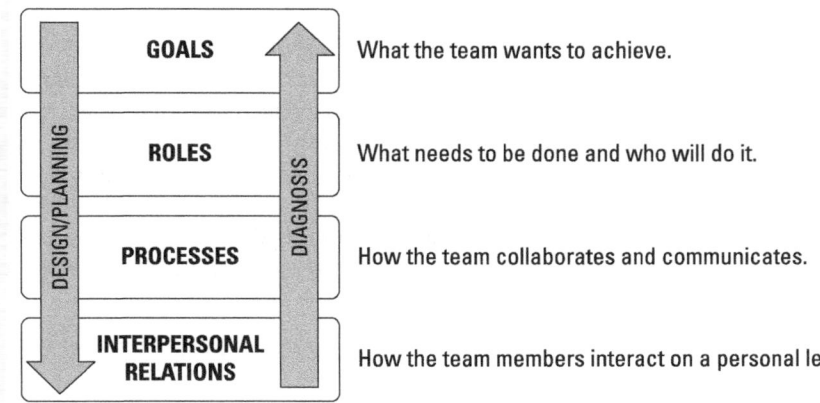

FIGURE 2-1:
GRPI model by
Richard Beckhard.

GOALS — What the team wants to achieve.

ROLES — What needs to be done and who will do it.

PROCESSES — How the team collaborates and communicates.

INTERPERSONAL RELATIONS — How the team members interact on a personal level.

DESIGN/PLANNING

DIAGNOSIS

Goals

Goals equate to the "common mission or specific objective" I mention earlier in this chapter where I define what a team is. The primary question associated with this facet of the model is, "What does the team want to achieve?" or, at a more basic level, "Why does this team exist?"

How a leader answers this question informs the answers to all the others. Does your team exist to market your organization's products? Create and sell a better dog food? Keep a performing arts organization well-funded? Improve a specific business process within your company? Defend your national borders? Your goal will determine how many skilled people you'll need to recruit, the types of skills they need to have, the discrete tasks to be completed, and the kind of culture you'll want to create to meet your goals.

Roles

The *R* in GRPI is for roles, or sometimes you'll see this facet of the model labeled roles and responsibilities. The primary questions here are not about who specifically you' need to recruit to be a part of your team. Instead, they concern what roles those people will inhabit. What kinds of skills and prior experience do they need to bring in? How will different roles interact (or be interdependent of one another) and, at the same time, what boundaries will exist between roles (to minimize unnecessary conflict and disputes later on)? Does everyone on your team understand their own role (both its breadth and its limitations) and how it contributes to the team's goals?

It's important to think of roles before thinking about specific people. Often, when creating a startup or designing a brand-new team, a leader will already have an idea about some of the people they want to work with. When this happens, a role might be created around the skill set and personality of that individual. This might work in the short term, but if that person should need to be replaced eventually, their role might be so unique that it becomes difficult to fill. While it's always a good idea to take advantage of an individual's unique talents or motivations once they join your team, designing a role with one person in mind can cause unnecessary trouble later on.

Processes

Processes are the work that the people in the roles will do to achieve the goals. The primary question associated with this facet of the GRPI model is, "How will people collaborate and communicate?"

You don't want to start with this question because you need to get clear on the goals and roles first. Once you're clear on these things, figuring out how the team will do the work is indeed the next step. Here are some questions you need to consider:

>> Will some people on your team crave a certain amount of autonomy? If so, how much?

>> Is it important that everyone on the team know about the decisions that are being made elsewhere on the team? If so, how will this information be conveyed, and how often?

Interpersonal relations

Interpersonal relations are connected to the process of doing the work but is somewhat less formal. A team's interpersonal relations are a window into the team's culture. Some people describe it as a team's "mood" or "vibe." The primary question associated with this facet of the model is, "How do team members treat each other?"

It might seem like a given that all team members, on any team, should treat each other with kindness and respect. A bully anywhere on a team can destroy morale and derail a team from its common purpose. At the same time, there's a lot of room for variance here, depending on goals, roles, and process. A group of creative professionals who typically generate ideas through brainstorming and general consensus will naturally interact very differently than a surgical team who perform operations on patients, where the slightest misstep could have fatal con-sequences. When you examine the goal of your team, the roles necessary to realize that goal, and processes you've put in place to enable the work, what kind of mood, vibe, or culture is going to be the most beneficial for your particular team?

REMEMBER

Team culture doesn't just happen. It's created when certain kinds of people interact in certain kinds of ways. And while it's true that any member of your team, from the most senior professional to the newest intern, can impact a team's culture, you as a leader have an outsized influence on this. Leaders help create the culture they desire by doing the following things:

>> Talking about culture and setting clear and measurable expectations. I cover this in Chapter 12.

>> Role modeling the kinds of behaviors they're looking for from others. (See Chapter 5.)

Diagnosing team issues

The GRPI model helps a leader design a team where goals, roles, processes, and interpersonal relations are aligned and all are working to support each other, but it can also be used to diagnose team issues. Notice in Figure 2-1 that the "Design/planning" arrow points down and has its point of origin in goals. As we've dis-cussed, the first question you should ask yourself is about goals, roles, and so on.

However, when you're diagnosing team issues, problems are often first visible in the area of interpersonal relations. While conflict on a team could be creative or generative in nature, when conflict is unresolved or people are quarreling over seemingly petty stakes, the team feels dysfunctional, and people no longer enjoy their work. At such moments, it's important for a leader to step in and mediate.

Consequently, when in diagnosis mode, it's helpful to use the model in reverse. Start with interpersonal relations (where the trouble often bubbles up). Are people behaving in alignment with your stated cultural values? If not, why not? Don't be afraid to examine yourself and consider whether you've done an adequate job of role modeling the kinds of behaviors you want others to emulate.

If the squabbles aren't because of individual bad actors, move up the model one rung and examine the team's processes. Are the petty fights the result of poor communication, or have some individuals not been collaborating as they ought to? If so, you might have to do some work strengthening the norms of your team.

If he work isn't the issue, move up again and examine roles. Are members of your team fulfilling their roles adequately? Are they perhaps doing more than they ought and infringing on someone else's role?

If you've yet to diagnose your issue, the answer might lie at the top of the model — in your team's goals. Ask these questions:

>> Are the goals still working for your team, or do they need to be re-examined?

>> If you asked each individual on your team to state the team's goals, would their answers resemble each other?

>> Is everyone on your team truly committed to the same goals, or are some of them working at odds with one another?

Richard Hackman's Five Factor Model

In 2002, renowned psychologist Richard Hackman developed a model for team effectiveness. It contains some of the elements that may seem familiar if you've read the earlier section about the GRPI model, but Hackman's work lists five factors of a successful team. This model is more of a checklist than a process; if your team can exhibit the five factors shown in Figure 2-2, then it's likely to be successful!

 **A real team**	 **Compelling direction**	 **Enabling structure**	 **Supportive context**	**Expert coaching**
A consistent, defined group that depends on each other to get things done.	A unifying mission that acts as a shared source of motivation.	A set of norms, processes and shared habits that help work happen smoothly.	Access to the tools, resources, information and incentives required to excel.	A leader that can coach and develop the team to continually improve.

FIGURE 2-2: Five factor model by Richard Hackman.

A "real" team

The first factor identified by Hackman separates the idea of a team from a random group of people. Much of this goes back to the working definition of team from the beginning of this chapter. Does the team perform interdependent tasks? Is their work aligned in a common direction?

However, Hackman introduces another important concept here, which is consistency. According to Hackman, a consistent team is one where membership is fairly stable. People may come and go, but in general, team members have the time and space to get to know each other and develop relationships.

A compelling direction

The second factor is concerned with the "common mission or specific direction," but again, Hackman provides an additional layer. The word *compelling* prompts the question of motivation among your team members. Are they driven to meet their defined purpose? If the direction is fuzzy, team members might be misaligned. If the goals are too ambitious, team members can easily feel overwhelmed or set up for failure.

If a leader not only dictates the desired end state but also micromanages every detail of the team's work, team members feel a lack of agency and a longing to break free. Whether a team is properly motivated can make the difference between a high-performing team and one that simply does adequate work.

An enabling structure

Hackman's view of structure is one that is aligned with the goals of the team. Hackman advocates for a team that is proactively designed to facilitate rather than impede teamwork, including an appropriate amount of feedback that allows for continuous improvement.

A supportive context

The supportive context factor is not only about the way people on the team treat each other but also includes systemic support systems such as rewards for excellent work, education, and training that allow team members to develop necessary skills. It also includes a work-life balance that supports employee's life both outside and inside the team.

Expert coaching

Hackman posits that team members will sometimes require someone who can mitigate conflict, provide feedback and advice, or simply listen to team members when they're feeling conflicted, unsure, or overwhelmed. Depending on the goals, structure, and unique personalities of your team, this might look like regularly scheduled team meetings, frequent one-on-one coaching sessions, education and training, or peer coaching within a team. While much of this responsibility will naturally fall to you, the team leader, note that expert coaching could also come from a variety of other folks, including training professionals, HR representatives, counselors, and even team members supporting each other.

Bruce Tuckman's Five Stages of Team Development

Just as a person goes through different stages of their life as they grow, mature, and manage change, the same is true for teams. Teams experience growing pains. The most common framework to illustrate the stages of team development was developed in the 1960s by American psychologist and researcher Bruce Tuckman. Originally, his model contained only four stages (forming, storming, norming, and performing). However, in 1977, he added a fifth stage: adjourning. (See Figure 2-3.)

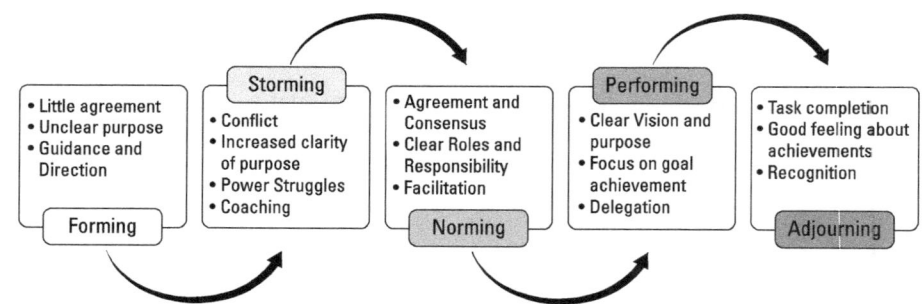

FIGURE 2-3: Tuckman's model of team development.

Forming

When teams first come together, there's often a lot of excitement and optimism. Team members are excited to be part of a new team and eager to get results and feel successful. This is the forming stage.

What is required of a leader during the forming stage is coordinating behaviors. Often, the leader is responsible for selecting the team. The leader's priority should be to clearly communicate the common goal or shared purpose of a team. It's also important to ensure that every member of your team feels valued and necessary to the team's success. This requires knowing each person's role and believing their role to be essential, but it also means that the leader is interested in each team member as a person, not just a function.

This requires knowing their role and believing that they matter in a way that conveys how integral their contribution is to the team. This helps the leader signal to each member of the team that they are seen, heard, and indispensable rather than transactional.

What a leader might observe during the forming stage are lots of questions from team members. At first, team members might happily work on their own or in small silos. They may be highly motivated but still unsure if they understand the common purpose of the team. Generally, people in this stage strive to make a good impression on leaders and colleagues. At the same time, their concern is for themselves first (Will I fit in? What's my role? Who can I trust?) and the team second. Since bonds of trust have yet to be formed, this is natural and to be expected. Team members are typically receptive to guidance from their leaders about group norms and processes at this early stage, so take advantage of that and communicate these expectations frequently.

TIP

During the Forming stage, most of the team's energy is on defining the team and its goals, so task accomplishment may be low at this stage. Unless you have prepared some very easy "quick wins" for the team to complete and immediately celebrate, you can set the team up for success by allowing them to build trust without a long list of tasks to complete right away.

WARNING

Be aware that while the overall mood is happy when a team is forming, some team members may experience some anxiety as well. They might wonder if they'll be accepted by the rest of the team or if their performance will meet everyone else's standards. Leaders should stay attuned to shifts in team members' moods and comfort levels, watching for signs of uncertainty or stress so they can offer reassurance and support early on.

REMEMBER

Enjoy the Forming stage while it lasts. It's a lovely place to be, but it's temporary! Teams will move on from forming eventually.

Storming

During the storming stage, the initial excitement and optimism of the team begin to fade as people settle into a predictable routine. However, as the name suggests, storming can often be characterized by frustration, conflict, and anger. This is to be expected; as team members start to put more energy into their work, they naturally put less energy into gaining everyone else's approval. When people's authentic selves begin to show, there are going to be disagreements on processes, boundaries, norms, and habits. Most people (especially leaders) don't particularly enjoy this stage and may secretly wish for the pleasant, polite days of the forming stage to come back. However, seasoned leaders know that storming is necessary for a team to establish trust and build authentic relationships.

What a leader might observe during the storming stage are behaviors that indicate frustration. For some, this might be an outward expression, but for others, it could look like stewing silently in a private corner. As the work naturally slows down and colleagues aren't responding as quickly and happily as they used to, some team members might feel that the work isn't happening fast enough. Often, the leader becomes a scapegoat because they have "allowed" the team to devolve into bickering and constant irritation.

The first trait required of a leader during the storming stage is patience. Leaders who have lived through this stage many times have come to expect it. They don't blame themselves when the first signs of conflict arise, and they're able to smile and listen to the team, even when the members aren't behaving quite as nicely as they were a short time ago. Moreover, leaders who are shepherding a team through storming do a lot of coaching. They must be a trusted resource to everyone on the team (even those who place blame the decrease in civility at the leader's door!), and coach the team to place more trust in each other. When conflict arises during the storming stage, a leader's job is not to take sides but to facilitate a way for the two parties to resolve it together.

TIP

When the team looks like it might be splintering apart, it's helpful to assist everyone in refocusing on their goals. One way to do this is to break the goals into smaller achievable steps. While it can be wonderful for a team that is form-ing to think about what they can accomplish in a year or two, a team that is storming will be much better served by knowing what needs to happen by the end of the week.

WARNING

It's especially important during the storming stage to keep an eye on your team members who might already feel set apart or isolated from the group for any rea-son (for example, the only woman on the team, the youngest member, or the only one with a more "senior" job title). You'll want to ensure they're not feeling the effects of this volatile stage more than other people on the team. While this stage should be temporary, it might remind some team members of previous toxic work environments or even isolated experiences of discrimination they encountered in the past.

Norming

When and if the norming stage is reached, team members will find a balance between their personal needs and expectations and what the team needs and expects from them. I say "if" because, unlike storming, there's no guarantee that a team will reach this stage. However, if the team and its leader can effectively build norms that are flexible and inclusive, there should come a time when every-one on the team experiences a sense of safety in expressing their authentic selves.

This includes asking questions, offering new ideas, or even challenging the team's work. (See Chapter 3 for more on psychological safety.)

What leaders might notice, if they're observant, is that team members are knocking on their doors less often and resolving conflicts on their own without many signs of outward conflict. This is because they trust their team members to hear them out and are much more willing to assume positive intent when something doesn't go as planned. Often, teams in this stage will begin developing their own inside jokes, and certain team members might be given nicknames.

What is required of a leader during the norming stage are empowering behaviors. As team members build bonds of trust among each other, they want to know that their leader trusts them as well. Check in, get feedback, and reward team members for a job well done, but resist the urge to micromanage and allow the natural leaders on your team to take ownership of their work.

WARNING

If things seem to be going well during this stage, it's mostly due to the team trusting each other. It doesn't necessarily mean that the norms and processes the team created or agreed to during the forming stage are the best ones for this specific team. At the very least, leaders should be open to feedback regarding different or better ways of doing things. Even better, be proactive. Ask the team what improvements they'd like to see.

Performing

When a team is making visible progress and members begin to see the effects of their hard work, it enters the performing stage. Here, members are acutely aware of the strengths and weakness of all team members (including themselves), and the team is finally greater than the sum of its parts. All members feel valued and included.

What a leader might notice during the performing stage is that the role definitions, which the team worked so hard to create during the forming stage, have become much more fluid. Team members are willing to stray from their job descriptions, and sometimes their colleagues are not threatened or territorial in response. Dissent is expected and handled so collegially that an outside observer might not notice it.

What is required of a leader during the performing stage is very similar to what the team needed from them during norming. Listening and receiving feedback are still critical. However, as the team begins to self-manage regarding their tasks, the leader should set aside some time to foster continued team engagement. This might seem unnecessary, but the performing stage should not be taken for granted because it isn't guaranteed to last forever.

While it's possible for a team to remain in performing mode for a long time, change can and will happen. Key members of the team (including leaders) may leave, they may or may not be replaced, priorities might shift, changes in the marketplace may demand new ways of working, or external factors may have a huge impact on the way a team works together, as we saw in response to the COVID-19 pandemic. When these things happen, it's likely that the team will cycle through the stages of team development again. If you're a new leader on an established team, you will likely be welcomed by many friendly faces who hang on your every word. This is a repeat of the forming stage, and you will likely experience some storming and norming before you can once again lead a performing team. However, if the bonds of the team are strong and they're used to engaging as a performing team, the cycle should move very quickly. But much of this depends on you being the type of leader that the team needs during each phase of the cycle.

Adjourning

They say nothing lasts forever, and that can be true for some teams. If a team has completed its work or is disbanding for some reason (the company is restructuring or closing its doors, or there's a monumental change such as a large layoff that will necessitate a return to the forming stage), the team goes through a process of adjourning. During this phase, the team either completes its task and celebrates its success or decides what will be finished and what not before all or most of the team says goodbye. Even if the team is dissolving for the very best of reasons (such as if the task was successfully completed and its success has been recognized, and the leader received a big promotion based on the team's exemplary work), there's often an air of sadness about the team breaking up or changing.

What a leader might notice during the adjourning stage could be as varied as the team members themselves. Some might become anxious and less focused on their tasks, whereas others could find that hyperfocusing helps them deal with the impending sense of loss. There will often be a strong desire to reminisce. If the future of the individual team members is unclear (for example, if many must look for their next job), they could begin to separate prematurely as a form of emotional protection.

What is needed from a leader during the adjourning stage is to help the team to acknowledge its upcoming transition. Obviously, if there are still deliverables that are required during this time, they should be attended to. If possible, time should also be spent evaluating the team's work, allowing each member to take some lessons learned with them. Even if the reasons for the team's dissolution don't feel very celebratory (a reduction in force or a company shutting down), encourage your team to celebrate each other and whatever successes you achieved together. Let each team member know what you value about them, so they can take that into their next chapter.

As with any transition in life, there's no one correct way to adapt or mourn. As a team prepares to break apart, allow for a range of different reactions. Obviously, if a team member seems to be in abject denial, a leader can help by gently reminding them of the upcoming closure. If a team member is acting out in ways that are having a negative impact on the entire team, some coaching may be necessary. Otherwise, allow people to grieve and separate in the ways that feel the best to them. It's entirely appropriate and predictable that individuals return to a self-focused outlook during this stage, and there's no real benefit in transitioning into an intact group.

UNDERSTANDING YOUR TEAM'S DEVELOPMENT STAGE

Where is your team? Teams who have just come together will almost certainly find themselves in the forming stage. The storming stage is almost certain to follow. If the team disbands or goes through a big change, the adjourning stage will certainly happen, but the stages of norming and performing aren't guaranteed.

Teams that could be accurately described as toxic or dysfunctional might be permanently stuck in the storming stage. Other teams that feel much more pleasant but never reach their full potential might be in the norming stage but not able to break through into performing. Even teams that are performing at their peak (performing) could cycle through the process again when a significant upset forces them to regroup and create new ways of doing things.

That said, your team isn't guaranteed to be in the performing stage just because you've been together for a while. Much of this has to do with how much trust your team members have in you, their leader, and in each other.

If you're having trouble deciding which stage best describes your team, ask yourself the following:

- How much negative conflict (squabbling, territorialism, gossip) do you notice?
- Is it possible that negative conflict exists but is being hidden from you?
- How much positive conflict (respectful dissent, collaborative problem solving) do you see?
- Does your team perform their tasks with high quality? Are they able to do this on time and under budget?
- Does your team take pride in their work?
- Do they readily recognize and celebrate the accomplishments of others?

The T7 Model of Team Effectiveness

Developed by Korn Ferry Institute in 2012, the T7 Model of Team Effectiveness is a thorough tool for assessing the performance of your team.

As its name suggests, the T7 model has seven components, each beginning with the letter T. (See Figure 2-4.) They are

>> **Thrust:** Shared purpose or common goal

>> **Trust:** A culture of mutual confidence and respect

>> **Talent:** Aptitude and experience of team members

>> **Teaming skills:** The ability to collaborate effectively

>> **Task skills:** The ability to execute quality work

>> **Team leader fit:** How well the leader supports and facilitates the work

>> **Team support from the organization:** How well the larger organization supports the team

FIGURE 2-4: Korn Ferry's T7 Model of Team Effectiveness.

Thrust

As depicted in many of the models we've already discussed, the T7 model recognizes that a unifying, common purpose or goal is necessary for a team to be high-performing. Team members need to both understand the goal and be properly motivated by it.

Trust

In addition to the motivation that comes from a goal, individual team members should also find drive in their confidence in each other. Trust is dependent upon leaders who act with integrity and team members who pull their weight so that everyone can do their best.

Talent

Talent refers to the experience team members bring to the group effort, as well as their aptitude and willingness to learn. In this model, talent is better described as capability than ability, and it's an indicator of long-term, sustainable high performance. This component also includes how talent is acquired, developed, allocated, and deployed.

Task skills

These are the skills (or the ability) that team members can apply to their work at present. When teams possess both talent and task skills, they can do what needs to be done today and can be prepared for what needs to be done months or years into the future.

Teaming skills

Teaming skills are the interpersonal skills that team members must exhibit in addition to the skills that are germane to their job description. These skills encompass not only how to work effectively in any team but how to manage the unique personalities of their specific team. The skills include collaborative decision-making, conflict management, managing processes, and supporting a healthy work culture.

Team leader fit and team support from the organization

As suggested by the name, this part of the model is only partly concerned with a team leader's competencies. It also examines how well the leader fits with their specific team. Some teams require more autonomy than others, while other teams might crave more interaction. Some teams are on a steep learning curve and require enough coaching to maintain the quality of their work but not so much that they feel micromanaged. This part of the model is usually depicted as a large circle surrounding the first five components of the model (refer to Figure 2-4).

Finally, when a team exists within the context of a larger organization, the support that they receive (or the lack of support) can have an enormous impact on the effectiveness of that team.

Which Model Is Best?

Ultimately, the models you choose to employ to design a team, diagnose its current state, or measure its effectiveness are entirely up to you. I like all of these models and employ each depending on the kind of team I'm working with and the issues that specific team is facing. Rather than advocating for one model being superior to all the others, I argue that a capable and flexible leader is able to understand and employ more than a single theory to better understand their team.

TIP

Of course, models are theoretical, and people are far more complex than a simple model can easily capture. But simple models can be especially helpful when dealing with complex issues, as you, the leader, struggle to ask the right questions in the right order. Models like these can help a task-centered leader remember to consider their people, and a people-centered leader remember to stay focused on tasks and goals. The goal of a good model is to help a leader ask the right questions, not arrive at a quick answer.

Common Types of Work Teams

In addition to the theoretical models that help you understand your team, there are also several practical, tangible functions a team performs. Each one asks for something a little different from its leader. As you apply the models we've discussed, think about what kind of team you're leading and let that also guide your approach.

Intact teams

If your team is one that regularly works together in a common physical space, has formed strong bonds, and knows each other so well that it has come to rely on the various strengths and communication styles found on the team, you're probably working on what's called an *intact team.*

Intact teams are usually fairly stable, with low turnover over time. Team members are familiar with one another, so much so that patterns and rituals have sprung up, often without being prompted by the team leader. Intact teams often represent core functional units within an organization, like a finance department, a production team, or a group of engineers working on a specific long-term project.

The benefits of working on an intact team include the improved coordination and enhanced collaboration that derive from the close working relationships found there. These dynamics can come in very handy when the team experiences high-pressure situations or must react to big external changes. Intact teams can often learn new things and adapt to change more quickly than other kinds of teams. Moreover, they typically experience less turnover than remote or hybrid teams.

What's needed from the leader of intact teams is a mix of approachability and appropriate distance. Because an intact team is co-located, leaders have physical access to team members very often. Leaders with a tendency to micromanage, therefore, can easily do too much in this regard, and team members can often feel suffocated. Leaders of intact teams need to learn to trust the members of their team but maintain approachability so that when problems arise, team members don't hesitate to bring the leader into an important conversation.

TIP

One great way to strike this balance is to work on developing appropriate personal relationships with your team. Get to know them as people, learn about their families and hobbies, and celebrate their birthdays (all dependent upon the organization's culture, of course). Because you enjoy such physical proximity with your team, you have the opportunity to make deeper and more personal connections, especially if it can prevent you from managing every little step of your team members' jobs.

Remote/hybrid teams

When a significant portion of your team works at a significant distance (either a work-from-home arrangement or a different corporate office elsewhere in the world), then you work on a hybrid team. If the entire team works in separate locations (perhaps everyone works from a home office), then your team is fully remote.

Remote and hybrid teams increased in popularity after the COVID-19 pandemic. Teams that were formerly intact were forced to become remote — almost overnight. Many teams found that they functioned surprisingly well, and many team members found that they were hesitant to return to a co-located space, even when it was once again safe to do so. Whether they were introverted and enjoyed working in a quieter and calmer environment, were happy to skip a daily commute in rush hour traffic, or found they could get more done when large team meetings were less frequent and more efficient, working in an individualized space suited them. Some company leaders also discovered that leasing corporate office space, once an expense taken for granted, would garner huge savings for their company if more people worked outside a physical office.

Since the emergence of the COVID vaccine, many organizations mandated a return to the office, in deference to the benefits of intact teams as described in the preceding section. But many teams found that their working relationships were just as solid in a remote or hybrid situation, especially if they had already worked alongside their colleagues for years. Now, the further we get from the days of global quarantine, the challenges of working remotely have come into sharper focus.

What's needed from leaders of remote teams is availability and frequent contact with team members. This is not a free pass to micromanage your team! In fact, many people who prefer to work remotely do so specifically because they feel like they have more autonomy and agency than they did when sharing a physical space with their leaders. And leaders of remote teams can sometimes be too distant. When working in a shared office, leaders can keep their doors open when they're willing to be interrupted; this is necessarily more difficult in a remote setup. So, it might be necessary to schedule ongoing one-on-one meetings with team members. If you lead with questions like "How are you this week? How can I support you?" rather than "Tell me what you're working on so I can keep tabs on you," these meetings need not dampen the enthusiasm of your most talented workers. These meetings might need to be more frequent for newer members of your team, tapering off over time.

REMEMBER

It's still possible (and preferable!) to develop appropriate personal relationships with your remote team members. You can still celebrate birthdays! But the ways in which these relationships are formed and milestones are recognized will necessarily be different in a remote setup.

What's needed from leaders of hybrid teams is fairness and inclusion. It will likely be your primary challenge to ensure that the team members you work next to feel the same amount of personal agency that your distanced team members do and that your distanced team members feel a similar sense of belonging as your co-located team members do. It might be impossible for these disparate experiences to ever be the same, but it's nonetheless a good goal to strive for!

Project teams

If your team has come together to work on a discrete project with a defined end state, then you're leading a project team. Project teams are easily identifiable based on a clearly defined scope, a discrete set of objectives, and often a predetermined start and end date. The primary focus of a project team is delivering a specific and often tangible outcome, such as a new software application, a product prototype, a short marketing campaign, or a website launch. Once the project is completed, a project team will typically disband.

What's needed from leaders of project teams is a particular focus on the task at hand. Success on a project team is often measured by the delivery of a particular product on a particular date. Tasks such as creating the project plan, managing the budget, managing the schedule, delegating tasks to appropriate team members, managing all product deliverables, and communicating with outside stakeholders all fall to the team leader. On a more long-term team, it could be possible to share some of those responsibilities with your high-potential team members, but on a discrete project team, this is unlikely.

REMEMBER

Fortunately, project teams often require less management in the realm of interpersonal dynamics. Of course, when working with a limited project lifespan, major conflicts could be a big disruptor, so you'll always want to be looking out for team members who are misaligned on project goals or overstepping their prescribed roles, just in case.

Cross-functional teams

When the people you manage are a group from different functional areas within an organization who have been brought together toward a common mission, then you're working on a cross-functional team. Because of their diverse perspectives and skill sets, cross-functional teams make it possible to harness increased creativity and innovation. Within a larger organization, the presence of a cross-functional team facilitates better communication and collaboration between entire departments, reducing misunderstandings and improving overall organizational efficiency. The quality of solutions proposed by a cross-functional team is often enhanced by receiving input from people who, collectively, have fewer "blind spots" than a team with more similar backgrounds.

Cross-functional teams might be project teams with a short lifespan and predetermined end date. However, they're often process improvement teams, whose common mission is dedicated to identifying and implementing improvements within a specific business process, like improving customer service or streamlining internal communications. These teams might be permanent within an organization, but because of their cross-functional nature, they may see more turnover than your typical team as team members transfer from and return to their original departments on a rotating schedule.

What's needed from the leader of a cross-functional team is a clear and motivating mission, and the leader needs the ability (or willingness) to communicate and overcommunicate this early and often to team members. Goal misalignment can be more common on a cross-functional team because they're made of people from different disciplines, often with different definitions of what constitutes successful work. Leaders of cross-functional teams often have to keep an eye on power dynamics as well. Often, team members have wide disparities of age, tenure, experience, and seniority within the company. Younger or newer employees may welcome the idea of working in a "flatter" team structure where they can contribute ideas more freely, but older, more experienced employees may resist giving up some of the influence they enjoyed on their prior team.

Sometimes, membership on a cross-functional team coincides with work on a departmental team. For example, an employee is expected to dedicate 25 percent of their time to the cross-functional team while still working 75 percent of their hours on their original team. In these cases, team leaders might be called upon to coach their team members on how to set effective boundaries, both within their cross-functional team and back in their departments.

TIP

Because of their diverse nature, cross-functional teams are more prone to conflict. A team leader should expect this but should resist the urge to eliminate conflicts as soon as they arrive. Frame conflict as a given, but also, realize that if it's managed well, it can be a generative source of creativity and innovation. This might be counterintuitive to a conflict-averse leader, but remember, all those different perspectives were likely the reason the cross-functional team was created in the first place!

Management teams

If you're a CEO or a C-suite level leader in a large organization, chances are your team is a management team. That is, your team members are leaders who guide and manage large groups of people. Management teams are often defined by a C-suite (a group of people who all have the words *chief* or *officer* in their titles, such as chief human resources officer, chief financial officer, or chief operations officer). Management teams are responsible for strategic planning, operational management, and ensuring the company's goals are met. These teams make critical decisions for a department or an entire organization. If your management team is a C-suite, then by definition, your team is also a cross-functional team (see the preceding section).

What's needed from the leader of a management team varies widely based on the size of the team and the organization, industry, and the workplace culture. But what is necessary no matter what kind of management team you're leading is an unwavering commitment to your organization's values. And if "integrity" isn't specifically called out in your company's core values, add it to the list. The art of leading leaders is one of gaining their respect. These are very likely highly successful people in their own right. The act of leading people is not foreign to them, and they can much more easily spot deficits in their own leaders. So, the leader of a management team who plays favorites, says one thing in public and the opposite in private, shirks responsibility for one's own actions, fears conflict, lacks vision, micromanages, or ignores feedback when any of these deficiencies are brought to their attention will likely lose the respect of their team, resulting in entire departments or sub-teams within an organization working at cross-purposes.

Chapter **3**

Identifying Key Attributes of High-Performance Teams

Whether in global corporations, nonprofit organizations, or entrepreneurial startups, the world's best teams share foundational attributes that drive extraordinary results and foster environments where every member feels valued, heard, and empowered. These attributes are not mere buzzwords but are rooted in intentional practices, shared values, and a collective commitment to excellence. While every team will look different depending on its context, there are common attributes that distinguish between those that thrive and consistently exceed expectations.

This chapter delves into the practical and psychological foundations that underpin high-performance teams. It explores how shared leadership serves as a catalyst for engagement, retention, and innovation. Additionally, I highlight how communication, trust, clarity of roles, diversity, resilience, accountability, psychological safety, and other qualities can create dynamic teams capable of exceeding expectations in any environment.

Exploring the Role of Shared Leadership

Effective leadership sits at the heart of every high-performing team. In my years of consulting with Fortune 500 companies, I've seen that leaders who combine competence with character elevate not only performance, but also engagement and loyalty. Research has shown that leaders who demonstrate both technical expertise and emotional intelligence score twice as high on engagement metrics and are 1.7 times more likely to be rated as world-class.

Effective leadership isn't confined to title or authority. It's about influence, vision, and the ability to unlock potential within every team member. In today's workplace, leaders must be emotionally intelligent, agile, culturally competent, and able to lead diverse teams across geographies and generations. They also need to be fluent in digital literacy, ethics, and inclusive practices that prepare teams to work with new technologies in a global context.

As an author for Microsoft's LinkedIn Learning, I've had the opportunity to observe their company's culture first hand. Their CEO has shifted it from a competitive, siloed environment to one that is infused with empathy, collaboration, and a growth mindset. It celebrates learning and shared success. This cultural transformation led to increased innovation, accelerated market growth, and a dramatic improvement in employee morale.

REMEMBER

Leadership is not a title, it's a practice. However, it's also a shared responsibility, as I discuss in the next section.

Leadership should never be limited to a single individual. High-performing teams recognize that leadership is most powerful when it's shared, distributed, and cultivated at all levels. Shared leadership is a proven driver of performance, sparking innovation, agility, and ownership across the team. The Center for Creative Leadership (CCL) reports that teams that embrace shared leadership generate 23 percent higher innovation and demonstrate significantly greater agility during times of disruption. The reason is that when leadership is shared, the responsibility for success is spread among many, creating a collective commitment to the mission rather than reliance on one leader at the top. McKinsey's 2024 study on organizational agility found that leaders in "fast-moving organizations," when compared with peers in slower companies, reported 2.1 times higher operational resilience. The same group also reports 2.5 times higher financial performance.

Empowering individuals to make real-time decisions based on their knowledge and proximity to the work, builds speed and responsiveness. It also instills confidence because employees feel trusted and valued for their contributions.

One of the best examples of this principle in practice is W.L. Gore, the company behind Gore-Tex. Gore intentionally minimizes hierarchy and operates on a lattice structure where employees step into leadership roles based on their expertise and passion rather than rank or title. This system encourages individuals to take ownership of solutions, collaborate across boundaries, and lead projects from where they are. The results — breakthrough innovations and a track record of resilience in volatile markets — speak for themselves.

TIP

When leadership is shared, ideas flow more freely, creativity is unleashed, and accountability is distributed in ways that make the team stronger and more adaptive.

For shared leadership to thrive, organizations must intentionally create environments where authority is delegated, strengths are recognized, and peer mentoring is encouraged. Leaders can establish rotational leadership roles that allow different team members to guide projects, lead meetings, or represent the group in cross-functional forums. Decision rights should be clearly defined so that expertise drives solutions rather than hierarchy. When teams see that leadership is fluid, based on the situation and the skill set required, they are more willing to step up, take initiative, and own results. At its core, shared leadership shifts the mindset from "me" to "we."

Embedding shared leadership also requires recognition and celebration of collective wins. Too often, organizations spotlight individual star performers while overlooking the power of the team. High-performing teams highlight how collaboration and distributed leadership produced success. They tell the stories of how different members stepped forward at critical moments, how expertise from unexpected places solved complex problems, and how shared responsibility accelerated progress. These narratives reinforce the belief that leadership is everyone's job, not just the responsibility of a few.

Shared Purpose

A compelling shared purpose is the anchor that unites high-performing teams and propels them toward extraordinary achievement. Purpose provides clarity, meaning, and motivation, fueling perseverance even in the face of adversity. PwC's 2023 Global Workforce Survey found that nearly 80 percent of leaders believe purpose is a key driver of success, yet only one-third have fully embedded it within their teams. This gap reveals that while most leaders understand the importance of purpose, far fewer know how to translate it into the everyday actions and culture of their teams.

When purpose is authentically embedded into the fabric of work, it shifts from being a lofty slogan to becoming the compass that directs behaviors, decisions, and performance. In my book, *Living Beyond What If* (Berrett-Koehler Publishers, 2021), I remind readers that purpose is not simply about having a job; it's about having a mission that pulls you forward and inspires you to give your best even in times of challenge. The same is true for teams. When teams discover their collective *why*, they find renewed energy, deeper collaboration, and the resilience to navigate uncertainty. Purpose becomes the glue that holds them together when circumstances try to pull them apart.

Consider Patagonia, which has become a global example of purpose-driven culture. Its unwavering commitment to environmental sustainability does more than attract passionate employees; it drives breakthrough innovations in product design and inspires collaboration across departments. Employees know that every design choice, manufacturing process, and advocacy campaign contributes to the larger mission of protecting the planet. Purpose is not confined to a statement on the website. It's present in brainstorming sessions, product launches, and advocacy efforts, and it creates a culture where teams see their work as both urgent and meaningful.

Other global organizations such as Unilever and Tata Group in India have shown that embedding purpose not only drives social good but also business growth. Unilever has tied its strategy to sustainable development goals, and its purpose-led brands consistently outperform others in growth and customer loyalty. Tata Group has long integrated values of social responsibility into its operations, and its reputation for purpose-driven leadership continues to attract top talent across industries. These examples illustrate that when organizations place purpose at the center, teams feel more engaged, customers become more loyal, and innovation accelerates.

And just as leadership must be shared (as I describe earlier in this chapter in the "Shared Leadership" section), purpose must be cocreated, not dictated from the top down. When leaders invite teams into the process of defining their mission and values, buy-in is authentic, and commitment is sustainable. Leaders should create intentional spaces, such as facilitated workshops or retreats, where teams reflect on what truly matters to them and how their individual strengths contribute to the greater good. This practice ensures that purpose remains current, relevant, and aligned with both organizational goals and global realities.

Aligning individual goals with a shared mission strengthens team cohesion. Employees want to know that their contributions matter. Recognizing team members not just for their output but for how their work advances the mission makes recognition more meaningful and powerful. When individuals clearly see the connection between their daily responsibilities and the organization's broader vision, they show up with greater passion, energy, and accountability.

Storytelling is a powerful tool for sustaining purpose. Leaders who regularly connect daily tasks to the larger impact help team members internalize the importance of their work. Whether a story is about how a product improved a customer's life, how a service helped a community thrive, or how a solution contributed to tackling climate change or health inequities, the narrative transforms routine work into mission-driven contributions.

In today's global context, where industries are being reshaped by challenges such as climate change, social unrest, political polarization, and rapid technological disruption, revisiting and refining team purpose is essential. High-performing teams are those that stay anchored in meaning and relevance, continuously asking not just "What are we achieving?" but "Why does it matter?"

Ultimately, purpose is more than an organizational strategy. It's a human need. Just as individuals thrive when they find meaning in their lives, teams thrive when they share a purpose that inspires them to work together with unity and resolve. When organizations embrace this truth and intentionally build purpose into the DNA of their culture, they not only elevate performance but also create a legacy of impact that endures.

Mutual Accountability

One of the defining characteristics of high-performing teams is mutual accountability. It is not enough for individuals to simply complete their assigned tasks. High performance requires that every member of the team takes responsibility not only for their own contributions but also for the overall success of the group. When accountability is shared, trust deepens, collaboration strengthens, and results improve.

Research continues to affirm the value of accountability in driving team effectiveness. A recent study by Culture Partners (formerly Partners In Leadership) revealed that organizations with strong accountability cultures are 2.5 times more likely to achieve high performance and meet their strategic goals. Similarly, Gallup's global survey on workplace engagement found that teams with clear accountability practices report 27 percent higher performance outcomes. These findings reinforce that accountability is not a soft skill but a business imperative.

In my LinkedIn Learning course "Practical Tips for Demonstrating Accountability," I emphasize that accountability is not about blame or finger-pointing. It's about ownership, transparency, and follow-through. Teams that excel in accountability practice open communication, set clear expectations, and establish shared goals. They celebrate successes together and learn collectively from setbacks.

Importantly, they hold each other to high standards in a respectful and supportive way, understanding that accountability is a gift we give each other to ensure we all succeed.

For leaders, cultivating mutual accountability starts when they model the behavior for the rest of the team. This includes keeping commitments, providing timely feedback, and creating a safe environment where individuals feel empowered to speak up when commitments are not met. Teams should establish clear agreements, revisit them regularly, and hold open conversations about progress. When accountability becomes a shared value rather than a top-down demand, teams not only meet expectations but often exceed them, propelling themselves toward sustained excellence.

A compelling example comes from Toyota's legendary "andon cord" system. On the assembly line, any worker has the authority to pull the cord if they notice a defect, a safety concern, or a problem that could compromise quality. This action immediately stops production until the issue is resolved. The system demonstrates that accountability is not reserved for leaders or managers; it's distributed across the entire team. Each person is empowered to protect quality and uphold shared standards. Rather than being punished for slowing the process, team members are recognized for taking ownership. The andon cord represents a culture where accountability is seen as an act of courage and commitment to excellence.

WARNING

Accountability without psychological safety leads to fear and anxiety, not ownership. I cover this topic a bit more in the "Trust and Psychological Safety" section later in this chapter and also in Chapters 3 and 5.

Continuous Improvement

High-performing teams are never satisfied with the status quo. They see continuous improvement not as an occasional initiative but as a way of thinking and operating every day. This mindset requires humility to acknowledge there's always room to grow, courage to rethink what's been done before, and curiosity to explore innovative ideas. McKinsey's 2024 report found that organizations that embed continuous learning into their culture are 32 percent more likely to meet or exceed their strategic goals. In other words, continuous improvement is not just an aspiration; it's a proven pathway to sustained success.

A long-term colleague of mine works as a senior executive at Amazon and told me about a practice they have called the "Day 1" mindset. By treating every day as if it were the company's first, Amazon encourages experimentation, rapid iteration, and an openness to change. Teams are empowered to test new ideas, learn quickly from what works and what doesn't, and build on those insights. This approach keeps innovation alive and prevents complacency. Teams that embrace a similar philosophy continually reinvent themselves, and in doing so, they remain resilient and relevant in fast-changing markets.

Continuous improvement also thrives on feedback. High-performing teams create safe environments where feedback is welcomed, not feared, and where missteps are viewed as opportunities to learn rather than reasons for blame. Retrospectives, idea-sharing forums, and cross-functional collaborations are critical practices that allow teams to reflect on what went well, what needs refining, and what should be tried next. By celebrating small wins and recognizing effort as well as outcomes, leaders build momentum and sustain motivation for long-term growth.

Technology has become a powerful accelerator of this mindset. Teams that leverage AI-powered analytics, predictive modeling, and real-time data are able to spot trends, adapt to disruption, and seize opportunities faster than competitors. One of my previous clients, Johnson & Johnson's clinical research teams, exemplify this by routinely reviewing protocols with input from diverse perspectives. Their willingness to revisit and refine their processes has led to breakthroughs in medicine and patient care, demonstrating how continuous improvement fuels innovation and advances outcomes that matter on a global scale.

For teams to truly embody this value, organizations must invest in professional development, digital upskilling, and coaching. Employees should be encouraged to pilot new approaches, test bold ideas, and iterate without the fear of failure holding them back. Leaders can reinforce this by modeling curiosity, asking reflective questions, and highlighting lessons learned even when results fall short. This shifts the focus from perfection to progress, which is the heart of continuous improvement.

Improvement is a journey, not a sprint. Celebrate small wins along the way.

REMEMBER Improvement is about creating a culture where every team member feels responsible for moving the organization forward one step at a time. Recognizing incremental progress and celebrating the learning that happens along the way ensures that energy is sustained.

Diverse and Complementary Skills

Diversity is more than a moral imperative; it's a strategic advantage that fuels the success of high-performing teams. Deloitte's 2023 Global Human Capital Trends report confirms that inclusive teams outperform peers by up to 80 percent. When teams intentionally integrate people with different skills, perspectives, and life experiences, they expand their capacity to see problems from multiple angles and to create solutions that are both innovative and relevant. Importantly, diversity extends beyond demographics to include diversity of thought, professional expertise, cognitive styles, and problem-solving approaches. The blending of these differences sparks creativity, accelerates learning, and builds resilience.

Google's Project Aristotle revealed that cognitive diversity, or the presence of different ways of thinking and problem-solving, is one of the strongest predictors of team effectiveness. These findings from Google and Deloitte show that diversity is not about checking boxes; it's about intentionally cultivating a mix of capabilities that makes the team stronger, smarter, and more adaptable.

TIP

To fully leverage diversity, inclusion must be intentional and embedded into the daily fabric of the team's operations. Without equity in recruitment, assignments, recognition, and development, the benefits of a multitalented and diverse team can be diminished. Equally important is creating a culture where all voices are welcomed, respected, and valued. Teams that encourage healthy debate and varying points of view avoid groupthink and surface blind spots that might otherwise derail progress. Leaders can set the tone by modeling inclusive behaviors such as asking quieter members to contribute, ensuring credit is shared fairly, and creating safe spaces where individuals can express ideas without fear of judgment. When team members experience this level of inclusion, they bring more of their authentic selves to the table, which amplifies collaboration and strengthens trust.

The most successful teams also recognize that diversity is not static; it must evolve as the organization and its challenges evolve. As industries face new demands from technology, globalization, and shifting demographics, teams should regularly revisit their composition to ensure that the mix of skills, perspectives, and experiences is still aligned with the goals ahead. By cultivating a workforce that is both diverse and complementary, organizations position themselves to anticipate trends, respond to disruption, and innovate for the future.

Effective Communication

Communication is the lifeblood of high-performing teams. When I say "communication," I mean more than the exchange of information. Communication is the foundation for clarity, collaboration, and trust. The Project Management Institute reports that nearly one-third of project failures can be traced back to poor communication, making it one of the most significant risks to team success. Companies like Salesforce model what strong communication looks like by ensuring that leaders share strategies, challenges, and successes openly, setting the tone for transparency across the organization.

REMEMBER

Effective communication requires clarity, consistency, and active listening. It also demands that teams are equipped with the right tools and skills to collaborate across time zones, cultures, and functions. Digital platforms enable global connectivity, while training in intercultural competence ensures that messages are both delivered and received with respect. Emerging AI-powered technologies now offer another layer of support by analyzing communication patterns and identifying breakdowns before they escalate. These innovations are valuable, but they work best when paired with human-centered practices such as empathy, curiosity, and a willingness to adapt.

Creative organizations like Pixar remind us of the power of dialogue through their "brain trust" sessions, where candid feedback and constructive challenge are welcomed. These practices demonstrate that effective communicators do more than share their ideas; they also listen deeply, seek to understand, and create space for every voice to be heard. Leaders can reinforce this culture by implementing regular check-ins, daily huddles, and ongoing team dialogues. Training in active listening and cross-cultural communication helps prevent misunderstandings, while encouraging feedback ensures that issues are raised and resolved quickly.

Ultimately, communication is not a one-time event but a continuous process. When leaders model transparency and responsiveness, and when teams engage in meaningful dialogue with one another, they unlock the full potential of collaboration. The result is stronger relationships, faster execution, and the kind of innovation that sets high-performing teams apart.

Defined Roles and Responsibilities

Clarity around roles and responsibilities is essential for focus, accountability, and executing on performance goals. When team members know exactly what is expected of them, they can direct their energy toward results rather than confusion or duplicated efforts. Slack's research shows that teams with clearly defined roles consistently deliver projects on time and within budget, underscoring how structure drives both efficiency and confidence. NASA also models this discipline by ensuring every team member understands their precise role during critical missions, while still cross-training for flexibility and resilience in high-stakes environments. This balance of precision and preparedness helps avoid costly mistakes and builds confidence across the team.

One of the most effective tools for creating role clarity is the RACI model (see Figure 3-1), which defines who is responsible, accountable, consulted, and informed for each task or decision.

What are the **RACI** roles?

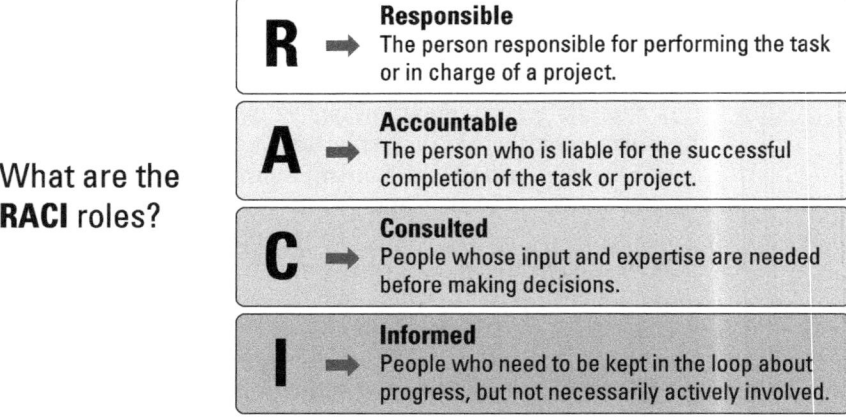

R →	**Responsible**	The person responsible for performing the task or in charge of a project.
A →	**Accountable**	The person who is liable for the successful completion of the task or project.
C →	**Consulted**	People whose input and expertise are needed before making decisions.
I →	**Informed**	People who need to be kept in the loop about progress, but not necessarily actively involved.

FIGURE 3-1:
The RACI model.

The person who is *responsible* owns the execution, while the one who is *accountable* ensures outcomes are achieved. *Consulted* individuals provide expertise or input, and those who are *informed* stay updated on progress. When applied consistently, a RACI matrix reduces overlap, prevents missed handoffs, and ensures that no task falls through the cracks. For example, in a product launch, marketing may be responsible for the campaign rollout, the project manager may be accountable for overall delivery, legal may be consulted on compliance issues, and executives may be informed of key milestones. By mapping responsibilities this way, teams minimize ambiguity and build trust in one another's contributions.

REMEMBER

Roles should not be static. As strategies shift and goals evolve, responsibilities must also adapt. Leaders should regularly review and adjust the RACI framework to ensure alignment with organizational priorities. At the same time, cross-training team members develops agility and resilience, equipping them to step in when unexpected challenges arise. A practical reminder is to revisit role assignments during major project transitions or after significant organizational changes to avoid gaps or bottlenecks. And a valuable tip is to openly communicate any changes in responsibilities to the entire team to maintain transparency and avoid assumptions.

TIP

Ultimately, the goal is to balance clarity with adaptability. Too much rigidity can stifle innovation, whereas too much flexibility can breed chaos. By combining the discipline of tools like the RACI model with a mindset of agility and continuous review, leaders create environments where roles are clear, execution is strong, and teams can confidently deliver results.

Trust and Psychological Safety

Trust is a nonnegotiable foundation for high-performing teams. It's established through honesty, transparency, and fairness. Once broken, trust is notoriously difficult to restore. That's why leaders and team members alike must safeguard it by keeping commitments, avoiding favoritism, and addressing issues promptly and equitably.

According to the 2024 *Edelman Trust Barometer*, an impressive 79 percent of employees worldwide expressed that they trust their employers, a level surpassing trust in nongovernmental organizations (NGOs) (57 percent), government (55 percent), and media (52 percent). This finding captures the profound authority and credibility that organizations hold in the minds of employees and underscores the critical role of trust within internal workplace dynamics.

Yet, trust alone is not enough. In today's workplace, psychological safety (the assurance that one can express ideas, ask questions, or admit mistakes without fear), is increasingly recognized as the most critical attribute of effective teams.

Recent global research, including studies highlighted by *Harvard Business Review* in 2024, shows that teams with high psychological safety outperform their peers by as much as 35 percent on key business metrics. These teams innovate more, retain talent longer, and maintain higher levels of engagement and resilience.

Google's Project Aristotle identified psychological safety as the number one predictor of high performance, while Microsoft's culture of growth mindset demonstrates how organizations thrive when people are encouraged to experiment, learn from failures, and share openly with colleagues.

TIP

What we learn from these and other teams that have high trust and psychological safety is that they model transparency in decision-making, ensure fair recognition and reward systems, and address breaches of trust swiftly and respectfully. Additionally, leaders invite feedback, questions, and dissenting voices in meetings, as well as modeling vulnerability themselves. And there is an investment in coaching, mentoring, and ongoing dialogue to foster psychological safety as a strategic imperative.

Healthy Conflict Resolution

When people with different experiences, perspectives, and ideas come together to solve complex challenges, disagreements are inevitable. High-performing teams recognize that conflict, when addressed constructively, can become a powerful driver of innovation, creativity, and growth. When ignored or mismanaged, it can erode trust, create division, and compromise performance. Research from CPP Global estimates that workplace conflict costs U.S. companies $359 billion annually in lost productivity, yet that same energy, if harnessed well, can strengthen collaboration and uncover solutions that might otherwise remain hidden.

REMEMBER

Healthy conflict focuses on issues rather than individuals. It directs attention toward ideas, processes, and outcomes rather than personalities or hidden agendas. It occurs in environments where psychological safety is strong, where team members feel safe to voice concerns, and where different perspectives are welcomed. (See the "Trust and Psychological Safety" section earlier in this chapter.) In these settings, conflict sharpens thinking, broadens understanding, and fosters collaboration. Unhealthy conflict, in contrast, often becomes personal, emotional, or divisive. It thrives in teams with weak trust, unclear communication, or unchecked biases, leading to resentment, disengagement, and lower performance.

Several practices help ensure conflict strengthens rather than weakens a team. Teams that establish clear ground rules for dialogue are better equipped to navigate differences. Frameworks such as "Start, Stop, Continue" allow members to raise concerns in constructive ways, creating climates where respectful challenge leads to breakthroughs and stronger bonds. This framework is a simple way of asking the following questions:

>> What new ideas, activities or behaviors should we initiate?

>> What ineffective, harmful, or unnecessary actions or behaviors should we avoid?

>> What is working well that the team should keep practicing?

Leaders who normalize disagreement and actively seek diverse perspectives reduce the stigma of conflict and reinforce that it's a healthy and necessary part of growth. Approaching differences with curiosity instead of judgment transforms conflict into a chance to learn and evolve.

TIP

Conflict is not a sign of dysfunction. When managed with respect and curiosity, it's one of the strongest indicators that a team is engaged and committed to growth.

Every team member also plays a role in sustaining healthy conflict. The following steps provide practical ways to ensure that conflict becomes a constructive force:

1. **Practice active listening.**

   Demonstrate respect by fully hearing others before responding. This reduces misunderstandings and ensures that everyone feels valued.

2. **Speak with clarity and kindness.**

   Express concerns directly but respectfully, avoiding sarcasm or accusatory language.

3. **Acknowledge emotions.**

   It's natural to feel frustrated or passionate in moments of conflict. Naming emotions can prevent them from escalating into unproductive behaviors.

4. **Seek common ground.**

   Even in disagreement, identify shared goals or values that unite the team and keep the conversation focused on collective success.

5. **Commit to follow-through.**

   After conflict is resolved, ensure that agreements are honored and next steps are carried out consistently.

WARNING

Silence should never be mistaken for harmony. In fact, silence can be a warning sign of fear, disengagement, or unresolved tension that undermines performance.

Agility and Adaptability

The pace of change in our world is not slowing down, and teams that hope to succeed must learn how to bend without breaking. Every day brings new challenges, whether it's a shift in customer expectations, the emergence of new technologies, supply chain shortages, a global pandemic, or an economic crisis. What separates high-performance teams from the rest is their ability to adapt quickly and adjust gracefully, turning uncertainty into opportunity. Teams that remain rigid or overly attached to "the way things have always been done" often struggle to keep up. On the other hand, teams that embrace agility and adaptability not only survive but thrive. They respond quickly, adjust strategies effectively, and often find opportunities hidden within challenges.

Agility refers to a team's ability to move quickly and decisively in response to new information or external pressures. Adaptability speaks to the willingness and capacity to adjust mindsets, processes, and strategies to fit changing conditions. Together, these qualities enable teams to anticipate disruption, pivot when necessary, and continue to deliver results even in uncertain times. High-performance teams excel because they treat change not as a threat but as a natural and expected part of the journey.

One powerful example of agility and adaptability can be seen in the healthcare sector. When the COVID-19 pandemic struck, hospitals and medical teams across the world were forced to reimagine their workflows, staffing models, and even their physical spaces. Teams that had already cultivated a culture of collaboration and continuous learning were able to adapt more quickly. They shifted to telemedicine, restructured emergency departments, and shared resources across networks to meet unprecedented demands. While the circumstances were extraordinary, the underlying principle was clear. Teams that embraced agility and adaptability could transform adversity into action.

TIP

To cultivate agility and adaptability, teams must first foster a mindset that sees change as opportunity. Leaders can encourage this by modeling openness, curiosity, and resilience. When leaders demonstrate that they're willing to experiment, learn from setbacks, and adjust their course, it gives permission for team members to do the same. Teams also need structures that support fast decision-making and cross-functional collaboration. Clear communication channels, defined roles, and trust among members allow them to respond swiftly without unnecessary bottlenecks.

Another key driver of agility is continuous learning. Teams that make learning a daily habit are better prepared for disruption. They invest in upskilling, embrace new technologies, and seek diverse perspectives that expand their problem-solving capacity. Adaptability also requires emotional intelligence. Teams that acknowledge stress, uncertainty, and resistance to change are better able to support one another and build resilience. Psychological safety plays an important role here, as it encourages members to voice concerns, suggest new approaches, and admit mistakes without fear of blame.

High-performance teams that master agility and adaptability are those that remain both flexible and focused. They do not resist change, nor do they chase it aimlessly. Instead, they align every adjustment with their shared purpose and long-term goals. They balance speed with thoughtful decision-making and adapt without losing sight of their values. In doing so, they stay resilient, innovative, and capable of seizing opportunities even in the midst of disruption.

Celebration and Appreciation

High-performance teams know that success is not only measured by goals achieved but also by the way those achievements are recognized and celebrated. Celebration and appreciation are more than feel-good activities. They are strategic practices that build morale, strengthen relationships, and sustain motivation over the long term. When teams pause to acknowledge their progress and express gratitude for each other's contributions, they reinforce the behaviors and values that lead to excellence.

REMEMBER

Do not wait for only big milestones to celebrate. Small wins, consistent effort, and everyday contributions matter just as much as the big ones and recognizing them helps sustain motivation and build a culture of gratitude.

Celebration can take many forms. Some teams hold regular recognition meetings where milestones are highlighted and team members are publicly thanked. Others create rituals such as ringing a bell when a project is completed, sending handwritten notes of appreciation, or sharing stories of success at the start of meetings. These moments create a culture of positivity and belonging, where individuals feel seen and valued. Even small gestures, like a shoutout on a digital platform or a thoughtful email, can have a significant impact on morale and engagement.

Appreciation is equally critical. When team members take time to recognize not only results but also the effort, creativity, and resilience that went into achieving them, it fosters trust and deepens commitment. Gratitude strengthens the bond between colleagues and reminds them that they are part of something larger than themselves. In my work with organizations, I have seen that when teams consistently practice appreciation, they experience higher engagement and lower turnover because people feel motivated to contribute their best because their contributions are acknowledged.

TIP

Make celebration timely and specific. Recognize achievements as close to the moment as possible and highlight exactly what was done well.

Chapter **4**

Detailing the Business Benefits of Exceptional Teams

The most successful leaders I've coached, consulted with, or trained over the years all share one thing in common: They didn't stumble into high performance. They cultivated it. They modeled the behaviors they wanted to see. They mastered the soft skills that build trust, inspire engagement, drive innovation, and promote a sense of belonging. Most importantly, they knew that a high-performing team doesn't just happen because you hire the smartest people. It happens because you develop the right skills, competencies, and behaviors to harness people's strengths, navigate their differences, and align them toward a shared goal.

This chapter draws on the latest research and best practices from the field to take a deep dive into the tangible business benefits that arise when organizations invest in cultivating exceptional teams.

Building Organizational Proficiency

When team members are brought together with complementary skills and empowered to collaborate, organizational proficiency soars. According to a 2023 Gallup study, companies with highly engaged teams demonstrate a 21 percent increase in profitability and a 17 percent increase in productivity compared to their peers. This is no coincidence. Teams that are aligned and well-trained can execute strategies with precision, respond effectively to change, and consistently deliver high-quality outcomes.

TIP

Proficiency is not simply about knowing how to do the job. It's about raising the level of excellence so that individuals and teams can deliver at their very best every day. High-performing teams understand that proficiency means continuously improving, adapting to new technologies, and building the interpersonal trust that allows for seamless collaboration. When this happens, the organization becomes more agile and resilient in the face of challenges.

Consider these examples of clients I've served over the years. Disney approaches proficiency through their culture of excellence. Every employee, from frontline cast members to senior executives, goes through extensive training to understand not just the technical aspects of their roles but also the company's standards of service. Disney calls this "creating magical moments." By aligning skills with a larger purpose, they increase both individual capability and collective impact. The result is an experience that has kept millions of visitors loyal to the brand for decades.

Another great example comes from Salesforce. Known for its innovation and strong team culture, Salesforce invests heavily in continuous learning through its Trailhead platform. This online learning hub equips employees with technical expertise, leadership skills, and customer engagement strategies. By democratizing learning and making it accessible to everyone, Salesforce ensures that teams are always building new competencies, closing skill gaps, and staying ahead of market changes. That level of proficiency translates into stronger customer relationships and a consistent position as a global market leader in cloud solutions.

Proficient teams also understand the importance of cross-functional collaboration. At Schreiber Foods, for example, team members from operations, logistics, and customer service come together to solve supply chain challenges. This collaborative model has allowed the company to maintain efficiency even in times of disruption, such as during the COVID-19 pandemic. Because employees were cross-trained and proficient in understanding more than just their own roles, they were able to adapt quickly and keep the business running smoothly while competitors struggled.

TIP

Invest in continuous learning and cross-training. Equip your team not only with technical skills, but also with interpersonal and leadership capabilities that enable them to thrive in today's complex environment. Consider microlearning, ongoing workshops, and rotational assignments to keep everyone's skills sharp.

One strategy that has worked for my team and a few other clients is creating "learning circles" inside the team. The team breaks into small groups that meet regularly to share insights, best practices, and lessons learned from projects and from learning assignments. The learning circles build collective intelligence and give employees ownership over their growth. They also create safe spaces for asking questions, exploring new ideas, getting to know each other in a deeper way, and accelerating proficiency at a team level rather than relying solely on individual development plans. We found that these learning circles leveraged each individual's strengths, bridged skill gaps, and fostered a culture of mutual support, respect, and belonging.

Proficiency is a journey, not a destination. It requires intentional leadership, consistent investment, and a culture that rewards curiosity and learning.

REMEMBER

Never assume that proficiency will happen on its own. It's your role to create the conditions where learning is celebrated, mistakes are treated as opportunities, and every team member feels supported in growing their skills. When you model this mindset, your team will follow your lead, and together you will elevate the entire organization's capacity to perform at a higher level.

Sparking Innovation and Continuous Growth

Innovation is the lifeblood of any organization that wants to stay relevant, competitive, and positioned for long-term success. High-performing teams are especially powerful engines of innovation because they bring together diverse backgrounds, perspectives, and experiences that serve as incubators for creative ideas and disruptive solutions. Inclusive organizations consistently outperform others in driving innovation and successfully entering new markets.

When people with different worldviews come together in an environment that values their input, groupthink is disrupted, and new possibilities emerge. Teams that embrace diversity of thought and experiences are able to brainstorm more dynamically, identify unmet needs more effectively, and craft fresh solutions that others may overlook. The most exceptional teams also provide a safe space where every voice matters, and where ideas can be tested without fear of failure.

Psychological safety is at the core of this process. I talked more about this in Chapter 3. As Dr. Amy Edmondson's research has proven, when team members feel free to take risks, share bold ideas, and challenge the status quo without the risk of ridicule or punishment, innovation becomes a natural byproduct. Leaders play a vital role here by modeling openness and curiosity, encouraging idea sharing, and creating consistent opportunities for experimentation. Regular forums such as innovation labs, hackathons, or "what if" sessions are practical ways to spark creativity and cross-pollinate ideas. Equally important is celebrating the lessons that come from failed experiments and treating them as stepping stones to breakthrough success rather than setbacks.

A global manufacturing company I worked with did this. They launched an internal Innovation Lab that invited employees from various departments (engineers, marketers, HR professionals, and customer service representatives) to collaborate on solving business challenges. The results were extraordinary. Not only did they see a 50 percent increase in patent submissions, but they also experienced a measurable boost in employee engagement. Why? Because people felt that their ideas mattered and their contributions had impact.

TIP

Leaders should never underestimate the value of simply asking questions like, "What have we never tried?" or "How might we serve our customers better if there were no limits?" These prompts open the door to creative thinking and remind teams that no idea is too small or too unconventional. In fact, some of the most successful products and services in the world began as casual, even humorous, suggestions in brainstorming sessions. Leaders must also model the behaviors they want to see by sharing their own stories of risk-taking, acknowledging when they do not have all the answers, and giving credit generously. Recognition is one of the most powerful accelerators of innovative thinking.

Finally, remember that innovation is not only about disruptive, headline-making ideas. It is just as much about the small, incremental improvements that make daily processes more effective and inclusive. Whether it's designing a better way to run meetings, creating a smarter onboarding process, or finding a new approach to developing talent, small acts of creativity can transform an organization's culture.

REMEMBER

When you empower your team to treat innovation as a habit rather than a one-time event, you begin to build a culture where every individual feels a sense of ownership and possibility. High-performing teams thrive in this environment because they know their ideas matter, their voices are valued, and their creativity fuels progress. In a world that is moving faster than ever, innovation cannot be an option. It must be the standard that drives your team forward.

Delivering Better Problem-Solving

Today's challenges rarely have simple solutions, and no single individual has all the answers. That is why the collective intelligence of a diverse team always outperforms the brilliance of any one person. Research confirms this. The World Economic Forum's 2023 *Future of Jobs Report* lists complex problem-solving as one of the most in-demand skills globally, and companies that invest in collaborative practices for problem-solving are 33 percent more likely to outperform their competitors in customer satisfaction and market agility. Likewise, a 2024 McKinsey report found that organizations that emphasize collaborative problem-solving achieve a 30 percent improvement in both the speed and quality of their solutions. In other words, collaboration is not optional; it's essential.

Exceptional teams know how to harness their diversity of thought, background, and expertise to dissect challenges and uncover root causes. They bring together different perspectives, ask probing questions, and generate a wider range of potential solutions than any one person could devise. They also lean into structured frameworks like design thinking or the Six Thinking Hats approach to ensure that every angle — logical, creative, emotional, and practical — is carefully explored.

TIP

Want to strengthen your team's collaborative problem-solving skills? Try Edward de Bono's *Six Thinking Hats* framework. It guides teams to look at problems from six distinct perspectives (for example, logic, emotion, caution, optimism, creativity, and process), helping balance analysis with innovation. You can also explore resources on *design thinking* from IDEO or the Hasso Plattner Institute of Design at Stanford University for additional hands-on tools.

From my own consulting work, I've seen the value of creating what I call "problem-solving pit stops." These are dedicated sessions where teams reflect on recently completed projects, identify what worked well, and analyze what could have been done differently. One of our healthcare clients adopted this practice through monthly "learning huddles," where leaders and frontline staff came together to share lessons learned. Over the course of a year, they achieved double-digit reductions in patient wait times while also boosting employee engagement. When organizations make learning a habit, problem-solving becomes faster, smarter, and more sustainable.

REMEMBER

It isn't enough to hire smart people and put them on a team. You must create the right environment for them to thrive — one that encourages safe spaces for dissent, structured collaboration, and a relentless focus on learning. That means assigning a "devil's advocate" to challenge assumptions, encouraging constructive dissent rather than forced consensus, and celebrating the breakthroughs that emerge when every voice is valued. When you commit to these practices, you do not just solve problems more effectively, we build stronger, more resilient organizations capable of winning in any environment.

Making More Informed Decisions

When leaders make decisions without sufficient information, they increase the risk of costly mistakes, missed opportunities, and diminished trust from their teams. On the other hand, when decisions are grounded in accurate data, diverse perspectives, and sound analysis, they inspire confidence, strengthen collaboration, and accelerate performance. High-performing teams thrive in environments where every member feels empowered to contribute insights, ask critical questions, and weigh alternatives before moving forward. This shared responsibility for making smart decisions not only improves outcomes but also deepens engagement and ownership.

To strengthen informed decision-making, leaders should start by gathering both quantitative data and qualitative input. Numbers can tell part of the story, but insights from employees, customers, and stakeholders add valuable context. Another strategy is to create a decision-making framework that includes clarifying the problem, exploring multiple solutions, evaluating risks, and anticipating long-term implications. Leaders should also build trust so that team members feel free to challenge assumptions and share honest feedback. Finally, practicing transparency by communicating the rationale behind decisions helps reinforce trust and alignment.

Informed decision-making also requires a culture that values open dialogue, constructive debate, and ongoing refinement. It isn't enough to make a decision and move on; high-performing teams continuously evaluate what works, what does not, and how they can improve the process.

WARNING

Of course, even the most talented teams must remain vigilant about unconscious biases that can cloud judgment. Leaders play a critical role in equipping their teams with the tools and frameworks that help mitigate bias and ensure fairness in decision-making. This includes documenting the rationale behind decisions so that every member understands not only what was decided but also why. That level of transparency strengthens accountability and makes implementation smoother because people are more likely to commit to a decision they helped shape and fully understand.

In the end, making more informed decisions is one of the most powerful business benefits of high-performing teams. When leaders establish clear processes, create space for dissenting voices, and foster an environment where all perspectives are valued, the team becomes more agile, more innovative, and more resilient. And when team members see their ideas, concerns, and expertise shaping the path forward, they are more engaged and more invested in the success of the organization.

Realizing Positive Customer Service Results

Exceptional teams drive exceptional customer experiences. When your employees feel connected, empowered, and valued, they bring energy and commitment to every client interaction. Research continuously underscores the direct link between strong internal teamwork and positive customer outcomes. A 2022 Gallup study revealed that businesses ranking in the top quartile for employee engagement, closely tied to team effectiveness, outperformed competitors by 21 percent in profitability and 10 percent in customer ratings. Similarly, research published in *Harvard Business Review* (2023) showed that companies with robust cross-functional teams resolved customer issues 30 percent faster and saw a 17 percent increase in repeat business compared to those with siloed departments.

Lastly, according to the 2024 American Customer Satisfaction Index, organizations with high team cohesion report a 15 percent higher customer satisfaction rating and a 22 percent reduction in service-related complaints.

Exceptional teams are quick to respond to customer needs, collaborate across functions to resolve issues, and proactively seek feedback to fuel continuous improvement. They understand that customer service is not a department; it's an attitude and a collective responsibility.

TIP

Regularly share customer success stories and testimonials with your team; not just to celebrate the win but *also* to learn from it. When teams see the real impact of their work, it reinforces purpose and strengthens their connection to the customer experience. Take time to celebrate achievements collectively, then review feedback together to identify patterns, uncover opportunities, and cocreate action plans for improvement. This practice builds trust, boosts morale, and turns customer insights into continuous performance gains.

Companies like Zappos and Ritz-Carlton exemplify the power of exceptional teams in action. Zappos, renowned for its customer-first philosophy, empowers its teams to make decisions on the spot to delight customers, resulting in an industry-leading Net Promoter Score (NPS) and consistently high customer loyalty. Ritz-Carlton, a global leader in hospitality, attributes its legendary service to the autonomy and trust it places in its teams. Every employee is authorized to spend up to $2,000 to resolve a guest issue without seeking managerial approval. This trust has cemented the brand's reputation for service excellence and driven remarkable guest satisfaction.

REMEMBER

Happy teams = happy customers. By investing in your team's well-being, you create a ripple effect that drives loyalty and business growth.

Improving Worker Retention

Exceptional teams are magnets for talent. Today's workforce, particularly the younger generations, seek organizations where they can belong, contribute meaningfully, and grow. A 2023 SHRM (Society for Human Resource Management) study found that companies with strong team cultures have 40 percent lower turnover rates than their industry average.

Team environments that foster trust, recognition, and open communication keep employees engaged and motivated. Mentorship programs, peer-to-peer recognition, and clear career progression pathways are all proven strategies to boost retention.

TIP

Leaders play a critical role by modeling inclusivity, giving regular feedback, and facilitating team bonding activities to create an environment where people want to stay and build their careers.

Google's famed Project Aristotle unearthed the key ingredients of effective teams and retaining employees, with psychological safety emerging as the most critical factor. By empowering employees to share ideas, take risks, and learn from failure without fear, Google has created a culture where innovation flourishes and people feel valued. The company's supportive team environment is further reinforced by flexible work arrangements, extensive professional development opportunities, and peer-driven feedback systems, all of which contribute to consistently low turnover and an enviably high retention rate.

Another standout example is HubSpot, renowned for its transparent culture and employee-centric policies. HubSpot invests heavily in mentorship programs, clear career growth paths, and open communication forums where every voice is heard. The company's commitment to trust and autonomy empowers teams to act swiftly and creatively in pursuit of shared goals. As a result, HubSpot enjoys one of the highest employee satisfaction scores in its industry and is regularly featured on Best Places to Work lists. These organizations demonstrate that the key to attracting and retaining top talent lies in cultivating high-performance teams where people feel connected, supported, and inspired to achieve greatness together.

TIP

Conduct regular "stay interviews" to understand what keeps your employees engaged and address concerns before they become exit interviews. One of my best bosses used to do this regularly. I didn't know what it was called at the time, but I remember leaving his office feeling seen, heard, and valued. Every few months when we had our scheduled one-on-one meetings, he wouldn't focus on the projects that I was working on. Instead, he did a check-in on how I was feeling and experiencing the organization. I later found out that he was conducting stay interviews.

A *stay interview* is a proactive conversation between a leader and an employee with the goal of understanding what motivates the employee to stay with the organization, what might cause them to leave, and what can be done to make their work experience more fulfilling. Unlike an exit interview, which happens after an employee has already decided to leave, a stay interview is forward-looking. It helps leaders build trust, strengthen engagement, and address concerns before they become retention risks. It's one of the most effective tools in a leader's toolkit for reducing turnover and creating a culture where people feel valued and heard.

Here are a few common questions leaders might ask during a stay interview:

>> What do you look forward to most when you come to work each day?

>> What talents or skills are you not using in your current role that you'd like to apply?

>> What factors might cause you to consider leaving?

>> What can I do as your leader to better support you?

>> What would make your job more enjoyable or fulfilling?

>> How do you feel about your career growth and development opportunities here?

REMEMBER

Retention is not just an HR metric; it's a reflection of the health and vibrancy of your team and organizational culture.

2

Becoming a High-Performance Leader

Discover the foundational leadership competencies you need to inspire, develop, and sustain high-performing teams.

Build advanced skills like strategic thinking, problem-solving, coaching, and mentoring.

Learn how to move from a risk-averse to a risk-ready leader and guide your team through transition with confidence.

Guide your team through each stage of the change and transition process.

Chapter 5

Developing Core Leadership Competencies

The most successful leaders I've coached, consulted with, or trained over the years all share one thing in common: They didn't stumble into high performance. They cultivated it. They modeled the behaviors they wanted to see. They mastered the core competencies that build trust, inspire engagement, and promote inclusion. This chapter unpacks what those key skills and competencies are and how you, as a leader, can develop them in yourself and your team.

Moving from Managing to Leading

Across cultures, industries, and sectors, I've met professionals who proudly say, "I've been managing teams for ten years." That's commendable but managing requires skill, precision, and discipline. When I ask, "How have you developed as a leader in those ten years?" I often get silence or a puzzled look.

That silence speaks volumes.

REMEMBER

Managing is about oversight. It's ensuring that tasks are completed, deadlines are met, and goals are achieved. Managers are often evaluated based on efficiency, order, and process compliance. And all of that matters, especially in highly regulated environments or industries where consistency is key. But *leading* is about impact. It's about creating the conditions where people can thrive, stretch, and evolve. It's about lighting a fire in someone, not just checking boxes. Leaders don't just ask, "What are we doing?" They ask, "Why does this matter? Who are we becoming as a result of it?"

In one of my global leadership workshops, a participant from Singapore shared how she'd been promoted to manage a department of 40 people after a successful run as a project analyst. Her technical skills were exceptional, and she was always on time and under budget. However, once she got into the management role, she struggled. People weren't engaged. Morale was low. Turnover spiked. She said, "I thought I was doing everything right. But I realized that I was managing tasks, not leading people."

That realization is critical. What got you the promotion (your ability to *do*) is not what will make you successful at the next level. That requires learning to *empower* others to do and become more. You can be a great manager and a poor leader. You can also be a strong leader without having a formal title. Leadership is not confined to org charts. It's about behavior, mindset, and influence.

In Table 5-1, I make this distinction even clearer.

TABLE 5-1   **Managers versus Leaders**

Managers	Leaders
Maintain systems and status quo	Drive change and challenge the norm
Focus on tasks and processes	Focus on people and purpose
Rely on control and supervision	Inspire, coach, and empower
Solve problems in the moment	Anticipate the future and guide toward it
Seek compliance	Cultivate commitment

TIP

If you're spending most of your time in your inbox, reviewing status updates, and solving every small issue yourself, you're likely managing. If you're spending time developing your people, aligning around a vision, and shaping culture, you're leading.

Managers control, leaders cultivate

One of the most powerful shifts a professional can make is moving from control to cultivation. Managers often feel the need to control outcomes. They monitor, they correct, they approve every detail. But leaders focus on building capacity in others to deliver results on their own.

Here's an example of onboarding. A manager may check the box that new hire orientation was completed. A leader ensures that onboarding is a welcoming, inclusive, and inspiring experience that communicates the team's culture and values. The difference is getting someone *ready to work* rather than getting someone *excited to contribute.*

The difference between managing and leading plays out across every touchpoint (for example, how meetings are run, how decisions are made, how accountability is handled). In fact, studies across multinational companies have shown that teams led by people who demonstrate strong leadership behaviors, not just managerial attributes, report higher engagement, lower turnover, and greater innovation.

WARNING

If your team only performs when you're present, you're probably managing them. If they perform regardless of whether you're in the room, you've likely been leading them.

Leaders set the culture

Another critical distinction between managers and leaders is that managers may reinforce a company's culture, but leaders define it. Leaders set the culture regardless of whether they mean to.

Whether you lead a global department, a regional office, or a small project team, your behaviors set the tone. If you lead with transparency, you encourage honesty. If you lead with fear, you breed silence. If you lead with compassion, you foster loyalty. Every tone you set becomes a signal to your team of what is acceptable, expected, and valued.

As I often teach in my LinkedIn Learning courses, culture is not just what's on your wall; it's what walks down your hall. It's how people feel at the end of the meeting. It's how inclusive your decision-making is. It's the consistency between your actions and your words.

You don't need to have "Chief" in your title to influence culture. Leaders exist at every level of an organization — and so does their impact.

REMEMBER

The best teams don't follow leaders because they *have to.* They follow leaders because they *want to.* That difference is earned through credibility, consistency, and care.

Getting Clear on Purpose and Vision

One of the biggest differences between a manager and a leader is that leaders are anchored by a deep sense of purpose and a clear vision for the future. Managers can be highly skilled at overseeing tasks and meeting deadlines, but leaders operate from a bigger "why" and a compelling "where." They know what they stand for, where they're headed, and how to bring others along with them.

Effective leadership starts with leading yourself. Before you can inspire, guide, or influence others, you must be clear about who you are, why you exist, and what destination you are moving toward. In my work with leaders around the world, I have seen that this requires two essential anchors: purpose and vision.

Purpose

Purpose is knowing who you are and why you exist. It's the anchor that guides your decisions, shapes your behavior, and fuels your energy when challenges arise. It's your personal and professional "why," the reason you show up each day, the reason your team exists, and the reason your organization matters. Purpose not only helps you navigate the complexities of leadership, but it also inspires the people you lead.

My purpose statement is very clear: *To transform organizations and empower individuals by helping them to get a larger vision for themselves and to become a better version of who they are.* This purpose guides how I design my programs, choose my partnerships, and lead my teams. It reminds me that my role is not just about producing results but about unlocking potential in others and leaving a lasting impact.

A purpose-driven leader does not simply assign tasks; they connect the dots between each person's role and the greater mission. Instead of saying, "We need to hit this month's targets," they might say, "We are here to make a positive difference, to innovate in ways that create lasting value, and to be known for our integrity and excellence." That shift changes everything, moving work from a list of deliverables to a meaningful pursuit.

Vision

Vision is knowing where you want to go and who you want to become. It's the mental picture of your desired future, whether that is three, five, or ten years ahead. Vision provides clarity about what success looks like and directs your attention to the present actions needed to get there. If purpose is your "why," vision is your "where," and together they form a leadership compass that keeps you and your team moving forward with intention.

Here is my vision statement: *Be a world-renowned global thought leader who delivers transformational value in the areas of organizational leadership, high performance, and personal reinvention.* This vision keeps me focused not only on what I want to achieve but on the type of leader I need to be every day to move toward that future. It influences the opportunities I pursue, the skills I develop, and the relationships I cultivate.

The most effective visions are not vague aspirations like "Let's be the best." They're vivid, specific, and inclusive. They describe a destination people can see, feel, and get excited about. For example, *We will be recognized as the most trusted and innovative organization in our field, known for our diverse talent, collaborative culture, and exceptional results that benefit our communities.* A vision like this pulls people forward, especially during tough seasons, because it reminds them of the greater possibilities ahead.

REMEMBER

Purpose and vision statements cannot be written once and then forgotten. They must be lived daily. They show up in your actions, in the way you run meetings, in the goals you set, and in how you treat your people. When purpose and vision are consistent, they create trust, engagement, and a sense of belonging on the team.

Developing Your Purpose and Vision Statements

Purpose and vision are your leadership GPS. They tell you why you do what you do and where you're headed, giving you clarity for decisions, direction for action, and inspiration for your team. Creating them involves three steps:

1. **Identify your purpose.**
2. **Define your vision.**
3. **Make them actionable.**

Use the guide in the following sections to write your purpose and vision statements so you can lead with intention and confidence.

Identify your purpose

Your purpose answers the question, "Why do I exist as a leader?"

Reflect:

>> What motivates me to lead beyond a paycheck or title?

>> What positive difference do I want to make in the lives of others?

>> What strengths and passions do I bring that can transform people or organizations?

Write your purpose statement:

_____

_____

_____

Define your vision

Your vision answers the question, "Where am I going and what do I want to become?"

Reflect:

>> In three, five, or ten years, what do I want my leadership legacy to be?

>> What will success look like for my team, my organization, and myself?

>> How do I want to be recognized or remembered as a leader?

Write your vision statement:

_____

_____

_____

Make them actionable

Once you have your purpose and vision, integrate them into your daily leadership:

>> **Communicate:** Share them with your team and explain why they matter.

>> **Align:** Set goals and priorities that move you toward your vision.

>> **Live it:** Model behaviors and decisions that reflect your purpose every day.

Commitment prompt: One way I will live my purpose and vision this month is

_____

Purpose and vision are not meant to sit in a drawer. Revisit them regularly, adapt them as you grow, and let them guide both big decisions and small daily actions.

Modeling Integrity and Ethical Decision-Making

Leadership isn't just about having a title or making big-picture decisions. It's about being someone others can trust and respect.

So, what does this look like in practice? It means being honest and transparent in your communications. When you make a mistake, own it. When you don't know an answer, admit it and commit to finding out. Integrity isn't about being perfect; it's about being authentic and accountable.

Ethical decision-making is equally essential. It's easy to do the right thing when it's convenient, but true leadership shows up when the stakes are high or the path isn't clear. Before you decide, pause and reflect: Is this aligned with our values? How will this impact our team, organization, and community? Who might be affected, and what would I want if I were in their shoes?

Here are a few practical ways you can model integrity and ethical leadership each day:

>> **Lead by example:** Whether you're honoring commitments or treating everyone with respect, let your actions set the standard.

>> **Speak up:** Don't shy away from difficult conversations. If something doesn't feel right, raise the concern with a solutions-focused mindset.

>> **Prioritize fairness:** Make decisions using consistent criteria. Avoid favoritism and explain your reasoning when possible.

>> **Be courageous:** Sometimes, doing the right thing isn't popular. Stand firm on your values, even when it's uncomfortable.

REMEMBER

Integrity is like a muscle; the more you use it, the stronger it gets. When you consistently model ethical behavior, you not only earn trust, but you inspire those around you to step up and do the same. And that's the kind of leadership that transforms teams, organizations, and yes, even the world.

So, as you reflect on your purpose and vision, ask yourself, "How can I model integrity in my leadership journey this week?" Write down one specific action you'll take and then go do it! Your example matters more than you may ever know.

Your team, peers, and colleagues are always watching how you respond in moments of challenge, ambiguity, and even success. Modeling integrity means that your actions consistently align with your principles, even when no one else is looking.

Cultivating Trust and Psychological Safety on the Team

High-performing teams do three things consistently:

>> Learn faster than the problem changes

>> Coordinate work with minimal friction

>> Spot risk early so quality improves

Trust and psychological safety make all three possible. When people expect candor and care, they share information quickly, ask for help sooner, and challenge assumptions before a decision hardens. Energy that would have gone into self-protection gets redeployed into execution.

Trust is confidence in the character and competence of leaders and teammates. Psychological safety is the shared belief that the team is safe for interpersonal risk-taking (for example, asking questions, admitting mistakes, offering bold ideas, and debating direction). You need both: Trust anchors the people and safety sets the climate; performance is the result.

REMEMBER

Safety is not about being nice. It's about enabling candor, speed of learning, and higher standards.

According to Dr. Timothy Clark, author of *The 4 Stages of Psychological Safety* (Berrett-Koehler Publishers, 2020), each stage meets a basic human need and unlocks stronger performance:

» **Inclusion safety:** People feel accepted and respected so they can show up as themselves Make belonging the default. Set clear norms for respect, ban demeaning humor, and invite people to bring relevant parts of their identity and strengths to the work. Try these things:

- Open every project with a round of personal strengths and hidden skills relevant to the mission.

- Name and stop interruptions.

- Rotate facilitation and note-taking to balance voice and influence.

» **Learner safety:** Questions, feedback, first-time mistakes, and experiments are treated as part of growth and normalized. Provide specific, timely feedback and create low-risk practice fields. Try these things:

- Use dry runs, simulations, and peer reviews before launch.

- Debrief weekly with short retros focused on insights, not blame.

» **Contributor safety:** Individuals are trusted to apply their strengths, take ownership, and shape real work. Invite people to apply strengths beyond their job titles. Design interdependent work so collaboration is required, not optional.

- Uncover hidden talents — languages, domains, tools — and align them to workstreams.

- Share credit publicly; tie recognition to behaviors that reinforce team norms.

» **Challenger safety:** Allows people to question assumptions and propose better ways without fear of retaliation. Protect the right to question direction. Separate dissent from disrespect and reward well-reasoned challenges.

- Ask explicitly, "What are we missing? Who disagrees and why?"

- Model humility. Change your mind in public when evidence warrants it.

As teams progress through these stages, they learn faster, innovate more, and surface risks sooner — all hallmarks of high performance.

RECOGNIZING BEST PRACTICE COMPANIES

Organizations that institutionalize trust and safety embed these principles in strategy, systems, and stories. Here are four examples to adapt to your context.

- **Pixar, "Fail early and often":** Pixar's creative culture reframes mistakes as essential learning. Phrases like "fail fast" and "be wrong as soon as you can" encourage rapid experimentation and candid critique. Contributor and challenger safety are designed into the process, which keeps ideas flowing and quality rising.

- **Eileen Fisher, "Leadership is about listening":** Founder Eileen Fisher models deep listening and flexible agendas so real issues surface. Curiosity over control helps teams balance focus with adaptability and creates space for authentic voices.

- **Barry-Wehmiller, "What we do matters":** The company's people-centric leadership philosophy treats dignity as a design requirement. Leaders are taught to care tangibly. This includes recognizing contributions, coaching with empathy, and making decisions that honor both performance and people. Trust becomes the operating system.

- **X Development (Moonshots), "Aim for 10X":** X normalizes audacious goals and fast learning cycles. Teams fall in love with problems, test early in the real world, and celebrate learning — even when ideas are retired. These norms require and reinforce contributor and challenger safety.

REMEMBER

If even one person feels unsafe, the team's learning speed drops to the pace of the least-safe member.

REMEMBER

Trust and psychological safety are not soft extras. They are the hard edge of execution and the heartbeat of high-performance teams. Build them deliberately, measure them consistently, and protect them relentlessly.

Leaders cannot mandate safety; they must model it and reinforce it until it becomes habit. Here is a list of 10 proven practices that I use as a team leader and that I recommend to all leaders. Which do you practice consistently and effectively?

>> Tell the truth, especially when it's hard. Explain the "why" behind decisions and trade-offs.

>> Keep promises and when you can't, repair fast — notify early, apologize, and offer remedies.

>> Respond productively to errors: Separate intent from impact, correct issues, and protect dignity.

>> Start meetings with a 60-second scan for risks, blockers, and help needed; solve the biggest constraint first.

>> Invite the quietest voices first. Use round robins or written inputs to level airtime.

>> Replace blame with curiosity by asking "What made the right action hard?" and "What would make the right action easy?"

>> Make learning visible. Share your own mistakes and what you changed because of them.

>> Institutionalize feedback with monthly one-on-ones, peer feedback circles, and quarterly retros with decisions tracked.

>> Design for inclusion by rotating stretch assignments, pairing mentors across difference, and auditing recognition patterns.

>> Reward challenges that improve outcomes, even when they slow things down today to speed them up tomorrow.

TIP

When emotions spike, lower the temperature with questions. Curiosity is the shortest path back to problem-solving.

Demonstrating Emotional Intelligence and Empathy

If you want to lead a high-performing team, your technical skills and expertise will only get you so far. What really sets great leaders apart is their ability to connect with, inspire, and bring out the best in their people. That comes down to emotional intelligence.

Emotional intelligence, often called EQ, is your ability to recognize, regulate, and express your own emotions, while also being aware of and sensitive to the emotions of others. It's about managing yourself well in every situation and creating the kind of environment where others feel valued, understood, and motivated to contribute their best.

When leaders strengthen their EQ, they do more than manage projects or meet deadlines. They create teams where trust runs deep, communication is open, and challenges are met with resilience rather than resistance. And that is the kind of team that consistently performs at the highest levels.

Psychologist Daniel Goleman identifies five key components of emotional intelligence. The next sections explore them through the lens of leadership and high-performing teams.

Self-awareness

Self-awareness is knowing yourself well enough to understand how your emotions impact your behavior and your decisions. It's being aware of your triggers, your strengths, and where you have room to grow.

For leaders, self-awareness means you don't let a bad meeting or a tough email spill over into how you treat your team. It also means you are willing to listen when others point out blind spots and you view feedback as a gift, not a threat.

Actions to strengthen self-awareness:

>> Take a few moments each day to check in with yourself. Notice how you feel and why.

>> Keep a leadership journal to reflect on how you handle situations and what you might do differently next time.

>> Own your reactions. If you lose your cool, acknowledge it, apologize, and use it as a learning moment.

>> Celebrate your wins and growth. Recognizing progress builds your confidence and models self-reflection for your team.

Self-regulation

High-performing teams thrive in environments where leaders stay composed under pressure. Self-regulation is your ability to remain calm, adapt to change, and respond rather than react.

When you can regulate your emotions, your team feels safe bringing you bad news or offering an honest opinion. They trust that you will hear them out and respond thoughtfully, even in stressful moments.

Here are some actions to strengthen self-regulation:

>> Develop healthy outlets for stress. Exercise, meditate, laugh, rest, or find a space that recharges you. For me, it's the beach.

>> Pause before responding when emotions are high. Even a few deep breaths can help you choose your words carefully.

>> Pick your battles. Focus your energy on what matters most to the team's success.

>> Use a trusted peer or mentor as a sounding board before making big decisions in the heat of the moment.

Motivation

Motivated leaders inspire motivated teams. Motivation in the context of EQ is about knowing your "why" and acting in alignment with it. It's about staying focused and optimistic, even when things get tough.

When leaders demonstrate genuine passion for their work and commitment to the team's purpose, it creates contagious energy. That energy fuels perseverance, creativity, and a willingness to go the extra mile.

You can take these actions to strengthen motivation:

>> Keep your team connected to the "why" behind their work. Help them see the impact of what they do.

>> Set meaningful goals for yourself and your team and hold each other accountable.

>> Model a growth mindset. Treat setbacks as opportunities to learn and improve.

>> Encourage curiosity and continuous learning. The best teams are made up of people who are always growing.

Empathy

Empathy is the ability to truly understand and care about what others are experiencing. For leaders, empathy builds trust, strengthens loyalty, and creates a culture where people feel safe to share ideas and concerns.

When you lead with empathy, you do not just hear your team, you listen to understand. You see situations from their perspective, and you respond in ways that show you value their experiences and contributions.

Use these actions to strengthen empathy:

>> Take time to get to know your team members beyond their job titles.

>> Practice active listening. Give your full attention, ask clarifying questions, and avoid interrupting.

>> Assume positive intent before jumping to conclusions.

>> Keep an open-door policy so people feel comfortable approaching you with both opportunities and challenges.

Social skills

Social skills are how you put emotional intelligence into action. They're about building relationships, communicating clearly, resolving conflicts fairly, and creating a sense of belonging on the team.

Leaders with strong social skills know how to bring out the best in different personalities. They can navigate disagreements in a way that strengthens rather than strains relationships, and they make recognition a regular practice.

Here are some actions to strengthen social skills:

>> Be mindful of your tone, body language, and facial expressions. They communicate just as much as your words.

>> Learn from leaders who excel in relationship building. Observe their approach and adapt it to your style.

>> Expand your network inside and outside your organization to bring in fresh perspectives.

>> Recognize and celebrate the contributions of your team members often and sincerely.

Every high-performing team has one thing in common: a leader who knows how to connect with people. When you practice self-awareness, regulate your emotions, stay motivated, lead with empathy, and sharpen your social skills, you create the kind of environment where individuals feel seen, supported, and inspired to excel.

Emotional intelligence is not just about being "nice" or "understanding." It's a strategic leadership skill that directly impacts performance, retention, and results. If you want to elevate your team, start by elevating your EQ.

Chapter **6**

Advanced Skills and Strategic Behaviors for High Performance

The pace of change in today's workplace is faster than ever before. Leaders and teams are navigating shifting markets, disruptive technologies, evolving workforce expectations, and increasing pressure to deliver results with fewer resources. In this environment, simply managing day-to-day tasks is no longer enough. To thrive, leaders must upskill their approach and model strategic behaviors that inspire confidence, build resilience, and drive sustainable success.

Chapter 5 covers foundational skills. This chapter focuses on the advanced capabilities and competencies that distinguish average teams from truly great ones. By the end of this chapter, you will gain practical strategies for applying these capabilities to create a culture of excellence and high performance.

Mastering Strategic Thinking and Problem-Solving

Do you have the ability to paint a picture of the future? To offer ideas that will solve complex problems and set goals that achieve business results? And can you convey your ideas in a clear, concise, and compelling way that invokes buy-in, followship, and action?

If you answered yes, then you are demonstrating strategic thinking skills. At the heart of strategic thinking lies effective problem-solving for teams.

When it comes to leading a high-performance team, strategic thinking is a non-negotiable skill. In today's fast-paced business environment, team members are looking for leaders who possess vision, know how to deliver results, and understand the intricacies of their industry. But vision alone is not enough. Teams thrive with leaders who leverage strategic thought to solve problems collaboratively, turning obstacles into opportunities for growth. These leaders are committed to achieving outstanding outcomes and have the ability to inspire and guide their teams with clarity and purpose, especially when confronting complex challenges.

Strategic thinking involves the ability to envision the future and the art of formulating and executing strategies that position an organization for success in the long run. It goes beyond day-to-day problem-solving and focuses on shaping the future. However, developing effective solutions for immediate problems is also a vital building block of strategic leadership, especially when teams are involved. Leaders must foster an environment where team problem-solving is not only encouraged but expected, empowering every member to contribute their ideas and expertise to address emerging issues.

KPMG's 2023 *CEO Outlook* found that 92 percent of leaders believe strategic thinking is more important now than five years ago, especially in a world buffeted by rapid change and uncertainty. This finding underscores the need for leaders to integrate problem-solving into their strategic approach, ensuring that teams can adapt and innovate together. Here are some suggestions for practical steps for problem-solving:

>> Block out regular time for reflection and planning.

>> Set measurable goals aligned with broader organizational vision.

>> Encourage scenario planning and "what-if" exercises.

>> Foster a culture of curiosity; ask "why" and "what else?" often.

And here is some good news — This skill for strategic thinking and problem-solving can be developed by every leader at every level! In addition to KPMG's suggested steps, I suggest these steps to develop and demonstrate this skill:

1. **Start by surrounding yourself with individuals who are more experienced, knowledgeable, and successful within your organization or industry.**

   Observe how they approach challenges and opportunities, pay close attention to how they solve problems, and listen to the wisdom they share. By doing so, you create an environment where learning and growth are continuous, and where your perspective can expand beyond what you already know.

2. **Commit to thorough data gathering.**

   Dive into the details of the challenges your team faces and seek to understand the context behind any issues. Immerse yourself in the organization's vision, mission, and strategic operating plan, and consider the external forces that influence your work. The more informed you are, the more effectively you can generate ideas that are aligned with the goals of the team and that promote forward movement.

3. **In meetings, do not hesitate to ask thoughtful questions.**

   Strive for a deeper understanding of the matters at hand and evaluate the potential long-term and short-term impacts of decisions. Invite alternative viewpoints, especially those that challenge your thinking. This process not only broadens your perspective but strengthens your ability to anticipate trends and make informed, wise choices.

4. **Practice expressing your thoughts clearly, confidently, and passionately, so that your team feels energized and united in pursuit of common goals.**

   Communication, both verbal and nonverbal, is a pillar of strategic leadership. Having great ideas is only the beginning; articulating them in a way that inspires commitment and drives action is what sets high-performance leaders apart.

Take some time for honest reflection. Consider which of these steps you're already proficient in and where you have room to grow. Make a commitment to focus on those areas that will help close the gap and elevate your leadership effectiveness.

REMEMBER

Strategic thinking is not only a top-down approach needed at the executive ranks. It's a key skill set required at all leadership levels.

APPLYING STRATEGIC THINKING TO GLOBAL EXPANSION

I was working for a company that wanted to expand its global footprint to a number of European, African, and Asian countries. They assembled a task force to develop a growth strategy for how to successfully accomplish this objective. I was asked to serve on this task force as one who could bring HR/leadership development expertise and be sure that the talent and workplace culture lens was applied.

So, if you were asked to serve on this task force, how would you apply strategic thinking to help develop this global growth for your company?

The way that I tackled this project was first to understand several key questions:

- **Where are we now?** This involved a comprehensive analysis of the current state of the organization by conducting a SWOT (strengths, weaknesses, opportunities, and threats) analysis. As the HR expert, I reviewed employee data, trends, and the state of our workplace culture.

- **Where do we want to go?** Why are we expanding, and what's the end game? In my HR role, that meant understanding what skills and competencies were going to be needed and what were the demographics, culture, laws, languages, and norms so that we could secure the right talent, resources, policies, and programs to operate in each country in an inclusive and respectful way.

- **How will we get there?** I offered tactical steps and actions that would be needed from an HR perspective and presented them in both short-term and long-term activities.

- **What obstacles might we encounter, and how can we overcome them?** With my HR hat on, I thought about how this would impact every employee, what challenges and resistance we might get, and I devised response plans as well as contingency plans to address them.

I also benchmarked current business and industry trends. I studied the company's top five competitors to uncover what they were doing successfully, and I incorporated those findings into my recommendations.

Additionally, I did some scenario planning, which is a key tool for strategic planning. As the HR advisor, I was able to provide real-world employee scenarios that could occur regarding recruitment, pay, promotions, work schedules, violations of country laws, and, most importantly, workplace culture variations. It's been my experience that culture misalignment is one of the biggest obstacles to successful mergers, acquisitions, and expansion into other countries. All of these steps are what you can do to develop your strategic thinking from the role, position, or expertise you hold.

Providing Feedback, Coaching, and Mentoring

Coaching, mentoring, and giving feedback are not just "nice to have" skills for leaders; they're among the most powerful ways to harness the full potential of a diverse workforce. When done well, they boost employee engagement, drive productivity, strengthen retention, and foster a culture where people feel seen, heard, and valued. They also send a clear message: Your growth matters here.

I know this firsthand because early in my career, as a young, single woman of color, I had big dreams and the drive to climb the corporate ladder. I worked hard, delivered results, and consistently earned high marks in my performance reviews. But too often, I found myself being overlooked, undervalued, and passed over for promotions.

In several companies, I was even labeled a "high-potential employee" and "high performer," yet I was not given clear direction, constructive feedback, or the targeted coaching and mentoring I needed to advance, at least not as quickly as some of my male counterparts. It was frustrating and disheartening. And it was a missed opportunity for those organizations. They had someone on their team who was committed to going above and beyond, loved by clients, getting results, and eager to take on more complex and challenging assignments, yet they did not leverage me.

Unfortunately, my story is not unique. Many leaders avoid giving feedback, coaching, or mentoring because they feel unprepared, don't know how to approach it, or fear it will be uncomfortable. But the truth is, avoiding these practices costs organizations talent, innovation, and trust.

If you want to be the kind of leader who inspires growth and maximizes your team's potential, you must lean into this responsibility with both skill and sincerity. The next sections cover six strategies to help you do that.

Build trust and a deeper connection

Before you can coach or mentor effectively, you must earn the right to do so. People will not truly hear your feedback unless they believe you have their best interests at heart.

That means investing the time to get to know your team members beyond their job titles. Ask about their career aspirations, their passions, and even the challenges they face outside of work. Show genuine curiosity. Practice active listening, rather than just waiting for your turn to speak, by really hearing and understanding their perspective. Demonstrate empathy when they share a struggle.

When your team members know that you see them as people first, they're far more likely to receive your coaching and mentoring with an open mind and to act on it. Trust turns feedback from criticism into a gift.

Understand cultural context

Culture influences how people give, receive, and respond to feedback. Some cultures value direct, to-the-point conversations, whereas others view such an approach as abrasive. Some employees may expect regular check-ins, and others might interpret frequent feedback as a sign of poor performance.

As a leader, it's your responsibility to learn the communication styles, norms, and values of your diverse team. Ask questions. Seek to understand before making assumptions. Be aware of cultural holidays, traditions, and work styles. This awareness allows you to frame your coaching and mentoring in ways that feel respectful and inclusive, so your message is heard rather than resisted.

When you understand the cultural lens through which feedback is received, you can adapt your approach and avoid misunderstandings that damage trust.

Tailor feedback to individual needs

In the same way that no two fingerprints are alike, no two workers have the exact same development needs or learning styles.

Some people thrive with immediate, direct feedback. Others need time to process before they can act. Some respond best to public praise and private correction, whereas others may be motivated by having their wins celebrated in front of the team.

Pay attention to what makes each person tick. Notice how they respond in different situations. And when you coach or mentor, frame your feedback in a way that connects to their personal goals, strengths, and opportunities for growth.

Customized coaching and mentoring tell employees, "I see you. I understand how you operate. And I am committed to helping you succeed in your own way."

Deliver feedback with clarity and compassion

Feedback that's vague, overly critical, or sugar-coated is not helpful. Employees need to know exactly what they're doing well, what needs improvement, and how to bridge the gap. Be specific. Instead of saying, "You need to communicate better," you could say, "In last week's meeting, I noticed your updates were brief but lacked details on timelines and next steps. Including that information will help the team align more quickly."

Clarity gives employees something tangible to work with, while compassion ensures they do not feel attacked. Use a respectful and encouraging tone, and balance constructive points with recognition of what they're already doing well. This creates a safe space for honest dialogue and inspires the person to act on your feedback rather than shut down.

Make coaching and mentoring a consistent practice

Coaching and mentoring are not once-a-year events during the performance review cycle. They should be ongoing processes woven into your regular interactions. Short, timely conversations often have more impact than lengthy formal sessions that happen only occasionally.

Look for teachable moments in everyday work. If a team member does something well, acknowledge it immediately so the behavior is reinforced. If they make a mistake, address it as soon as possible so they can correct it and learn from the experience.

Consistency sends the message that development is a priority. It also helps to normalize feedback, so it becomes a regular part of the work culture, rather than something people dread or associate only with problems.

Hold people accountable while inspiring growth

The most effective coaching and mentoring strike a balance between support and accountability. Your role is to equip people with the tools, resources, and encouragement they need to succeed while also setting clear expectations and measuring progress.

Follow up on the feedback you give. Ask about progress, offer additional guidance when needed, and acknowledge improvements. When someone falls short, address it with firmness and fairness. Let them know you believe in their potential but that results matter, and everyone is expected to contribute at a high level. When employees feel both supported and challenged, they're more likely to stretch beyond their comfort zones, build new skills, and achieve higher levels of performance.

REMEMBER

Coaching, mentoring, and giving feedback are not optional for leaders who want to lead high-performing, engaged, and inclusive teams. They require intentionality, cultural awareness, consistency, and the courage to have honest conversations.

TIP

When you commit to mastering these skills, you're not just improving performance, but you're also shaping careers, strengthening trust, and building a legacy as a leader who truly invests in people. And in today's competitive and fast-changing workplace, that is the kind of leadership that wins every time.

Showing Empathy in Words and Actions

Imagine this. You're leading a virtual team meeting when you notice one of your high performers has their camera off for the third week in a row. Their normally vibrant voice is flat, and their contributions are minimal. After the meeting, you reach out to check in, and they share that they've been caring for an aging parent whose health is rapidly declining. They're exhausted, emotionally drained, and worried about falling behind at work.

In that moment, you have a choice: You can either keep the conversation strictly about deadlines and deliverables, or you can lean into one of the most powerful skills you can possess as a leader — empathy. And here's why empathy matters: the way you respond in moments like this directly impacts trust, morale, and ultimately the performance of your team.

For years, empathy was treated as a "soft skill" and a nice gesture rather than a measurable driver of business success, but times have changed. Research from *CEO World Magazine* and *Forbes* confirms that empathy now ranks among the most important leadership skills, and it's directly tied to better outcomes such as higher engagement, stronger collaboration, greater innovation, and reduced turnover.

In my firm's work over the past five years, we've conducted nearly 100 organizational assessments, focus groups, and listening sessions. One theme consistently rises to the top: *We want our leaders to demonstrate more empathy.*

This is not a generational preference or a passing workplace trend; empathy is a performance accelerator. When leaders fail to acknowledge the human side of work, engagement drops, collaboration falters, and innovation slows. But when leaders take time to truly understand their people, they create the trust and psychological safety that high-performance teams depend on.

What empathy looks like in leadership

Empathy is more than feeling sorry for someone. It's the ability to understand and value another person's perspective and their lived experience, and the ability to respond in ways that demonstrate that understanding. It's active, intentional, and often transformative for team performance.

Consider these real scenarios and in the spaces provided write out how you have responded/would respond.

Scenario 1: A team member loses a loved one after a long illness.

_____

_____

My response: "I am so sorry for your loss. I can only imagine how difficult this must be for you personally and professionally. I'm here to support you in any way I can."

This may seem simple, but it sends a clear message: _You matter to me beyond the work you produce._ In high-performance teams, that message builds loyalty and inspires discretionary effort once the employee is ready to return fully.

Scenario 2: Engagement survey results reveal employees feel overlooked and undervalued.

In a team meeting, how do you respond:

_____

_____

I coached my client to say: "I appreciate your honesty in letting us know we can do a better job of making sure you feel heard, valued, and appreciated. We're putting plans in place to close this gap, and we'd love your input to make it happen."

By inviting their ideas and involving them in the solution, you strengthen ownership and collaboration which are two non negotiables for sustained high performance.

Practical tips for demonstrating empathy every day

Empathy isn't limited to people in leadership roles. It's a skill that every team member can demonstrate in everyday interactions. Here are a few simple tips for how to do that:

TIP

>> **Listen to understand, not to reply:** In high-performance teams, listening is a competitive advantage. When someone shares a concern, give them your full attention. Ask clarifying questions, paraphrase what you've heard, and resist the urge to jump straight to solutions. Your goal is not just to hear the words, but to understand the emotions behind them. This deep listening not only validates the person but also surfaces insights that can improve team processes and outcomes.

>> **Acknowledge and follow through:** Empathy without action can feel performative. If a team member expresses a challenge, whether it's burnout, feeling unheard, or needing resources, leaders should acknowledge it in the moment and then follow through with tangible steps. Maybe it's adjusting timelines, redistributing workload, or arranging additional training. In high-performance cultures, leaders close the loop so employees see that their concerns lead to real change.

>> **Become familiar with the personal drivers of each team member:** Every high-performance team is made up of individuals with unique motivations, values, strengths, and challenges. Make time to find out what matters most to each person. You can do this through one-on-one meetings, informal check-ins, or team-building exercises. When you understand what drives someone, you can tailor your communication, recognition, and support in ways that maximize their contributions.

>> **Show empathy during change and uncertainty:** Periods of organizational change can rattle even the most resilient teams. Use empathy to keep performance from slipping. Acknowledge the discomfort, be transparent about what you know and don't know, and involve your team in problem-solving. This not only helps people adapt but also keeps morale high when you need it most.

>> **Model empathy for the team:** When leaders consistently show empathy, it becomes part of the team culture. Encourage peers to support one another, celebrate small wins, and check in on each other. In high-performance teams,

empathy flows laterally as well as from the top down, strengthening the sense of belonging and shared accountability.

>> **Check in when a team member seems disengaged:** If a team member seems unusually quiet during meetings or hesitant to share ideas, check in privately to see how they're doing. Ask open-ended questions like, "How are you feeling about the project?" or "Is there anything getting in the way of your work?" Listening without judgment and offering support — whether it's clarifying expectations or looping them into discussions — shows that you value their voice and well-being.

>> **Offer support when a colleague is overwhelmed:** If a colleague appears overwhelmed by deadlines or juggling multiple priorities, offer to collaborate on a task, share helpful resources, or simply acknowledge their effort. Saying, "I can tell you've been putting in a lot of work — how can I help lighten the load?" can go a long way in building trust and demonstrating empathy through action.

Leveraging Artificial Intelligence and Advanced Technology

In today's fast-paced and digitally connected world, the leaders who build and sustain high-performance teams are those who embrace, not resist, technology. We are in the midst of the Fourth Industrial Revolution, where artificial intelligence (AI), machine learning, automation, and other advanced technologies are reshaping how we live, work, and lead.

The leaders who master the integration of AI and advanced technology into their team strategy will gain a competitive advantage, whereas those who lag behind risk becoming irrelevant. Moreover, leveraging technology for high performance is not about replacing people with machines. It's about using technology to enhance human capability, amplify creativity, improve decision-making, and free up time for higher-value work.

I have experienced firsthand how AI can transform everything from hiring decisions to strategic planning to personalized coaching. It takes a leader who is willing to lean in, learn the language, understand the possibilities, and develop and lead their teams to high performance.

The following sections explore what this looks like in practice and identify the many ways that leaders are utilizing AI.

REMEMBER

Your team will model your attitude toward AI. If you show curiosity and openness, they will follow your lead.

Understanding AI in the context of leadership

Artificial intelligence is, at its core, the simulation of human intelligence processes by machines, including learning, reasoning, problem-solving, and decision-making. It isn't a futuristic fantasy anymore; it's already embedded in our daily lives. When your phone suggests the fastest route home, that's AI. When Netflix recommends your next binge-worthy series, that's AI. And when your HR software predicts which employees are at risk of burnout, that's also AI.

For leaders, the question is not "Should I use AI?" but "How can I use AI responsibly and strategically to make my team more effective?" High-performance teams thrive on clarity, agility, and innovation, and AI, when integrated thoughtfully, accelerates all three.

REMEMBER

It's important to dispel the myths. AI isn't a magical silver bullet, and it won't replace the need for human leadership, emotional intelligence, or ethical decision-making. Instead, think of AI as a powerful partner that can enhance, not erase, the human element.

The leader's role in an AI-enhanced workplace

In an AI-driven environment, leaders wear several hats: visionary, translator, strategist, and coach:

>> **As a leader, you must paint a clear picture for your team of why AI adoption matters.** People don't buy into technology; they buy into purpose. Connect the dots between AI and the team's goals, and show them how AI can remove roadblocks, improve processes, and create opportunities for growth.

>> **Become AI-literate yourself.** You don't need to be a data scientist, but you do need to understand enough about AI's capabilities and limitations to make informed choices. This means keeping up with trends, learning the basic terminology, and asking smart questions of your tech partners.

>> **Lead with empathy.** AI brings change and change often brings fear: fear of being replaced, fear of the unknown, fear of losing control. Your role is to acknowledge those fears, provide transparency, and create a culture where technology is seen as an enabler, not a threat.

>> **Uphold ethical standards.** AI systems can carry bias if the data they are trained on is biased. Leaders must hold vendors accountable, ensure diversity in data sets, and establish guardrails for fairness, transparency, and privacy. High performance is not just about results; it's about results achieved the right way.

AI for selecting and developing high performers

AI is already revolutionizing how we recruit, onboard, and develop talent. For example:

>> **Recruitment and talent matching:** AI-powered platforms can scan thousands of resumes in seconds to identify the best-fit candidates based on skills and experience and even flag potential for growth based on learning agility. This speeds up hiring while reducing human bias if implemented with ethical oversight.

>> **Onboarding:** Chatbots and virtual onboarding assistants can guide new hires through paperwork, answer common questions, and introduce them to company culture before their first day.

>> **Workforce planning:** Predictive analytics can identify skill gaps before they become critical, allowing leaders to upskill or hire in advance.

>> **Performance management:** AI tools can track performance metrics in real time, providing leaders with actionable insights rather than just annual review snapshots.

The result is that leaders can give less focus to administrative tasks and more to building relationships, coaching, and creating conditions for high performance.

Technology can streamline processes, but trust, motivation, and culture are still built human to human.

REMEMBER

AI in decision-making and strategic planning

High-performance teams thrive on smart, timely decisions. AI takes the guesswork out by processing vast amounts of data quickly, identifying patterns, and forecasting likely outcomes.

For example, AI can

» **Support scenario planning:** Simulate multiple "what-if" scenarios so leaders can evaluate potential risks and opportunities before making a move

» **Enhance competitive intelligence:** Monitor competitors, market shifts, and customer sentiment in real time

» **Drive innovation:** Spark new product ideas by analyzing gaps in the market or unmet customer needs

One leader I worked with used AI tools to analyze global market trends and discovered an emerging niche that competitors had overlooked. Their team launched a targeted product six months ahead of the competition, and it became their best seller. That's is the power of pairing human vision with AI precision.

As you find ways to incorporate AI into your role in leading a high-performance team, keep these things in mind:

TIP

» Use AI as one input in decision-making, not the only one.

» Pair AI forecasts with your team's experiential knowledge.

» Keep AI tools updated with fresh and relevant data for accurate insights.

AI and team development

A hallmark of high-performance teams is a commitment to continuous learning. AI-powered learning platforms take development to the next level in the following ways:

» **Personalized learning:** AI can recommend training modules based on an employee's current role, career aspirations, and learning style.

» **AI-driven coaching:** Some tools provide real-time feedback on communication, presentation, or leadership skills.

» **VR and simulation:** Advanced technology allows team members to practice scenarios such as crisis management or negotiations in a safe, immersive environment.

» **Skill tracking:** AI can track skill progression and prompt managers when an employee is ready for new challenges.

REMEMBER

Using AI for team development not only builds capability but also drives engagement. When people see that their development is prioritized, they are more likely to bring their best selves to the team.

Measuring the ROI of AI in teams

If you can't measure it, you can't manage it. Leaders must track how AI impacts productivity, innovation, and engagement. Key metrics might include

>> Cycle time reduction on key processes

>> Employee satisfaction and adoption rates of new tools

>> Increase in idea generation or innovation output

>> Reduced turnover or burnout rates

Also monitor the human side of ROI (are people more engaged, creative, and connected) because technology is reducing their stress and freeing their time? Numbers matter, but so do the stories behind them.

REMEMBER

People will accept AI more readily when they see how it helps them succeed, not just how it helps the organization succeed.

The high-performance teams of tomorrow will be human-led, AI-empowered, and relentlessly focused on impact. And the leaders who thrive will be the ones who understand that technology does not replace great leadership, it amplifies it.

Demonstrating Leadership Accountability Consistently

One of the greatest challenges threatening the success and sustainability of today's organizations is not just a lack of leadership; it's a lack of leadership accountability.

A global survey conducted by LHH (formerly Lee Hecht Harrison) and Dr. Vince Molinaro that was published in *The Leadership Accountability Gap* found that responses from more than 2,000 senior executives revealed only about 49 percent of leaders are considered truly accountable, meaning many fail to take personal ownership and instead defer decisions upward.

Leadership accountability is at the heart of any organization's ability to achieve optimal performance. At a time when we continue to experience accelerated change, workplace complexities, and shifting worker expectations, leadership accountability couldn't be more critical. Employees today place a higher premium on their leaders "walking the talk" and being more accountable. So, what is leadership accountability?

It means that as a leader, you accept responsibility for the outcomes expected of you, both good and bad. You don't blame others. And you don't blame the external environment. It's an important skill because it builds trust within teams, creates respect between leaders and employees, and promotes a sense of fairness that is essential to an engaged workforce.

REMEMBER

Without accountability, even the most brilliant, hard-working, well-intentioned leaders fail; they fail to meet their performance goals; they fail to develop their teams; they fail to hire top talent; they fail to coach their employees; they fail to communicate clearly; they fail to optimize performance; and they fail the business overall.

Moreover, leadership accountability matters for organizational performance, culture, and sustainability. Here are a few examples:

>> **Trust and culture:** Inconsistent accountability undermines trust and harms culture. Consistent accountability, by contrast, sets a standard of integrity.

>> **Performance and innovation:** LinkedIn research shows that companies with strong accountability outperform peers and enjoy better leader satisfaction.

>> **Retention and talent flow:** Workers, especially Millennials, expect clarity, growth, and purpose. Leadership deficiencies in these areas lead to turnover and difficulty in attracting talent.

REMEMBER

Organizations must foster a culture of accountability by setting clear expectations, defining metrics, and holding leaders responsible through transparent evaluation and consequences. They must also strengthen leadership pipelines through succession planning, mentoring, rotational leadership programs, and skills development. And finally, they must ensure psychological safety and trust are demonstrated so that everyone feels safe to admit mistakes, learn, and hold one another accountable without fear.

IN THIS CHAPTER

» Explaining the key drivers of
risk aversion

» Knowing the consequences of being
risk averse

» Determining your tolerance for
risk-taking

» Encouraging your team to be
risk ready

» Evaluating the benefits of risk-taking

Chapter **7**

Moving from Being Risk Averse to Risk Ready

E very organization and leader faces constant tension between risk and reward. On one hand, playing it safe may feel comfortable, but it often leads to stagnation and missed opportunities. On the other hand, embracing risk can unlock innovation, competitive advantage, and long-term growth. Many leaders and teams struggle to strike the right balance because of deeply ingrained tendencies toward risk aversion.

This chapter explores how to shift from a mindset of fear and avoidance to one of readiness and resilience. I reveal the key drivers of risk aversion and uncover the psychological, organizational, and cultural factors that cause individuals and companies to hold back. This chapter also explores the consequences of being risk averse and helps you determine your tolerance level for risk-taking through self-reflection and practical tools so you can identify your natural tendencies and where you may need to grow.

Lastly, I reveal the payoff of risk-taking in organizations and identify the risk-ready behaviors that leaders and teams can take to foster a culture of experimentation, learning, and adaptability.

Revealing the Key Drivers of Risk Aversion

Risk aversion doesn't come from nowhere. It often develops from a mix of emotions, organizational experiences, and leadership mindsets. To move toward becoming risk ready, leaders must first understand what drives their hesitation. In this section, I reveal six of the most common drivers.

Fear

Fear is perhaps the most universal driver of risk aversion. Leaders may fear failure, rejection, or reputational harm. Sometimes the fear is tied to financial loss, while at other times, it's about disappointing stakeholders or losing credibility. Neuroscience research reminds us that the human brain is hardwired to prioritize safety. When the amygdala detects a potential threat, even in the form of uncertainty, it triggers a "fight, flight, or freeze" response. Many leaders unknowingly live in this freeze mode, where they avoid action altogether.

Consider a manager who has a bold idea for restructuring the team to increase efficiency. The data suggests it would work, but the fear of disrupting current performance or facing backlash from colleagues leads the manager to stay silent. Over time, these moments accumulate and create cultures where new ideas never surface. Fear, left unchecked, becomes the silent killer of innovation.

Past experience

History influences how people view risk. Leaders who've been burned by failed initiatives or poor investments often carry those scars into future decision-making. They often live inside the trauma of that experience. While learning from experience is important, living in the shadow of old mistakes can trap leaders in caution.

I recall an executive who once championed a product launch that failed spectacularly. Instead of reframing that failure as a valuable lesson, the executive interpreted it as proof that bold moves are too risky. As a result, future opportunities were dismissed before they were fully explored. Organizations led by such individuals may find themselves falling behind competitors who are willing to experiment, fail fast, and adapt.

A healthier approach for that executive would have been to separate the *event* from the *identity*. Failure should never define a leader, but it should inform wiser choices going forward. The most risk-ready leaders are those who take past lessons and use them as springboards, not barriers.

Lack of trust

Trust is the soil in which risk-taking grows. When trust (trust in oneself, in team members, or in senior leadership) is missing, the appetite for risk diminishes significantly. Leaders who do not trust their employees tend to micromanage, avoid delegation, and shy away from decisions that require collective buy-in. Similarly, employees who do not trust their leaders are unlikely to take initiative for fear of being blamed or punished.

Research from Gallup has shown that high-trust cultures report significantly higher engagement, productivity, and innovation. Without trust, the opposite is true: Collaboration stalls, creativity dries up, and people play it safe. Imagine a team where employees believe that even small mistakes will be held against them. In such an environment, risk aversion becomes the default because no one feels secure enough to stretch beyond the obvious.

Building trust requires transparency, consistency, and accountability. Leaders who model openness, own their mistakes, and empower their teams create conditions where risk feels less like a gamble and more like a shared journey.

Comfort zone

The comfort zone is a deceptively attractive place. Leaders who have achieved success using familiar strategies often resist leaving the routines that worked in the past. The problem is that comfort breeds complacency. In rapidly changing markets, what worked yesterday will not necessarily work tomorrow.

Consider the story of Kodak, once the global leader in photography. Its executives stayed within their comfort zone, focused on film, and resisted digital innovation even though the company's own researchers had invented the first digital camera. Their refusal to step beyond the comfort zone ultimately led to bankruptcy.

The comfort zone does not just affect large corporations, it shows up in leaders at every level. A manager may continue using outdated technology because it's familiar, even though better tools exist. Or an HR director may avoid redesigning a broken process because "we've always done it this way." Leaders who remain in their comfort zones may preserve short-term stability but sacrifice long-term success.

Need for control

Control provides the illusion of safety. Leaders who crave control often find themselves micromanaging, overplanning, and resisting delegation. Although structure is valuable, excessive control prevents teams from experimenting and diminishes employees' confidence.

A need for control is often rooted in insecurity. Leaders may fear being judged for poor results, so they attempt to own every decision. But this stifles creativity and slows execution. Imagine a marketing director who insists on approving every social media post before it goes live. While the intention is to protect the brand, the result is missed opportunities, bottlenecks, and frustrated employees.

REMEMBER

Risk-ready leaders learn to release control strategically. They empower others to take ownership, encourage small bets, and accept that not every outcome can be predicted. By focusing on guiding principles instead of rigid rules, they build teams that are capable of acting swiftly in uncertain situations.

Analysis paralysis

Analysis paralysis is the tendency to overthink and overengineer every possibility until momentum disappears. Leaders stuck in this pattern are constantly gathering data, running scenarios, and waiting for the "perfect" moment to act. In reality, that moment rarely arrives.

In volatile environments, speed can often outweigh certainty. While careful planning has its place, excessive analysis leads to lost opportunities and competitive disadvantages. For example, by the time a company finally approves a new digital platform after months of deliberation, a competitor may have already captured the market.

TIP

Risk-ready leaders recognize when analysis shifts from being helpful to being harmful. They balance the need for information with the discipline of action. Instead of waiting for all the lights to turn green, they move forward when there is enough evidence to justify a reasonable decision. They treat risk as a process of iteration rather than a one-time leap.

Detailing the Consequences of Remaining Risk Averse

A number of studies reveal just how risk aversion continues to dominate organizational decision-making. According to a 2023 McKinsey survey, nearly 72 percent of executives admitted their organizations are more risk averse than risk ready, citing fear of failure, regulatory concerns, and shareholder pressure as primary reasons. Deloitte's 2024 Global Human Capital Trends report also found that while 87 percent of leaders agree that innovation requires taking risks, only 29 percent said their organizations actively encourage it.

The consequences of this widespread caution are measurable. Gartner's 2023 research on innovation showed that companies that are overly risk-averse are 25 percent less likely to meet their growth targets compared to competitors who cultivate risk tolerance. Risk aversion is not just about avoiding potential losses; it often leads to missed opportunities, slower decision-making, and diminished employee engagement.

Risk aversion may feel safe in the moment, but over time it becomes a silent barrier to progress that results in suppressing innovation, slowing adaptability, and weakening employee engagement. When leaders avoid taking calculated risks, they send a signal that experimentation is dangerous, and that failure is unforgivable. The result is predictable: Agility fades, creativity dries up, and the organization loses its competitive edge.

This section explores what happens when leaders and organizations let fear, comfort, or overcaution drive decision-making. This section also examines how excessive caution leads to stifled innovation, reduced agility, lower employee engagement, and missed market opportunities. Lastly, it exposes how forward-thinking leaders can recognize these warning signs before they become irreversible.

Stifled innovation

One of the most significant consequences of risk aversion is the stifling of innovation. When organizations default to "playing it safe," they discourage experimentation, limit creativity, and ultimately undermine their ability to stay relevant in a rapidly evolving marketplace. A risk-averse culture often rewards predictability and punishes failure, which sends a strong signal to employees that new ideas are too dangerous to pursue. Over time, this leads to a climate of caution where creativity is suppressed, and innovation becomes stagnant.

Blockbuster is a striking case. The company dominated the video rental industry for years. Despite early opportunities to invest in streaming technology and even purchase Netflix, Blockbuster doubled down on its brick-and-mortar model. Its risk aversion kept it tied to a familiar strategy, even as consumer behavior shifted dramatically. In contrast, Netflix embraced the risks of streaming and went on to transform how entertainment is consumed globally. Blockbuster's reluctance to innovate eventually led to its downfall.

Retail provides similar lessons. Companies like Sears, JCPenney, and Toys "R" Us were once household names with strong brand loyalty and national presence. Yet their hesitation to aggressively invest in e-commerce left them vulnerable. While online competitors captured the growing digital shopping market, these retailers clung to outdated strategies because they were fearful of disrupting their in-store businesses. By the time they attempted to catch up, consumer expectations had already shifted, and their delays cost them market share, profitability, and, in many cases, survival.

Reduced agility

In an environment where disruption is constant, agility is nonnegotiable. Risk-averse organizations often become rigid in their structures and processes, making them slow to respond to external shocks such as economic downturns, supply chain disruptions, or shifts in consumer behavior.

Consider Nokia, once the global leader in mobile phones. Its reluctance to pivot toward smartphones, despite early warnings about changing consumer preferences, left it vulnerable. While companies like Apple and Samsung took bold risks in developing touchscreen and app-driven devices, Nokia clung to its existing operating system and product models. By the time it attempted to adapt, the market had shifted dramatically, and its decline was irreversible.

Similarly, BlackBerry once defined business communication with its secure mobile devices. However, its risk-averse approach to consumer-focused innovation caused it to miss the smartphone wave. Its lack of agility, tied to overconfidence in existing strengths, eventually relegated it to a niche market rather than the global powerhouse it once was.

REMEMBER

These examples illustrate that organizational agility is not about protecting the status quo but about embracing change before it becomes unavoidable. Companies that are unwilling to take calculated risks are often outpaced by competitors who move faster, innovate sooner, and adapt more effectively to new realities.

Lower employee engagement

Employees quickly sense when their organization values conformity over creativity. Gallup's 2023 *State of the Workplace* report noted that in organizations where leaders discourage risk-taking, employee engagement is 30 percent lower. This disengagement translates into reduced productivity, higher turnover, and missed opportunities for innovation at all levels.

For instance, a large retail bank known for its rigid systems and a culture of fear contributed to one of the largest banking scandals in recent history. Employees, under intense pressure to meet unrealistic sales goals, were discouraged from raising concerns or suggesting new approaches. The lack of psychological safety not only disengaged employees but also caused reputational and financial damage on a massive scale.

By contrast, companies that empower employees to take calculated risks often see much higher engagement. For example, Google's early culture of encouraging "20 percent time" projects led employees to pursue innovative ideas like Gmail and Google Maps. This freedom to experiment cultivated excitement, ownership, and a sense of purpose, showing how risk tolerance directly fuels engagement and creativity.

Missed market opportunities

Organizations that fail to take calculated risks often miss out on transformative opportunities. Sears, for example, had the infrastructure, brand recognition, and customer loyalty to dominate e-commerce. Yet its reluctance to fully invest in digital transformation allowed Amazon to capture the space Sears should have led. By failing to embrace the risks associated with changing consumer behavior, Sears lost relevance and market share, ultimately leading to bankruptcy.

In a similar vein, Toys "R" Us signed an exclusive online partnership with Amazon rather than building its own robust e-commerce platform. While it seemed like a safe strategy at the time, the decision prevented the company from developing digital capabilities and engaging directly with its customers online. When the partnership ended, Toys "R" Us struggled to catch up, missing the market opportunity that competitors capitalized on.

Conversely, companies that embrace risk often redefine industries. Netflix is an example of how bold risk-taking can pay off, transforming from DVD rentals to streaming, and then into original content production. The willingness to pivot into uncharted territory positioned it as a global leader in entertainment. These contrasts highlight how avoiding risks may feel safe, but in reality, it often creates greater vulnerability.

Leaders as transformation catalysts

Leadership transformation often starts at an individual level. A leader's mindset sets the tone for the entire organization, influencing how challenges are approached and decisions are made. One key aspect of this transformation is developing a growth mindset. Leaders need to cultivate a belief that challenges are opportunities for learning and growth rather than insurmountable obstacles.

Satya Nadella's leadership at Microsoft offers a clear example. When he became CEO, Microsoft was seen as lagging behind more innovative competitors. Nadella shifted the company culture from one of rigid certainty to one of curiosity and learning — what he called moving from a "know-it-all" to a "learn-it-all" organization. This cultural transformation not only revitalized innovation but also re-engaged employees who now felt their ideas mattered.

REMEMBER

Leaders who adopt transparent communication, actively listen to diverse perspectives, and encourage open dialogue help dismantle cultures of fear. When leaders model a willingness to learn and to view mistakes as growth opportunities, they create a ripple effect that shifts the culture away from risk aversion. Howard Schultz at Starbucks, for example, consistently encouraged experimentation with store concepts, customer experiences, and digital engagement. Even when some initiatives failed, the willingness to take risks strengthened the company's adaptability and growth trajectory.

Ultimately, leaders who embrace risk-ready behaviors set the stage for cultural transformation. By showing employees that risks are not only acceptable but expected when pursued thoughtfully, they turn organizations into places where innovation thrives, and resilience becomes the norm.

Fostering a Risk-Ready Workplace Culture

Leadership is the spark, but the culture that grows from that determines whether risk readiness becomes a lived reality. Here are a few strategies that organizations can employ to foster risk readiness:

>> **Foster a culture of continuous learning:** Organizations that encourage employees to dedicate time to experimenting and pursuing passion projects often see breakthrough innovations emerge.

>> **Promote inclusive decision-making:** When cross-functional teams are formed and diverse perspectives are sought, risks are evaluated more thoroughly, and opportunities are more accurately identified.

>> **Empowerment through responsibility:** Workplaces that delegate real decision-making authority to employees create environments where individuals feel ownership and accountability, which fosters smarter, calculated risk-taking.

>> **Celebrate learning:** Organizations that recognize both successes and lessons learned from setbacks help normalize experimentation and reduce fear of failure.

>> **Create cross-functional collaboration:** Breaking down silos ensures that different departments bring varied expertise to the table, resulting in more innovative and balanced approaches to addressing uncertainty.

Operating with a risk-ready mindset brings about numerous benefits for both leaders and organizations. These include enhanced innovation, resilience, and decision-making, as well as greater employee engagement, adaptability, organizational agility, and talent attraction. Research from *Harvard Business Review* (2024) shows that organizations with cultures supportive of calculated risk are 1.8 times more likely to be market leaders in their industry.

For example, organizations that are willing to test new business models or digital delivery methods often gain a competitive edge in saturated markets. Those that encourage employees to pitch bold ideas find themselves attracting top talent who value creativity and autonomy. In industries experiencing constant change, this willingness to embrace uncertainty makes the difference between thriving and merely surviving.

Assessing Your Tolerance Level for Risk-Taking

One of the most important steps in becoming a risk-ready leader is taking an honest look at your own comfort with risk. Every leader has a natural default when it comes to uncertainty. Some lean toward caution, preferring to stick with tried-and-true methods, whereas others thrive on bold moves and change. Neither extreme is inherently wrong, but failing to recognize where you fall on this spectrum can keep you from leading effectively and inspiring your team to innovate.

Risk tolerance is shaped by several factors that include your personal upbringing, your early career experiences, your organizational culture, and even your emotional resilience. For example, if you grew up in an environment where mistakes were punished rather than treated as learning opportunities, you may be more inclined to avoid risks as an adult leader. On the other hand, if you've been rewarded in the past for taking bold steps, you may be more willing to push the envelope in pursuit of growth.

I often remind leaders that you can't change what you don't first acknowledge. Assessing your risk tolerance begins with self-awareness. It requires pausing long enough to reflect on your thought patterns, decision-making tendencies, and even your fears. The more you understand yourself, the more intentional you can be in stretching beyond your comfort zone.

Here are a few reflection questions to help you assess your tolerance for risk-taking:

>> When was the last time I took a bold step that stretched me beyond my comfort zone? Did I lean into the opportunity, or did I find reasons to avoid it?

>> How do I typically respond to failure or setbacks? Do I see them as evidence that I should stop trying or as valuable lessons to apply in the future?

>> Do I tend to wait for perfect information before making a decision, or am I comfortable moving forward with uncertainty?

>> How do I react when my team suggests unconventional ideas? Do I encourage exploration, or do I default to "that won't work"?

>> If I imagine my ideal leadership legacy, is it defined more by playing it safe or by pursuing bold initiatives that created meaningful change?

Take a moment to answer these questions honestly. You may find that your responses reveal not only your natural risk tolerance but also areas where you may want to grow. For example, if you recognize that you often wait for perfect conditions before moving forward, you may need to practice making decisions with partial information. If you find yourself shutting down creative suggestions from your team, you may need to work on building more openness to experimentation.

REMEMBER

Risk tolerance is not fixed. It's like a muscle that can be developed. By gradually exposing yourself to calculated risks, celebrating progress rather than perfection, and reframing failure as feedback, you can expand your comfort zone over time. Leaders who take this step not only increase their own capacity for growth but also create environments where their teams feel empowered to innovate without fear.

The question is not whether you're risk averse or risk ready. The real question is whether you're willing to stretch beyond where you are today to become the kind of leader who embraces change and creates new possibilities.

Evaluating the Payoff of Risk-Taking in Organizations

Taking risks is not about leaping without thought and preparation. It's about making intentional, informed choices that position an organization for growth. When leaders move from risk averse to risk ready, they shift the conversation from "What if it fails?" to "What might we gain?" The payoffs are both measurable and cultural.

Innovation and competitive edge

Organizations that take calculated risks are often the ones that lead in innovation. They're more willing to test new ideas, adapt to trends, and pursue opportunities before competitors. Research from McKinsey shows that companies that make bold moves during times of uncertainty outperform more cautious peers by as much as 30 percent in market capitalization growth. One powerful example is Apple's decision to launch the iPhone — a risk that reshaped an entire industry and created one of the most profitable product lines in history.

Engagement and retention

Risk-taking also strengthens the employee experience. When leaders create an environment where it's safe to try new things, employees feel trusted, valued, and engaged. Gallup's research has found that highly engaged teams are significantly more productive and profitable than disengaged ones. Leaders who encourage experimentation signal to employees that their contributions matter, which in turn reduces turnover and builds loyalty.

Financial growth and resilience

Beyond innovation and engagement, there is a financial payoff. Deloitte's studies have shown that organizations that integrate risk intelligence into their decision-making not only achieve stronger returns but also rebound faster in downturns. One clear example is Amazon's early investment in cloud computing, which was seen as risky but has since become one of the company's most profitable ventures and is a pillar of its resilience.

Agility and adaptability

Risk-ready organizations are also more agile. They can pivot faster during disruption and seize opportunities that risk-averse organizations miss. The pandemic highlighted this reality as companies that quickly adapted to remote work and digital platforms thrived while others struggled to adjust. Agility has now become one of the most important indicators of long-term organizational success.

Building a learning culture

Perhaps the greatest payoff is cultural. Each risk, regardless of its success, creates an opportunity for learning. Leaders who normalize risk-taking build teams that are more resilient, creative, and confident. Over time, the organization develops a growth mindset that encourages continuous improvement and positions it to thrive in a rapidly changing world.

Behaviors for shifting to risk readiness

Moving from risk-averse to risk-ready leadership involves more than mindset; it's demonstrated through daily behaviors. In the following list, I discuss several that distinguish leaders who thrive amid uncertainty:

>> **Ask "What if?" instead of "What could go wrong?"** Risk-ready leaders reframe their questions. They imagine possibilities before they anticipate problems. This forward-looking approach invites creativity and reduces fear-based decision-making.

>> **Encourage experimentation and quick learning.** They create safe spaces for testing new ideas — using pilot programs, prototypes, or "beta" projects — and celebrate the insights gained, even when outcomes differ from expectations.

>> **Replace perfectionism with progress.** Instead of delaying action until every variable is known, they model agility — launching, learning, and improving in motion.

>> **Reward curiosity and initiative.** Risk-ready leaders publicly recognize those who ask bold questions or challenge assumptions. They make learning visible and normalize the discomfort that comes with growth.

>> **Model vulnerability and transparency.** When leaders admit mistakes or uncertainty, they build psychological safety across their teams. This openness encourages others to take smart risks without fear of retribution.

>> **Balance optimism with data.** They don't leap blindly. They use analytics, trend forecasts, and scenario planning to make informed choices. This ensures that risks are strategic, not reckless.

>> **Encourage dissent and debate.** Instead of surrounding themselves with agreement, they seek out opposing views. Constructive tension sharpens decision quality and widens perspective.

Chapter **8**

Leading the Team through Change and Transitions

" **C**hange is the only constant in life." This piece of wisdom is usually credited to the ancient Greek philosopher Heraclitus, who was born in the 6th century, B.C.E., and yet, 'the concept is just as true today as it was then. At work and in life, we can't always accurately predict the changes that come our way, but we can know for certain that nothing stays the same for long.

Therefore, one of the key competencies of any leader is to navigate their team through times of change. Whether that change is desired and planned or is thrust upon a team by external circumstances, leaders must decide the best direction and know how to get everyone moving in that new direction. Fortunately, with a little knowledge of team dynamics, a positive attitude, and a healthy dose of patience, these skills can be attained and strengthened.

Comparing Change and Transition

For the purposes of this chapter, I'm going to make a clear distinction between the word *change* and the word *transition*, using the definitions first coined by William Bridges, author of *Transitions: Making Sense of Life's Changes* (Balance, 2019). According to Bridges, change is an external event or a situational shift. It's a concrete, tangible modification that can be identified and marked on a calendar. Examples include a new job, a company merger, or a global pandemic that forces everyone to quarantine. A transition, on the other hand, is the internal psychological process individuals go through in response to change. It's about people's feelings, thoughts, and behaviors as they adapt to the new situation and internalize the change.

In his book, Bridges created a famous model for helping teams and especially leaders manage the transitional process. He famously reverses the traditional story structure of beginning-middle-end and introduces change management as a series of endings, followed by exploration, and ending with new beginnings. (See Figure 8-1.)

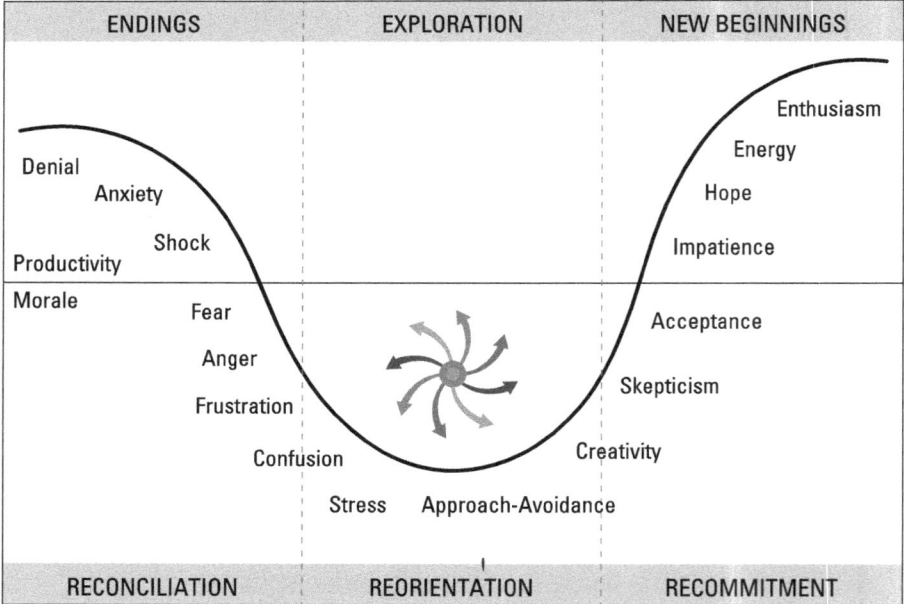

FIGURE 8-1: The Bridges Transitions Model.

That idea makes sense, when you think about it. If your team or organization is moving through a change-management process, the first step is never immediately doing things in a new way. Rather, an individual or team has to learn to let go of the old ways. It's a process of saying goodbye, which is why this phase is called Endings.

The next phase, Exploration (sometimes called the Neutral Zone), is an in-between time when the old is gone but the new isn't fully operational. The main value of Bridges's model is found in this phase of the process. Whenever the Transitions model is depicted graphically (as in Figure 8-1), the most notable feature of the journey is a rather severe dip in both morale and productivity at its center. The model isn't entirely pessimistic; both productivity and morale are higher at the end of the journey than they were at the beginning. However, Bridges wisely tells change practitioners to expect the process of change to be a little painful. Those who embark on a change process using the Bridges model for guidance and direction know to expect that the journey will not be easy but will ultimately be worth it.

The last phase is New Beginnings. If the transition process was successful and the new ways of doing things are working, people see the value in the change process. There's a palpable feeling of renewal as the team finds their footing and moves ahead with confidence.

According to Bridges, change succeeds when leaders recognize and support the inner journey people go through, not just the external shifts. Organizations that focus only on structural change but ignore the human transition miss the chance to turn disruption into innovation.

In addition to those three major stages, there are smaller steps within a typical change effort:

>> **Denial:** "We don't believe that change is possible."

>> **Anxiety:** "We can't possibly lose what we have; it's all we know."

>> **Shock:** "It looks like this is really happening, and we don't feel prepared."

>> **Fear:** "We've lost a lot and can't quite see yet what we've gained."

>> **Anger:** "How dare they do this to us?"

>> **Frustration:** "Why couldn't we just leave things alone?"

>> **Confusion:** "We can't go back but still can't see the way forward."

>> **Stress:** "Life was so much easier before this whole process started."

>> **Approach-Avoidance:** "We're seeing some benefits, but not enough."

>> **Creativity:** "Maybe we could do it this way . . ."

>> **Skepticism:** "Is this really working? Some us still have doubts."

>> **Acceptance:** "Apparently, this is the way it is now; we might as well get used to it."

>> **Impatience:** "Okay, we're all on board. When does the magic happen?"

>> **Hope:** "We're beginning to breathe a little easier now."

>> **Energy:** "Wow, this is so much better than it used to be."

>> **Enthusiasm:** "What took us so long?"

Of course, these steps are not a given. Arriving at a place of energy and enthusiasm is the result of hard work, determination, and a refusal to give up when bogged down during the most chaotic days of your journey. But the strain that inevitably happens when going through change is much easier to bear if you expect it, and that's the beauty of using this model.

Managing Personal Change

Change isn't always easy. When in the valley of the Bridges Transitions Model or John Kotter's Change Management model (read more later in this chapter in "Navigating Your Team through the Change-Management Process"), teams that are struggling often look to their leaders to be a steady bulwark of strength and support. This is possible only when the leader has adequately prepared themselves for the change, is absolutely committed to the change process, and can harness an optimistic spirit, even on the most difficult days.

Before you embark on a change process with your team, ask yourself the following questions and reflect on a response:

>> Why is this change happening?

>> Why is the change happening right now?

>> How will I communicate these "whys" to my team?

>> Am I on board with the change? If not, what could cause me to embrace it?

>> Am I prepared to "fake it 'til I make it" if necessary?

>> What are the risks involved if you don't change?

>> Why am I personally motivated to support this change?

>> What external forces are driving this change, and can they be mitigated?

>> How can I demonstrate through words and actions that I've fully embraced the change effort?

>> What challenges or barriers can I expect along the way? Have I planned for this?

>> Will my team (or certain members of the team) be resistant? How will I respond to resistance when it occurs?

>> What is needed to make the change stick?

>> What personal rewards will come my way if the change is successful?

>> What organizational rewards will benefit my team if the change works?

>> What are some likely consequences if the change effort fails?

If your change process isn't mandatory (for example, restructuring a department rather than complying with new government regulations), then answering these questions might reveal that the change either isn't the right move or simply isn't the right time. If you have the flexibility to adjust or postpone the change, doing so may be better for everyone. If, however, the change must happen (the entire company is adopting the new software, or the company is experiencing a merger whether you like it or not), these questions can help you communicate this urgency to your team, prepare you to be fully on board with the change, and plan for the challenges ahead.

Steering the Change-Management Process

Another pioneer and thought leader of change management is Dr. John Kotter. He's a former professor at Harvard University, as well as the best-selling author of *Leading Change* (Harvard Business Review Press, 2012). I've been using Kotter's change model for more than 20 years to help organizations navigate change and build more inclusive and high-performing teams. In the following sections, I describe what I believe to be the most important first steps to leading change in organizations and provide real-world examples of how I implemented them. As you review them, conduct an informal analysis of how many of these competencies you demonstrate as a consistent practice in your organization.

John Kotter's eight-step process (see Figure 8-2) is an excellent "how-to" framework that leaders can use to plan ahead.

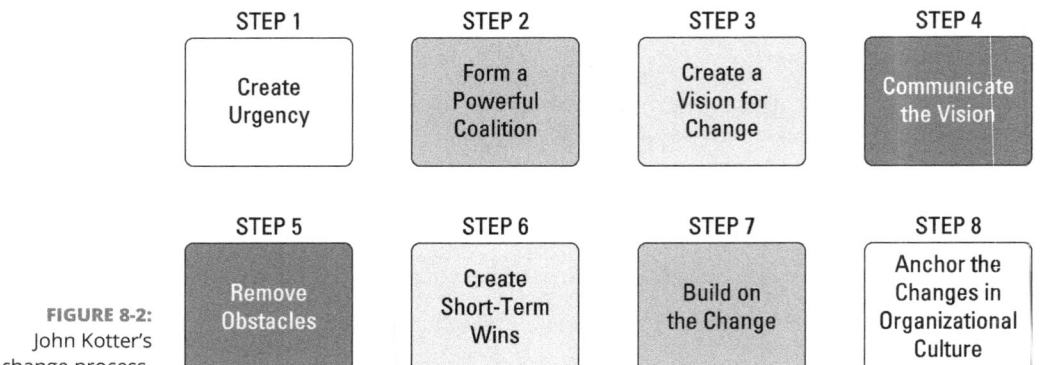

John Kotter's 8-Step Change Process
(Leading Change, 1995)

STEP 1	STEP 2	STEP 3	STEP 4
Create Urgency	Form a Powerful Coalition	Create a Vision for Change	Communicate the Vision

STEP 5	STEP 6	STEP 7	STEP 8
Remove Obstacles	Create Short-Term Wins	Build on the Change	Anchor the Changes in Organizational Culture

FIGURE 8-2:
John Kotter's
change process.

The following sections describe the eight steps of the process.

Create urgency

Before anyone commits to the arduous process of change, they must understand why it's happening and feel a genuine sense of urgency to act. Quite frankly, if most people in an organization don't see a compelling reason to change, they'll default to keeping things as they are. When external forces demand a shift to the status quo, people may comply on the surface but quietly resist in ways that can undermine progress. Without urgency, momentum stalls before transformation even begins.

In recent years, organizations across the globe have faced unprecedented scrutiny and resistance regarding their diversity, equity, and inclusion (DEI) strategies. In 2024 and 2025 especially, a wave of legislative rollbacks, public backlash, and misinformation campaigns created confusion, fear, and hesitation among employees and leaders alike. This climate made it harder, but also more essential than ever, to create a sense of urgency around why DEI work must continue and evolve.

One of my clients, a large multinational healthcare company, reached out when their executive leadership team began receiving pressure from board members and external stakeholders to "pause" or "rebrand" their DEI efforts in response to these attacks. Internally, the workforce was anxious. Employees from historically marginalized groups feared that their progress, voices, and psychological safety might be erased overnight. The DEI team was demoralized, and leaders were uncertain about how to communicate their commitments without risking reputational or political backlash.

This was a defining moment, not just for their business, but for their culture.

I was brought in to facilitate a series of strategic leadership sessions and employee town halls to help the organization respond with purpose and resolve. The first step was to reignite a sense of urgency by reconnecting leaders and employees to the deeper why behind their DEI investments. We clarified how inclusion was not merely a social initiative but a business imperative that directly impacted innovation, trust, and long-term performance.

From there, we evolved the strategy rather than retreating from it. Together, we built a future-focused, data-informed framework for inclusive leadership, embedded accountability into every leader's role, and shifted the narrative from "check-the-box compliance" to "culture transformation." I coached the team to communicate this vision with confidence, courage, and consistency, keeping urgency at the forefront to maintain momentum and buy-in.

The result was powerful: greater employee trust, stronger engagement across teams, and a renewed commitment to building a workplace where everyone feels valued, respected, and supported to thrive.

REMEMBER

Change is inevitable, but progress is a choice. As a leader, you must help your teams make the right one.

Form a powerful coalition

No one person, no matter how charismatic or hard-working they may be, can pull off an organizational change effort alone. They need allies (people throughout the organization with power and influence) who believe in the necessity of the change and can help execute the strategy. This coalition should include people with acknowledged expertise and informal leaders. They must be influential and well-respected so that those affected by the change will trust the process.

When I was implementing a change during a merger and acquisition for a utility company, I was tasked with assessing how the cultures of both companies would align, how they would clash, and what significant changes would need to be made once the merger took place. There was no way that I could be successful at this task alone, so I assembled a coalition of leaders from both companies and across various departments and locations. We all had varying degrees of functional expertise, tenure, and levels of authority with our respective companies, but all of us agreed on one thing: We wanted the merger to be a success with as little interruption as possible.

When thinking about who should join your coalition, look first to the people inside your team who are most likely to support the change enthusiastically and those whose support will go a long way to convincing others. But don't stop there: Your change coalition could include people outside your team, even people outside your organization. Anyone who can support the transition process, answer questions when people are confused, or champion the necessity of the change effort would be worth considering.

Create a vision for change

Your messaging shouldn't sound like doom and gloom. You should be inspiring a sense of hope by creating a vision of how things could be. To get anywhere, it helps to know exactly where you're going. Casting a clear vision is much more than sharing vague notions or positing grandiose ideas. Change can be scary, and many people resist or choose the status quo, so you must paint the picture of the future and describe the reason why it's important to create that future or to go in such a direction. You must also take it a step further and identify the steps to getting there and the benefits that will be enjoyed as a result of the change. Despite that, change will probably be a challenging and difficult process for most.

A national financial services client reached out to me when their return-to-office mandate caused a wave of employee disengagement and turnover. Despite two years of strong remote performance, leaders believed in-office visibility equaled productivity.

I helped them rethink that mindset. Through strategy sessions, we reviewed employee feedback, productivity data, and company values. I guided them in shifting from a rigid policy to a flexible, hybrid model centered on trust, performance, and well-being. We trained managers on leading hybrid teams and the skills needed to ensure connection, consistency, and continuity, and then we created communication protocols and aligned expectations across the board.

Leaders began to understand that flexibility isn't a perk, it's a powerful business strategy. When change is led with clarity of vision and purpose, and transparency, people don't just comply; they commit.

Communicate the vision

V vision that sits on a shelf helps no one. Communicating the vision is so obviously necessary, it almost goes without saying. However, it's called out as its own "step" in the process because most leaders woefully underestimate how much communication is necessary. To create an environment that welcomes change, the vision must be communicated, overcommunicated, and then communicated some more to be effective. When you think you're finished, you're about halfway there.

Recently my firm was completing an all-staff employee experience survey, and one of the questions asked was whether they felt that the company's new compensation structure and policy was clear. More than 80 percent of the staff responded, "What compensation policy?" Most of them had never been told about it. Needless to say, one of our key recommendations back to the HR committee was that they needed to socialize the plan across the organization if they wanted staff to buy into it and participate in fostering a culture of transparency and openness. You can't expect anyone to do anything if nothing has been communicated to them with clarity, consistency, and a compelling reason for the change.

REMEMBER

Not everyone on the team knows or understands new policies and changes; don't assume that because one person knows, everyone else knows. It's also not necessarily true that because one person agrees, every other team member agrees. Always be willing to communicate over and over, even when it appears obvious or unnecessary.

Just as communicating the vision can feel like a natural continuation of Step 3, it's also an opportunity to build on Step 2, forming a coalition. The communication process should include, as its own goal, the creation of what Kotter calls a "volunteer army" — people who will not only champion the change but become active participants in the change process.

Remove obstacles

Organizational change can feel very heavy. A wise way to begin the process, therefore, is to locate and isolate your biggest obstacles to change. What's standing in your way? Can you remove that obstacle or go around it for an easier path to success?

WARNING

Obstacles can show up in the form of powerful people who are resistant (or actively against) your change strategy, cultural norms, outdated policies and procedures, or environmental factors. An obstacle that is often overlooked is a lack of knowledge, which is easily overcome by providing training on the vision so that everyone is appropriately "upskilled" when the change takes effect. Not all obstacles can be so easily rid of, but planning this way is usually better than attempting to move through the immovable.

Create short-term wins

As you map out your change strategy, isolate those items that are highly visible but require comparably low effort. Plan to execute some of these first, and, if possible, sprinkle the rest throughout your process. Change is difficult, but being able to celebrate lots of small wins along the way makes it much easier. If necessary, just being halfway toward a goal can be made into a milestone worth celebrating!

Other examples of short-term wins could include discrete goals that go a long way to cutting back costs, improving efficiency, increasing profits, and so on.

REMEMBER

Part of celebrating short-term wins is rewarding the people who made them possible. If your culture supports it, try to reward individuals in a public way and celebrating their contributions. However, make sure you don't overlook anyone who played a large role in the team's success, or some folks will undoubtedly feel slighted, which will work against your ultimate goals.

Build on the change

Using the energy that's created from those short-term wins, the more difficult portions of your strategy now become possible. Remember to track lessons learned from the inevitable missteps and continue to reward people who are endorsing the change, leading the effort, or overcoming their own resistance.

TIP

One effective way to prevent your team from prematurely declaring victory while maintaining their commitment to the change process is to revisit Step 6, creating and celebrating short-term wins, and add a step, where the team reflects on what they learned on the way to this minor victory. The important part of doing this is determining how the lessons can be applied going forward. In this way, you're instilling a culture of continuous learning in a celebratory way while gently reminding your team that the journey isn't over.

Anchor changes in organizational culture

Leaving the process too soon might invite the organization to slip back — perhaps unconsciously — to the old way of doing things. Therefore, before declaring success, take some final steps to anchor the change in the culture. Just as you worked to remove obstacles in Step 5, this step can be thought of as instituting obstacles against backward movement. New policies or procedures and real accountability measures for noncompliance are often the first anchors you might create as the new way of doing things become old habits.

Before you put a formal end to your change efforts, ask yourself the following:

>> Does everyone understand the importance of the new changes and the benefits they bring?

>> Have you instituted norms and values that reinforce the change, as well as tangible rewards and/or consequences for compliance or lack thereof?

>> Are these new norms and values highly visible to job seekers and employees when selecting and hiring new talent, promoting employees, and so on?

>> Do you require new training and development programs to help employees develop necessary skills and competencies relevant to the new changes?

>> Have you improved or eliminated organizational processes that don't align with the new system?

>> Is everyone on board with the new way of doing things? If not, can individuals be coached or developed to ensure their commitment?

John Kotter reports that 70 percent of his clients who used his model eventually achieved their desired results. This might not sound like a lot, but I believe that this statistic doesn't reveal a weakness in the model. Rather, it simply reinforces the idea that change is difficult, and organizational change is even harder. Also, sometimes a change effort will be overtaken by other changes. If you were midway through an important change effort in March 2020 when COVID forced everyone to work from home, chances are that change effort was dropped, at least temporarily, while more substantial and disruptive changes were attended to. Given how difficult and precarious this work is, 70 percent is actually a very high number, which speaks to the wisdom of good planning and a clear-eyed approach to change management work.

OTHER MODELS FOR CHANGE MANAGEMENT

Kurt Lewin created a model of change with only three steps, which might be a good choice is your change effort is a bit smaller or simpler. The stages of the Lewin model mirror the transitions model of William Bridges:

- **Unfreezing**, which involves preparing people for change by addressing resistance and creating a need for it

- **Changing**, which involves implementing the new behaviors, processes, or beliefs

- **Refreezing**, which involves solidifying the change to make it permanent

Unfreeze, Change, Refreeze

UNFREEZE	CHANGE	REFREEZE
Begin by preparing for the change.	Implement the change.	Embed the change into the organization.

Handing Resistance to Change

As stated previously, there will always be resistance to a change effort. Even if you're sure that everyone hates the current state of things and would therefore welcome anything different, the process of change always brings up feelings of loss, and there's always a process of letting go. So even if you're not sensing any resistance at the outset, just wait! At some point in the change process, someone will be frustrated and long for the old days.

REMEMBER

Even if you're a wonderful and approachable leader, power dynamics can also get in the way of people being upfront about their resistance to change, especially if you're personally very excited about the changes to come. While I would encourage you to be an enthusiastic champion of your change process, know that this sometimes comes at a cost. Try to be both an eager advocate of change and a safe space where your team members can speak about their fears, concerns, and even things they like about your current state.

Resistance to change is why teams take such a dip in morale and productivity in the middle of the Bridges Transition Model, and it's the reason behind most of the steps in the Kotter process. I wish I could tell you there was a way to eliminate resistance, but I've never found that magic recipe in all my years of consulting. Even if I had, I might not trust it. The fact is, if no one is resisting the change, what's actually happening is that no one is really changing. Instead, they're just saying and doing what their leader wants to hear and see without letting go of anything. Just as aches and pains after exercising your body are proof that the exercise is accomplishing something, resistance to organizational change is evidence that something is working.

The Beckhard-Harris Change Equation

In the 1960s, management consultant David Gleicher created a "Formula for Change," which was later rebranded as an equation by Richard Beckhard and Reuben T. Harris. This simple formula is a way of predicting the success or failure of a change process, and it provides some tips on how to ready your organization for the hard work of transformation.

The equation is presented in simple mathematical terms. Essentially R must be less than the product of D, V, and F. (See Figure 8-3.)

Resistance to change	Dissatisfaction with the status quo	A compelling Vision for the future	Easily understood First Steps

$$R \quad < \quad D \quad \times \quad V \quad \times \quad F$$

This number is never zero

If any of these numbers equal zero, then everything turns to zero

FIGURE 8-3: The Beckhard-Harris change equation.

R, in this case, is the resistance to any change effort. Notice that R is always greater than zero because there is always some resistance to change. That's because change is hard, and no one would do it without proper motivation. Likewise, there may be pockets of deep resistance in your organization that a leader might underestimate or be unaware of. Before setting out to make change, a change leader should investigate and uncover things that could become unwelcome surprises later on.

Essential motivation comes from the opposite side of the equation. These three items (D, V, and F) are presented as being multiplied by one another to imply an important dynamic: If any of these equal zero, then the product is also zero. In other words, all three are vital to a successful change effort.

D is dissatisfaction with the way things currently are. If everyone is happy with the status quo, then there will be no successful changes made. Often, this lack of dissatisfaction is better characterized as ignorance than happiness (for example, customers are unhappy but leadership doesn't know it or employees are longing for more flexibility but reluctant to say so out loud). In such cases, it will be necessary to educate your organization on the need for change before beginning. If your strategy is to succeed, you'll need to stoke that dissatisfaction. Perhaps everything is working well now, but changes in your industry or environment mean that change will be necessary to be sustainable in the long term. If this is the case, you'll need to convince those in power before you can begin. This part of the Beckhard-Harris Change Model is very much aligned with "Step 1: Create urgency" from earlier in this chapter.

REMEMBER

This can be more difficult than it sounds. Especially if you're conflict-averse, the very idea of stoking dissatisfaction can be extremely counter intuitive. Most leaders make great efforts to do just the opposite, to make their team members and customers satisfied and happy. But no one who loves everything the way it is will help you change things.

V stands for vision — more accurately, a compelling vision of the future. If you're worried about creating dissatisfaction in your organization to spark change, this part of the equation provides a counterbalance wherein you can also spark hope and enthusiasm for a better day ahead. Your vision should demonstrate how your team, company, or industry will be tangibly and measurably different after undergoing a change process. This part of the Beckhard–Harris Change Model is aligned with "Step 3: Create a vision for change" from earlier in this chapter.

Finally, F stands for first steps. To embrace change and overcome its inevitable resistance, people in your organization must understand what to do about it. But what's especially profound about this part of the model is what it leaves out. People in your organization don't need to understand your entire strategy from beginning to end. If they are appropriately dissatisfied with the way things are, and they have been inspired by your vision of the future, they only need to understand what is necessary to do first. If they're very eager to begin, it's best not to dampen their enthusiasm by too much information at the outset. Your strategy should be open and accessible to anyone inside the organization who wants to see it, but most will only be interested in what they should do now or in the immediate future.

Before embarking on any kind of change initiative, a leader should check their team and any immediate stakeholders against this important equation, and ask themselves the following questions:

>> Are people dissatisfied with the way things are? Are those in power aware of the level of dissatisfaction that exists?

>> Do I possess an inspiring vision of the way things could be? Have I adequately communicated this vision throughout the organization, especially to the people who can create change?

>> Do I have easy-to-understand first steps ready for people to take? Will I be able to quickly and universally communicate these when necessary?

If the answer to any of these questions is "no," there might be some important work to do before embarking on the work of organizational transformation.

3

Recruiting, Selecting, and Onboarding a High-Performance Team

Find out how changing demographics will reshape the workforce of the future.

Spot and minimize bias in hiring and selection so that you can make fairer decisions.

Design onboarding experiences that help new team members succeed and integrate quickly.

IN THIS CHAPTER

» **Connecting more effectively in a global environment**

» **Embracing flexible work options**

» **Contributing diverse backgrounds, perspectives, and experiences**

» **Facing rising levels of stress, burnout, and disengagement**

» **Seeking greater inclusion, belonging, accessibility, and advancement**

Chapter **9**

Getting Clear on Changing Workforce Demographics and Needs

C hange is inevitable for the world outside your organization, but it's also true inside, up to and including who makes up the workforce. The workforce of today, and — crucially — the workforce of tomorrow looks different, comes to work with different assumptions, and is demanding a different kind of workplace than the workers of a generation ago experienced.

If these demographic trends are seen as a nuisance or a disruption, they can take you by surprise as you find yourself unprepared to lead a workplace you didn't expect. The good news is that while these shifts (which are sometimes seismic) often mean you'll have to lead differently, they can generally be expected and planned for, if you're paying attention.

This chapter takes a look at some key ways the workforce has changed and is continuing to change, so that you'll be ready to lead throughout your career.

Becoming More Globally Connected

Globalization occurs when a business operates in a country outside its original location. Globalization allows for business growth because it provides a platform for companies to offer products in many locales, regions, and countries. Labor costs and the price of manufacturing vary all over the globe, and countries often offer economic incentives such as tax breaks and land grants to win international business. Expanding to another country presents an opportunity to employ labor from that particular location, which creates both short-term challenges and long-term opportunities, as staff from a different culture adapt to your organization as your organization adapts to them to ultimately (we hope) benefit from the different viewpoints and solutions that cultural diversity can provide.

As companies expand their global footprints, their global workforces expand as well. But this process isn't as simple as it may sound. Essentially, successful global expansion hinges on the following:

>> **Knowledge management:** What does the company know about the countries it wants to expand to or the country where it employs workers? How is the company utilizing that information?

>> **Skillfulness and acumen:** How is the organization using its data analytics to develop and execute strategy for the production stream, operations, and people management?

>> **Agility:** How quickly and appropriately is the company responding to market changes across the globe? And is your workforce mobile (can employees work from anywhere and move quickly)?

Capturing and then strategically utilizing appropriate data is an important factor in effective global expansion. This data should reveal information about the organization and its market. Also, optimizing your data infrastructure is something to consider when expanding globally. What are your current and future IT needs, and how will the necessary transition impact those needs while allowing you to grow?

Another important factor is having in-country talent and a knowledge base that ensures your organization's ability to enter or exit a market as business needs change. Establishing partnerships and alliances in the people management and talent development space allows you to meet human resource needs such as hiring, payroll, and performance management.

Many of today's employees want the ability to live anywhere and work anywhere. So how do you then attract the best talent from anywhere in the world to work anywhere in the world? What risks are present when you cross international borders, and how do you mitigate them?

Here are three important considerations for hiring globally:

>> Establish a legal presence in the locale through a foreign subsidiary.

>> Hire an independent contractor from overseas. This approach may be a more viable option until you're ready for a direct hire.

>> Manage compliance. Adhering to local and national laws of operations is essential, and to do so, you need talent onboard to manage this area.

If you're interested in recruiting talent to work globally, here are a few tips:

>> Provide the employee with a "best place to work" experience, beginning with the recruitment and onboarding processes.

>> Provide a diverse work community.

>> Establish excellent corporate social responsibility practices.

>> Offer comprehensive and competitive benefits and services.

>> Allow for flexibility in how and when workers work and get paid.

Seeking More Flexibility in How and Where Work Gets Done

A little over five years ago, the COVID-19 pandemic caused a workplace shift that, quite frankly, no one saw coming. Not since the Spanish Flu outbreak of 1918 had the entire globe been affected by a global health crisis of that magnitude. In a matter of weeks, some companies that had never truly supported the idea of remote employees were forced to shutter their offices and send everyone home. At the beginning of the pandemic, most people believed we'd be "back to normal" within a matter of months, but quarantining and social distancing were the norm for more than a year. Even after vaccines were developed and widely distributed and people safe to congregate again, there was no "normal" to go back to.

Workers had become very accustomed to reduced commutes, home offices, virtual meetings, and increased autonomy. Although some workers longed to return to an office setting, many workers dreaded it. Many in the global workforce had discovered a possibility they'd never considered. Even though some companies resumed old policies and norms, the workforce itself had forever changed.

Leaders were forced to change as well. Those who still equated visibility with value or insisted that an employee's physical presence in the workplace was a sign of their engagement to their work became less effective, while those who embraced the new norms of flexibility, autonomy, and employee agency were rewarded.

TIP

Look for ways to say yes to requests for working more flexibly versus finding ways to say no. I've found that workers perform better when allowed more autonomy because they don't want to lose this benefit.

Most companies now employ at least some employees who are fully remote; others ask their employees to come to an office space only two or three days per week. A data report by McKinsey & Company suggests that 20 to 25 percent of the workforce in advanced economies across the globe could easily work from home for three or more days a week — that is, if the work doesn't require being in close proximity to clients and/or colleagues. Employers have come to recognize that remote/virtual working has produced considerable cost savings for physically based operations. Another benefit for employers is being able to hire the best people, no matter where they live, without anyone footing the bill for an expensive relocation.

REMEMBER

Remote working isn't a one-size-fits-all solution. Working from home does have some drawbacks. Employees tend to work longer hours when working virtually, and they tend to experience greater levels of isolation, loneliness, and extra interruptions/distractions (from family members, pets, noises in the neighborhood, and weak Internet connections). Leaders have the added responsibility of figuring out how to lead a remote team and how to maintain a sense of belonging, team camaraderie, and connection.

Here, I list seven ways to keep remote workers engaged. Consider which of the following you currently demonstrate effectively and consistently:

>> **Establish clear expectations and goals:** Remote employees (who spend much of the day on their own) want to know exactly what's expected of them and what success looks like, possibly even more than employees who work in a traditional office space.

>> **Implement the right communication channels:** In yesterday's office, email was the default way for people to communicate. Email still works for some things, but virtual meetings, instant messaging, and document-sharing

platforms are also effective ways to communicate, depending on the problem or project.

>> **Put check-ins on the calendar:** Despite enjoying their increased autonomy, remote workers are still human beings and therefore likely to be creatures of habit. It's a good idea to schedule regularly occurring check-in times (both group and individual) and treat those meeting times as sacred, only rescheduling under extraordinary circumstances.

>> **Invest in mental health:** Research as shown that for every dollar an organization invests in workers' mental health, they get four dollars back in terms of engagement and productivity. Just because you can't see the fatigue on a remote worker's face doesn't mean they're not feeling it. In fact, remote workers tend to work longer hours and are less likely to completely disengage from work when they're on vacation. You should offer benefits related to mental health, encourage breaks, and share guidelines for self-care.

>> **Celebrate early and often:** A big challenge with remote work is the feeling of being disconnected, so look for every opportunity you can to celebrate. One best practice is to open each virtual meeting with a round of "kudos," where team members (and leaders!) can publicly appreciate others on their team and thank them for great work or support.

>> **Document everything:** Sadly, there's some truth to the old saying, "out of sight, out of mind." Keep notes during every meeting and check-in and create checklists for projects big and small. Most importantly, be transparent about your documentation. Share your notes with an employee after their check-ins to ensure you've captured everything and share important documents on the cloud where everyone can see them.

>> **Have fun!** In a recent survey of remote employees, 20 percent — that's one in five! — reported that their biggest struggle with working from home is loneliness. Humans are social creatures and have a need to connect with people in order to trust them. So in the midst of hard work, it's important to create opportunities to tell stories, laugh, and maybe even play games.

TIP

As a leader, you'll need to balance your remote workers' need to connect with you and their teammates with "camera fatigue," a real phenomenon in today's increasingly remote and hybrid workplaces. Camera fatigue can be heightened by more intense eye contact, increased self-consciousness and self-monitoring that happens when a person constantly sees themself on screen, and the cognitive load of processing nonverbal cues in a virtual format. Think about this when scheduling multiple meetings, and consider adding movement breaks, allowing team members to limit camera usage during certain meetings, and encouraging self-care in this regard.

Bringing a Variety of Backgrounds, Perspectives, Experiences, and Identities

Diversity is the collection of unique attributes, traits, and characteristics that make up individuals, including values, beliefs, experiences, backgrounds, preferences, behaviors, race, gender, abilities, socioeconomic status, physical appearance, age, and so on. Some of these traits are visible, and many others are invisible.

By nearly every metric, the workforce is increasingly more diverse, and this trend will continue. A more diverse workforce has different, often conflicting, needs and requires a different kind of leadership.

Generational diversity

In the year 2025, the workplace experienced a generational shift when millennials (those born between 1981 and 1996) represented 75 percent of the American workforce. We're in for more changes in the decade ahead. At the time I'm writing this book (2025), there are five generational cohorts in the workplace, but there will only be four by 2040. Traditionalists and baby boomers will have essentially exited the workforce by 2035, and Generation Alpha (born between 2010 and 2024) will be entering in greater numbers. This generation is projected to stay in school longer than previous generations, live at home longer, and will be the first generation to have been partially raised by screens (many given tablets as both educational aids and virtual babysitters from the youngest ages). We don't quite know yet all the ways in which Gen Alpha will change the workforce, but we can listen and learn and be ready to welcome them when they start looking for jobs.

However, when we talk about generational diversity, it's important to remember that the generational labels and timelines vary across countries and cultures. While many Western societies define generations by historical markers like postwar eras and economic shifts, other regions use cultural milestones or educational systems to define generational identity.

Table 9-1 provides a more global snapshot of generational cohorts.

In regions like Asia, Africa, and Latin America, generational traits are also heavily influenced by sociopolitical events, religious and cultural traditions, access to education, and technology adoption. For example, in many African and Southeast Asian nations, Gen Z and millennials are significantly younger, more mobile, and more entrepreneurial due to the rapid growth of digital infrastructure and mobile connectivity.

TABLE 9-1 **Snapshot of Generational Cohorts**

Generation Name	Approximate Birth Years	Global Context
Silent Generation, Traditionalists	1928–1945	Shaped by WWII, colonial transitions, and industrialization in many countries. Mostly retired.
Baby boomers	1946–1964	Experienced post-war growth in the West and decolonization and nation-building in Africa, Asia, and Latin America.
Generation X	1965–1980	Saw the increase in globalization, economic restructuring, technological shifts, and the rise of dual-income families.
Generation Y/millennials	1981–1996	Digital pioneers who grew up during tech boom, economic recessions, and shifting social norms worldwide.
Generation Z	1997–2012	True digital natives, shaped by climate crisis, social movements, and global interconnectedness.
Generation Alpha	2013–2029	Born into a world of AI, automation, and pandemic disruption; expected to live longer, study longer, and delay workforce entry.

According to a recent Deloitte Global Millennial and Gen Z Survey, younger generations across the world are unified by their prioritization of mental health, flexibility, purpose-driven work, and social justice. However, their access to opportunities varies greatly by geography, socioeconomic status, and systemic barriers.

What does this mean for leaders? It means we must build workplaces and teams where all members can thrive across all ages and stages of life, and where policies are designed to be flexible, inclusive, and responsive to both local culture and global standards. It's no longer enough to lead with a "one-size-fits-all" mindset. We must develop *intergenerational fluency*, which is the ability to effectively understand, engage with, and collaborate across different generational cohorts in the workplace. It goes beyond just knowing the names and birth years of generations; it's about developing the insight, empathy, and communication skills to bridge values, expectations, work styles, and experiences between employees of different ages.

Ethnic and racial diversity

We can also expect the U.S. workforce to grow more steadily diverse from a racial standpoint. Because of population growth, immigration, and the aging of the baby boomer generation, white non-Hispanics will decrease while other racial groups will grow. Here are some specifics:

>> **White non-Hispanics:** Their percentage of the workforce will decline in the next decade due to lower birth rates and less global migration. This group is expected to make up less than 50 percent of the U.S. population for the first time by 2045.

>> **Hispanics and Latinos:** In the United States, this group is projected to grow significantly, driven by high growth rates and a younger population on average.

>> **Asian Americans:** This group, while smaller than Hispanics, will experience a similar growth pattern, with immigration being a primary driver of growth.

>> **African Americans:** This group in the U.S., while larger than the Asian American cohort, will grow, but at a slightly slower rate than either Hispanics or Asians.

Racial diversity is also growing in many nations around the world. According to a recent survey conducted by Pew Research Center, approximately 69 percent of people surveyed across 27 nations said their respective country has grown more diverse over the last 20 years. Close to half of survey respondents say that they favor a more racially diverse nation. Even though racial diversity is still growing in some nations, other nations, such as Trinidad and Tobago, already have a very diverse population, including East Indians, Afro-Trinidadians, and mixed races. Belize is another country with racial diversity, with its population made up of Mestizos, Kriols, Mayans, East Indians, and other races.

REMEMBER

When considering racial and ethnic diversity with a global lens, keep in mind that many countries use tribal or ethnic identities that may be "invisible" to those with North American backgrounds. For example, most Americans couldn't make distinctions between Hutus and Tutsis, but these differences are very profound to people in Rwanda and Burundi.

Gender diversity

Gender diversity is often the first aspect of change when companies begin to examine diversity. A 2020 McKinsey & Company study showed that companies with more women in its executive ranks were 25 percent more likely to have above-average profitability than companies with less females in its executive ranks. Newer research is showing us that gender-diverse organizations tend to outperform both those that are male-dominated and those that are female-dominated with an ideal configuration anywhere between 60/40 and 40/60.

A 2023 Catalyst & Accenture report, "Women on the Front Line," highlights that women (especially in frontline roles) are navigating complex intersections of race, ethnicity, caregiving, and economic status. This signals that tailored support is critical to elevating and retaining women.

Additionally, Catalyst's 2021 "Women in Management" data showed women held about 35.6 percent of manager roles in Canada, while in the United States they filled 40.9 percent of managerial positions, yet women of color remained significantly underrepresented (Black and Latina women each at about 4.3 percent).

Unfortunately, only 52 CEOs of Fortune 500 companies in 2025 were women, about 10 percent. A 2023 S&P Global study of over 1,100 companies showed that women held about 25 percent of senior management or leadership roles, a long way from parity. However, the business case for gender equity is stronger than ever. McKinsey's "Diversity Wins" study revealed that companies in the top quartile for gender diversity on executive teams were 25 percent more likely to outperform on profitability. The sweet spot? A leadership gender mix between 40 percent and 60 percent — not all male, not all female, but balanced and inclusive.

Compounding the challenge, the COVID-19 pandemic disproportionately pushed women out of the workforce. Nearly 80, percent of those who left the workforce during 2020 were women, many of whom carried caregiving responsibilities and lacked organizational support. That loss is still felt today. However, women are earning more college and graduate degrees than men in many countries. The pipeline exists for women in the workforce and leadership exists. We just need to build better bridges through mentorship, sponsorship, allyship, flexibility, and inclusive policies to help women.

Other kinds of diversity

Today's workforce is not only multigenerational, multiethnic, and gender-diverse, it's multifaceted in every way. As I often say, "Diversity is not just about what we can see; it's also about what we experience, believe, value, and live."

The following sections look at a few key identity dimensions reshaping our workplaces.

LGBTQ+

While conversations about diversity often begin with race and gender, LGBTQ+ inclusion is an equally vital component that demands attention from organizational leaders around the world. Yet, despite some progress in certain countries, the data continues to reveal a concerning pattern of exclusion, invisibility, and underrepresentation for LGBTQ+ professionals globally.

A 2022 global survey by Out & Equal, in partnership with Edelman, offered one of the most comprehensive international views on workplace inclusion for LGBTQ+ employees across 17 countries. The findings were stark: More than 60 percent of LGBTQ+ workers reported experiencing exclusion, discrimination, or discomfort at work. In contrast, workplaces with active LGBTQ+ inclusive policies saw a 13 percent higher engagement score across employee populations, suggesting that the benefits of authentic inclusion are measurable and significant.

Further emphasizing the business case, the 2023 Stonewall Global Workplace Briefing highlighted that companies with strong allyship programs, visible LGBTQ+ leadership, and inclusive language in their corporate communications enjoyed significantly lower turnover rates (up to 20 percent less) among LGBTQ+ staff. However, the same report revealed that in countries with generally progressive policies like the United Kingdom, Canada, and Australia, up to 50 percent of LGBTQ+ employees still chose not to disclose their identities at work. This reality mirrors a long-standing global trend: Many LGBTQ+ professionals remain closeted due to fear of bias, lack of psychological safety, or cultural taboos.

These findings are consistent with a 2022 report by McKinsey & Company, which noted that companies with clearly stated pro-LGBTQ+ leadership policies experience a 15 percent improvement in retention. Industries such as finance, technology, and professional services particularly benefit from inclusive policies that support authenticity and belonging. However, McKinsey also found that inclusion is often unevenly implemented. It tends to be strong in headquarters or Western regions, but less visible in satellite offices in regions where LGBTQ+ rights are still limited or stigmatized.

Adding to this global analysis is the 2024 Equileap Public Equity Report, which reviewed 2,000 of the world's largest companies and found that only 12 percent had shown significant improvement in LGBTQ+ inclusion metrics between 2021 and 2023. The majority of organizations either stagnated or lacked robust data collection altogether. This highlights a troubling gap between stated values and measurable progress — particularly in parts of Asia, Eastern Europe, and the Middle East, where legal and social challenges continue to limit inclusive practices.

What these studies collectively reveal is that LGBTQ+ inclusion is not just a U.S.-centric issue. It's a global concern that impacts millions of workers across borders, languages, and cultures. Progress remains uneven; in many regions, the barriers LGBTQ+ workers face are deeply embedded in cultural, legal, or organizational norms that prevent them from fully participating in the workforce.

To move the needle, DEI leaders and executive teams must embed LGBTQ+ inclusion into every level of their global workforce strategy. This includes establishing nondiscrimination policies that clearly protect sexual orientation, gender identity, and gender expression that are applied consistently across regions. It also means developing and promoting visible allyship programs, offering benefits that include same-sex partner support and gender-affirming healthcare, and ensuring global employee resource groups (ERGs) include virtual and localized support for LGBTQ+ staff in regions where visibility may carry risks.

Moreover, organizations must recognize that many LGBTQ+ professionals remain invisible in their data. A 2019 Yale University study estimated that 83 percent of lesbians, gays, and bisexuals worldwide are closeted to all or most of the people in their lives. Without psychological safety and trust, many talented employees are unable to bring their full selves to work, which limits creativity, collaboration, and contribution. Employers should therefore prioritize culture audits, safe reporting channels, and inclusive leadership training that addresses unconscious bias and fosters empathy.

Neurodiversity

Neurodiversity isn't new. It's always been here, although this term has been recently introduced in the workplace and advances in diagnosing and supporting neurodivergent people have made this community more visible and more vocal. *Neurodiversity* describes a spectrum of differences such as ADHD, autism, dyslexia, bipolar disorder, OCD, and more. Globally, an estimated 10 percent to 20 percent of adults are neurodivergent (up to one in five people), yet they remain significantly underrepresented in the workforce. For example, in the United Kingdom, only about 31 percent of autistic adults are employed, and two-thirds are either unemployed or underemployed worldwide.

This reveals a colossal untapped talent pool. The World Economic Forum (2023) and Deloitte (2024) affirm that neuroinclusive workplaces generate up to 30 percent higher productivity and deliver a 28 percent revenue increase for organizations actively embracing cognitive diversity.

Tech companies and consulting firms have become pioneers in neuroinclusive hiring. For example, SAP, via its Autism at Work program, now spans 17 countries and has maintained a 90 percent retention rate among autistic hires.

Microsoft began its neurodiversity initiative in 2015 and has since hired about 300 neurodivergent employees, offering job coaches, quiet spaces, and sensory accommodations.

EY expanded its Neurodiversity Center of Excellence from the United States to Poland, pairing neurodiverse hires with trusted "buddies" and specialized recruitment and onboarding processes.

Other global leaders include Bank of America, Dell, HPE, and JPMorgan Chase, which each have deployed neuroinclusive practices and report improved accuracy, morale, and efficiency.

A few things that global leaders can do to better meet the needs and expectations of any team member that identifies as neurodiverse include the following:

>> **Educate and normalize:** Deliver training on neurodivergence to all levels and encourage organizational empathy.

>> **Adapt hiring practices:** Remove bias from job ads and assessments; include accommodations like extra reading time or sensory supports in interviews.

>> **Create support structures:** Offer job coaching, mentoring, quiet zones, noise-canceling options, flexible schedules, and clear communication tools globally.

>> **Redesign workspaces mindfully:** Integrate sensory-friendly architecture, adjust lighting, reduce noise, limit visual clutter, and rethink "culture fit" norms.

>> **Embed in DEI strategy:** Integrate neurodivergence in corporate policies, establish ERGs, collect self-identification data, and set measurable goals tied to advancing inclusive behaviors.

>> **Ensure legal and ethical protections:** Support disclosure with dignity, enforce accommodations consistently, and remain compliant with local disability laws worldwide.

Faith/religious beliefs

Religious and spiritual identity has become a vital aspect of workplace inclusion and belonging, and it spans far beyond Christianity and Islam. While each religion remains significant, the third-largest group globally is now the secular or nonaffiliated population. More than 80 percent of the world identifies with a religious faith, and this is projected to rise to 85 percent by 2050. This includes the rapid growth of Hindus, Muslims, Buddhists, and other faith traditions in emerging economies, revealing an even more pluralistic workforce landscape than ever before.

Notably, companies across the Fortune 500 are responding. According to the 2024 Religious Equity, Diversity & Inclusion (REDI) Index, 85.8 percent of these companies now reference religion or belief in their diversity commitments, which is more than double than in 2022. Additionally, 12.4 percent host faith-based employee resource groups, up from 7.4 percent, indicating a cultural shift in embracing spiritual identity at work. Leading global firms like Accenture, American Airlines, Dell, Equinix, Salesforce, and Intel are creating space for faith through prayer rooms, flexible holy-day scheduling, chaplaincy services, and religious literacy initiatives.

Having faith-inclusive policies isn't enough. Many employees still feel compelled to hide their spiritual selves. A Deseret News/HarrisX poll found nearly 40 percent of workers keep their religion private out of fear — suggesting that workplaces often shift from compliance to proactive belonging only on paper. This is where global organizational leaders must move beyond ticking boxes and open a dialogue grounded in cultural fluency and empathy.

To lead your team more effectively, consider these tips:

TIP

>> **Start with awareness:** Understand your workforce's religious and nonreligious demographics through annual, self-identified data gathering and listening sessions.

>> **Build faith literacy:** Train managers and colleagues to engage respectfully with a range of beliefs and secular practices, reducing misconceptions and micro-exclusions.

>> **Create genuine accommodations:** Offer flexible scheduling for holy days, prayer spaces, dietary options, and grooming practices (controls that affirm religious needs without penalizing others).

>> **Cultivate safe interfaith dialogue:** Celebrate World Religion Day or organize interfaith panels to open respectful exchanges and foster empathy across identities.

REMEMBER

Inclusion means making every part of a person feel welcomed, even parts others may not immediately see. By intentionally honoring faith, belief, and nonbelief, global leaders can build workplaces that are not merely diverse but deeply inclusive, empathetic, and authentically human.

A new kind of leader

The increase in diversity in the workforce has ramifications for all people who want to manage teams and lead people both now and in the future. To be an effective leader in an increasingly diverse organization and world, focus on the following:

- >> **Don't sidestep it.** You may have been taught to avoid topics like race, gender, sexual orientation, disability, or religion. As a leader, you need to be comfortable talking about these issues and model your ease for your entire team. After all, if you can't talk about it, you won't know how to create a welcoming team environment where everyone on your team feels a sense of belonging and is free to do their best work.

- >> **Practice empathy.** While it may not be possible to fully step into an experience that isn't yours and understand it completely, you can certainly make the effort to see issues from a different perspective. Moreover, you can believe people when they open up and tell you how the workplace impacts them, even if their stories don't align with your experience.

- >> **Foster respect.** Do your research about how to best show respect to others and accept feedback from people when they tell you how you've fallen short. Promote collaboration across cultural differences that may promote different communication styles and provide training that will equip team members with the knowledge and skills to work together effectively.

- >> **Address challenges head on.** Don't sweep conflicts under the rug. Instead, practice courage and face them, developing your conflict-resolution skills along the way. Diverse teams tend to experience more conflict than homogenous teams, but conflict doesn't have to be toxic. When handled well, it can be generative, helping a team be more creative and innovative.

- >> **Adapt your leadership style.** Some of your team members may react well to direct feedback; for others, it might need to be couched a bit more gently. Some might bristle at the idea of being micromanaged, whereas others might wait to receive specific direction before being comfortable beginning new work. You should be able to vary your leadership style to accommodate different cultures and also coach your team members toward ways they can adapt to be more successful at your organization.

TIP

For my comprehensive views on how to be a better leader for your diverse staff, check out my book *Inclusive Leadership For Dummies* (Wiley, 2024) and two of my popular LinkedIn Learning courses called "Leadership Foundations" and "Skills and Competencies for Leading Today's DEI Workforce."

Reporting More Stress, Burnout, and Disengagement

Today, workplace stress, burnout, and disengagement have emerged as pressing challenges that transcend industries, sectors, and borders.

According to the World Health Organization (WHO), workplace stress is now officially classified as an occupational phenomenon, and its consequences are staggering. Globally, factors including long hours, heavy workloads, changes within organizations, tight deadlines, and concerns about job security are causing workers to feel increased levels of stress. These feelings can manifest in physical challenges as well, including exhaustion and even increased risk of heart disease.

A 2023 global survey by McKinsey & Company found that 59 percent of workers reported feeling stressed daily, with many citing a lack of psychological safety and organizational support as contributing factors.

Unchecked, chronic stress often leads to burnout, a condition that goes beyond mere exhaustion. The WHO defines burnout as "a syndrome conceptualized as resulting from chronic workplace stress that has not been successfully managed." Burnout doesn't just leave employees physically and emotionally depleted; it fosters feelings of cynicism, reduced commitment, and diminished productivity. In a 2022 report by Gallup, burnout was linked to a 63 percent increase in absenteeism and a 13 percent decrease in organizational performance.

Coupled with burnout is worker disengagement, a silent epidemic that stifles innovation and drains organizational morale. Gallup's 2024 State of the Global Workplace report sounds a clear alarm for leaders: Global employee engagement dropped from 23 percent in 2023 to 21 percent in 2024, which is the second decline in 12 years. This results in a staggering $438 billion loss in productivity. What's driving this? One chief reason is manager disengagement, which directly impacts frontline performance, and serves as the single largest predictor of team engagement.

WARNING

Declining clarity of expectations, recognition, development opportunities, and daily care — elements that were once hallmarks of productive workplaces — are now rarely experienced by employees. For instance, in the United States, 31 percent of workers felt engaged — matching a 10-year low — while manager-led declines impacted younger and female managers most sharply. Engagement isn't a feel-good metric; it's a performance lever. Highly engaged teams are less likely to be absent, experience more profitability, have fewer quality defects, and greater well-being.

From a leadership perspective, these trends present a call to action to reimagine workplace culture and address the root causes of stress and disengagement. Toxic work environments, characterized by favoritism, gossip, retaliation, and poor leadership, exacerbate disengagement and fuel the vicious cycle of burnout. Additionally, perfectionists and high achievers (those who often shoulder the burden of picking up the slack) face a disproportionate risk of burnout, creating ripple effects across teams and departments.

WARNING

When some members of the team are disengaged, picking up the slack usually falls on a small number who refuse to disengage (usually through learned work ethic or a personality type that leans into hard work). As grateful as you may be for these people in the short-term, their contributions are often stifled by the eventual burnout they experience from shouldering too much responsibility, creating a vicious cycle.

TIP

The solution lies in creating environments where employees feel valued, supported, and empowered. Leaders must step up and engage with their teams through empathy and active listening. Simple yet powerful questions like, "What would have to change for you to feel energized about your work again?" can open the door to meaningful conversations and transformative change.

Here are a few more proven practices that will enhance engagement on your team:

TIP

>> **Invest in your people leaders.** Only 44 percent have ever received formal leadership training. Equip them with role clarity, coaching skills, and tools to navigate hybrid and AI-driven transformations.

>> **Prioritize meaningful connection.** People leaders should hold regular one-on-ones to set clear expectations, provide feedback, and reinforce employee strengths. Data show weekly feedback can result in more than three times the engagement.

>> **Embed well-being in culture.** With global stress and life dissatisfaction on the rise, leaders must create environments where work and mental health coexist positively. Engaged employees are two times more likely to feel psychologically safe and to thrive. Encourage self-care (breaks, getting a good night's sleep, taking a walk mid-day) and provide guidance or even formal training to drive the message home. Also, ensure that staff who are feeling overwhelmed can discuss their concerns with you or someone else, anonymously if necessary.

REMEMBER

Engagement is not an HR checkbox; it's a leadership imperative. Organizations that invest in manager capability, build trust, and show authentic care can reverse the engagement slide and become ecosystems of innovation, resilience, and human performance.

When stress, burnout and disengagement are addressed proactively, the benefits extend far beyond individual employees, they reverberate across teams, communities, and global organizations, propelling them toward greater innovation, productivity, and long-term success.

Insisting on Greater Inclusion, Belonging, and Accessibility

Earlier in this chapter, I mentioned that millennials are now 75 percent of the U.S. workforce. When asked what's important to them at work, it's clear from abundant research that "engagement" tops the list. Terms like *positive work culture*, a *sense of community*, *collaborative environments*, and *meaningful work* come up time and time again, and the message is clear: The largest cohort of employees working today would happily work harder and longer if they feel included, respected, and truly seen in the workplace.

Of course, inclusion, belonging, and accessibility are important to all generational cohorts. I don't mean to say that there aren't some workers of every generation who will choose the job with higher pay and higher status, but most of the talent that you will be competing for now and in the near future won't be willing to sacrifice workplace culture for the sake of a paycheck.

REMEMBER

I define *inclusion* as the degree to which an employee perceives that they're a valued member of the work group and encouraged to fully participate in the organization. While the term *inclusion* is often paired with *diversity*, these are different concepts. You can have diversity and not have inclusion. Diversity just is. Some groups are more diverse than others, but every group has some diversity because no two people are exactly the same. Inclusion is the environment and atmosphere people experience and work in. Recruiting and hiring the most qualified people regardless of identity isn't enough. You must also create an inclusive work environment where everyone feels valued and respected, with an equal shot at success, however they define it.

Becoming an effective leader of an inclusive team starts with self-work. To create the kind of culture where others feel like they belong, you must first look inward. Consider the following:

>> **Get clear on your purpose, vision, and values.** Do you know why you want to lead? Do you have a personal vision of the kind of leader you want to be? Why is inclusion and belongingness important to you?

>> **Minimizing your own biases and microaggressions.** Did you know that you don't have to consciously agree with a pervasive stereotype for it to interfere with your decision-making, especially if you're feeling rushed or stressed? Do you know how to mitigate these biases to ensure that you're treating people fairly?

>> **Being authentic and transparent.** Do you shy away from authenticity or transparency? If so, what's preventing you from being more open? What are you protecting by keeping information close to the vest? Have you ever worked for a leader you would describe as authentic or transparent? What was the impact of these qualities on you?

>> **Demonstrating empathy and emotional intelligence.** Are you able to see the world from a viewpoint that isn't your own? Are you able to recognize and regulate your own emotions when necessary? How do these skills impact those who work under your direction?

>> **Developing cross-cultural competence and cultural intelligence.** Are you aware of how your own cultural background has impacted your communication styles and core values? Are you able to bridge cultural differences effectively, or do you tend to focus mainly on commonalities between yourself and others?

After engaging in the required self-work, it's time to turn your focus on your interpersonal skills, particularly between you and those you are leading.

Here are a few essential leadership skills that make everyday interactions smoother and more effective:

>> **Dealing with many different kinds of people:** How do you find the best talent regardless of identity, and how do you acclimate new workers into your team? Can you lead teams through all four stages of development (see Chapter 2)? Are you aware of the benefits a diverse team provides, and have you figured out how to maximize those?

>> **Establishing trust and psychological safety:** Do your team members trust you? Can they be their authentic selves at work, or are they forced to assimilate in order to succeed? Can they ask questions when they need help, or

contribute their expertise? Can they challenge you if they don't agree with you about something without risking their place on the team?

>> **Coaching and giving feedback:** Do you understand the difference between coaching and feedback? When providing coaching and feedback, do you ignore or incorporate the cultural context between you and your employees? Are you adequately prepared for your coaching and feedback conversations?

>> **Communicating:** Are you aware of language that might inadvertently offend or hurt some members of your team so that you can avoid it? Are you aware of the preferred communication styles among your team members so that you can adapt when necessary?

>> **Dealing with conflict:** Are you afraid of conflict? Do you avoid it when possible? Or are you able to discuss uncomfortable topics with your team and mitigate conflicts when they arise?

These are obviously big topics, but all are important to consider when building a culture where everyone feels seen, heard, and respected. For more on leading inclusively, check out my book *Inclusive Leadership For Dummies.*

Demanding More Growth Opportunities

Even if an employee is challenged by their work but not overwhelmed, led by empathetic leaders who recognize their gifts and include them, welcomed by leaders and colleagues alike to be their authentic selves, and routinely praised for their contributions to the team, one surefire way to disengage them is to make them feel like they're not moving or growing.

When millennials were growing up, the "participation trophy" was a common metaphor others used to describe everything that was wrong with this younger generation. The complaint was that children were constantly being told that they were "special" and "remarkable." It was an era where "every child got a prize," even those who hadn't done anything but show up.

Mind you, most of the folks doing the complaining were simultaneously raising these children and protecting their "self-esteem" at every cost. I'm not interested in shaming anyone for the way they were raised or parents who were doing their best — but the result is that millennials, as a cohort, display a lot of confidence in themselves while other generations, particularly the older ones, are much less likely to "blow their own horn," even if they experience a strong belief in their own talents.

In my experience working with millennials, their confidence is not unearned. They do have a lot to offer, and they are very talented. The main difference between millennials and baby boomers or Generation X (my generation) is that millennials aren't hesitant to say so. I also happen to believe that millennials weren't fooled by any "participation trophies" they received as children. As adults, they're not interested in rewards for just showing up (although they would appreciate the occasional "thank you" for a job well done). Rather, they want to succeed, and they believe they can.

REMEMBER

Millennials are a big group, and not all of them will conform to the personality type I'm describing here. There are millennials who suffer from imposter syndrome or who aren't bursting with confidence. As always, get to know your employees as individuals, and adjust your leadership style appropriately. But I do believe that the pattern is strong and true enough of most of them that the advice I'm about to give is warranted.

What millennials (and most other employees, quite frankly) want is to grow. They don't want to feel stagnant in their careers. They want to look back each year and find tangible ways that they have acquired new skills, completed different kinds of tasks, and met challenges head-on. When I say that they want to grow in their careers, I'm not just talking about promotions (although millennials love that kind of vertical growth as much as anyone else). Rather, they (and most others) want to feel as though they're consistently improving, learning, and developing as professionals.

As a leader, it's partly your responsibility to ensure that your team members are engaged in professional development activities. This could be training and education, certificate programs, or learning on the job by working on cross-functional teams or expanding their role beyond their current job description. Even — perhaps especially — if a particular team member is not yet ready to be promoted, they are always in a position to gain new skills and perspectives. In many organizations, the performance assessment process is a way to formalize the professional development process, by creating specific and measurable goals for each member of your team.

TIP

Unless an employee is failing and their goals are remedial in nature, try to strike a balance between developing an employee's weak areas and building on their strengths. When one's entire scope of professional development is focused on doing things that one isn't very good at, the process can be demoralizing and not very fun. By allowing each employee some time to enhance what they're already good at (and probably enjoy), they'll be much more motivated to pursue professional development activities without much prodding from you.

Chapter **10**

Sourcing and Selecting Top Talent

G reat teams don't just happen. They're the product of thoughtful planning, intentional selection, and ongoing development. When leaders set out to build high-performing teams, the most important first step is to source talent from a wide pool of skills, backgrounds, and perspectives. Over the years, I've spoken with countless leaders who expressed frustration about not being able to find the right people. The reality is, qualified candidates are out there, but too often, organizations rely on familiar recruitment channels and outdated selection criteria. As a result, they see the same limited outcomes.

Today's competitive landscape demands that leaders widen their nets, modernize their requirements, and actively work to remove bias from their processes. By doing so, organizations will be better equipped to build teams that adapt quickly, innovate consistently, and deliver exceptional results.

This chapter will guide you through the foundational strategies of sourcing and assembling a dynamic team. It will identify practical approaches for broadening the search for candidates and making informed decisions that reflect the organization's goals. Whether you're refining your hiring process or rebuilding a team from the ground up, this chapter will offer actionable insights to ensure every selection supports long-term performance and cohesion.

Closing Gaps with a Variety of Skills, Experiences, and Perspectives

REMEMBER

Building a high-performing team begins with understanding the essential skills and competencies each member brings to the table. Team members should possess a balance of technical expertise, business acumen, collaboration, communication, and learning agility to meet project demands and adapt to evolving challenges.

It's important to start with assessing the current skills on the team. Each member should be able to identify their strengths and areas for growth across various domains. Technical proficiency is vital for those working on specialized projects, while strategic thinking and business understanding empower individuals to see how their work contributes to larger organizational goals. Having a diverse range of perspectives and backgrounds widens the team's problem-solving capacity and helps address gaps in customer or stakeholder needs. The following sections cover a few examples of the kinds of skills that are critical to have on any team.

TIP

When assessing skills on your team, ask each member to map their strengths to current project needs. This simple exercise often reveals hidden capabilities you can deploy immediately.

Technical and functional

Technical skills empower team members to carry out their responsibilities with precision and contribute fresh solutions to emerging challenges. Mastery of relevant tools, programming languages, analytical techniques, and industry-specific technologies allows individuals to achieve efficiency and excellence in project delivery. Within high-performing teams, members are encouraged not only to refine their existing technical abilities, but also to explore new advancements proactively. By sharing knowledge and mentoring one another, they help to create a collective environment of continuous improvement and adaptability.

Yet, technical expertise alone is not enough to drive superior team outcomes. It must be complemented by functional expertise, which is a deep understanding of the processes, standards, and best practices that govern the team's domain. Functional expertise ensures that technical solutions are not only innovative but also practical and aligned with organizational requirements. This dual focus empowers team members to anticipate challenges, comply with regulatory and industry frameworks, and integrate their work seamlessly into broader business operations.

The most effective teams blend technical and functional strengths, recruiting individuals who can bridge the gap between what is possible and what is necessary. These professionals excel at translating business needs into actionable technical solutions and can communicate effectively with both technical and nontechnical stakeholders. By cultivating this balance, organizations set the stage for scalable, resilient teams that can deliver lasting value.

REMEMBER

Technical expertise becomes far more valuable when paired with the ability to explain complex ideas simply. Prioritize candidates who can translate knowledge into action.

Business acumen

A well-rounded team includes individuals who understand the organization's mission, market dynamics, and industry trends. This strategic awareness enables team members to prioritize effectively, make informed decisions, and align their contributions with the company's objectives. Individuals with strong business acumen can spot opportunities, avoid pitfalls, and help steer projects in the right direction.

Developing business acumen within a team goes beyond knowledge of financial statements or market share. It requires cultivating an environment where members are encouraged to think about the bigger picture — how their daily tasks contribute to long-term organizational growth and sustainability. Leaders can foster this mindset by regularly sharing insights on company performance, competitive strategy, and shifts in customer expectations. Encouraging participation in cross-functional projects and exposing team members to different aspects of the business helps deepen their understanding and broaden their perspective.

Furthermore, business acumen empowers teams to be proactive rather than reactive. When individuals are attuned to industry trends and aware of the broader context, they can anticipate changes and initiate strategic adjustments ahead of time. This adaptability is especially valuable in rapidly evolving sectors, where timely decision-making can be the difference between innovation and obsolescence. By supporting continuous learning and critical thinking, organizations ensure that their teams remain agile, resourceful, and equipped to drive sustained success.

TIP

Build business awareness by rotating team members into cross-functional meetings once a quarter. Exposure accelerates strategic thinking.

Collaboration

Effective collaboration is a hallmark of high-performance teams. Team members must be able to work together, leveraging each other's unique experiences and talents to solve complex problems. Rotating responsibilities or partnering on projects encourages sharing of knowledge and builds cohesion. Open feedback and recognition of diverse viewpoints contribute to innovative solutions and foster a supportive work environment.

REMEMBER

Collaboration improves when everyone knows what "success" looks like. Revisit shared goals regularly to make sure the whole team is aligned.

To strengthen collaboration, teams benefit from establishing shared goals and clear expectations from the outset. When everyone understands the collective objectives and how their individual contributions fit into the larger vision, it encourages commitment and accountability. Regular workshops or brainstorming sessions create space for idea exchange and help uncover hidden strengths within the group. These collaborative practices not only improve workflow but also build trust, making it easier to navigate challenges together.

Modern collaboration often relies on digital tools that bridge physical distance and streamline teamwork. Platforms such as shared documents, project management software, and instant messaging applications enable seamless communication and coordination, even for remote or distributed teams. Embracing these technologies allows members to contribute asynchronously, track progress transparently, and resolve issues more quickly. By cultivating an environment where collaboration is supported by both interpersonal relationships and robust digital infrastructure, organizations set the stage for collective achievement and sustainable growth.

TIP

Use shared digital dashboards to visualize progress in real time. Transparency reduces duplicate work and increases accountability.

Communication

REMEMBER

Effective communication is the backbone of any successful team. It serves not only as a conduit for sharing information but also as a foundation for building mutual trust and understanding. Team members should consistently provide updates on their progress, articulate challenges they're facing, and request clarification when objectives or instructions are unclear. When everyone is informed, goals are easier to align, and responsibilities remain transparent.

REMEMBER

Clarity beats frequency. Rather than sending multiple messages, consolidate updates so your team stays informed without feeling overwhelmed.

Establishing regular check-ins creates opportunities for open dialogue. These touchpoints allow individuals to anticipate potential roadblocks early, brainstorm solutions collaboratively, and reinforce shared purpose. Beyond scheduled meetings, accessibility to digital channels for informal conversations encourages spontaneous problem-solving and swift knowledge exchange.

Constructive feedback is a vital component of the communication process. When team members offer observations in a respectful and solution-oriented manner, it helps others recognize strengths, identify areas for improvement, and fine-tune their approach. A culture that welcomes feedback also empowers individuals to voice new ideas and perspectives, sparking innovation and challenging the status quo.

TIP

Equally important is active listening. By engaging with what others are saying, acknowledging their viewpoints, asking thoughtful follow-up questions, and reflecting on the information received, team members foster a sense of inclusion and belonging. This practice reduces misunderstandings and ensures that diverse perspectives are valued and considered in decision-making.

REMEMBER

Pausing for two seconds before responding prevents accidental interruptions and shows genuine respect for the speaker's perspective.

Strong communication skills extend beyond internal interactions. Teams that can effectively share their achievements, challenges, and needs with external stakeholders, clients, or other departments enhance the organization's overall collaboration and reputation. The ability to tailor messages for different audiences, adjust tone appropriately, and communicate across cultural or linguistic divides is increasingly critical in today's interconnected work environment.

Technology and digitization

The accelerating pace of technological advancement presents both a challenge and an opportunity for modern teams. Embracing digitization allows organizations to streamline operations, improve efficiency, and unlock new avenues for creativity. From data analytics and automation to cloud computing and collaboration platforms, leveraging the right technology empowers teams to make more informed decisions, optimize workflows, and deliver high-quality outcomes. Those who integrate digital tools into daily practices not only enhance their proficiency but also foster an environment where innovation can flourish.

REMEMBER

Staying abreast of new and emerging technologies is equally crucial for maintaining a competitive edge. Teams that are curious and proactive about technological trends are better positioned to anticipate industry shifts, respond to evolving customer needs, and seize untapped opportunities. Ongoing education, experimentation with new solutions, and openness to change encourage a culture of agility and resilience. By investing in the development of digital literacy and supporting continuous learning, organizations ensure their teams remain adaptive and forward-thinking.

Ultimately, technology should be viewed not just as a means to an end, but as a catalyst for growth and transformation. By prioritizing digitization and cultivating an appetite for emerging tools, organizations equip their teams to tackle complex challenges, unlock breakthrough innovations, and consistently outperform expectations in a rapidly changing world.

Before adopting new tools, ask the team to identify their biggest workflow frustrations. Choose technology that solves real problems rather than picking only the tools that are trending.

Learning agility

Team members who demonstrate learning agility by actively seeking out new knowledge, adjusting seamlessly to evolving circumstances, and reflecting critically on both successes and setbacks provide their teams with a robust foundation for innovation and resilience. By cultivating curiosity and embracing a growth mindset, individuals transform obstacles into opportunities, driving the team forward even when faced with uncertainty.

When teams are empowered to learn from failure and iterate on processes, they're better equipped to respond swiftly to market changes and shifting priorities. This flexibility allows teams to pivot strategies, adopt new technologies, and refine best practices without losing momentum or morale.

In addition, fostering a spirit of lifelong learning within teams strengthens overall performance. By providing access to ongoing education, mentorship, and cross-functional experiences, organizations nurture the development of versatile skill sets among team members. This investment in professional growth translates to a more engaged workforce that's eager to tackle complex challenges and contribute fresh perspectives. As individuals expand their expertise, the team as a whole becomes more robust — capable of navigating ambiguity, seizing emerging opportunities, and sustaining long-term success.

Effective leaders play a crucial role in modeling learning agility. By demonstrating openness to feedback, celebrating experimentation, and facilitating knowledge sharing, leaders inspire their teams to remain adaptable and proactive. This approach not only bolsters team cohesion but also establishes a culture where change is embraced as an integral part of growth. In a rapidly evolving business landscape, such agility ensures that teams remain competitive, resilient, and primed for ongoing achievement.

Casting a Wider Net to Build a Strong Pipeline of Talent

When it comes to building a high-performing team, leaders cannot afford to fish in the same narrow ponds and expect different results. A strong pipeline requires intentionality, relationship-building, and visibility in places where top talent may not have traditionally looked for you. The goal is not only to increase the number of candidates, but to expand the range of perspectives, skills, and experiences represented on your team. In this section I show you how to broaden your recruiting channels and tap into new, high-potential talent pools that strengthen your overall pipeline.

Universities, colleges, and nontraditional talent sources

Building a truly diverse and high-performing team means widening the recruiting lenses far beyond conventional channels. Start by forging strategic partnerships with educational institutions dedicated to serving underrepresented communities such as Historically Black Colleges and Universities (HBCUs), Hispanic-serving institutions, tribal colleges, and community colleges. These schools have a rich track record of cultivating talented graduates who bring unique perspectives and experiences.

But don't stop there: tap into vocational schools and technical training centers, which prepare students with hands-on skills and practical problem-solving abilities. These candidates often offer fresh approaches and adaptability, critical assets for teams seeking innovation.

TIP

To truly make an impact, move beyond posting jobs and invest in comprehensive outreach by offering scholarships, internships, apprenticeships, and mentorship programs tailored to each institution's strengths. Build authentic relationships by engaging with faculty, attending career events, and consistently showing up as a sponsor or speaker. This visibility ensures your organization is recognized as an employer of choice well before graduation.

By embracing these varied and sometimes overlooked hiring sources, you unlock a broader pipeline of motivated, well-prepared talent. The result is a team enriched by a wide spectrum of skills, backgrounds, and perspectives, ready to excel in today's dynamic environment.

Professional associations and industry groups

Nearly every profession (from accounting to engineering, architecture to sales) has organizations dedicated to underrepresented professionals. Building long-term partnerships with these groups is essential, but high-performing teams can cast an even wider net by engaging with networks serving veterans, career returners, neurodiverse talent, individuals with disabilities, and candidates from alternative education pathways.

Developing these relationships goes beyond simply sponsoring conferences or career fairs. Offer employees as speakers or mentors, collaborate on industry panels, host skill-building workshops, and create opportunities for meaningful networking and connection. By authentically showing up and investing in these communities, you pave the way for candidates with a variety of perspectives and life experiences to find pathways into your organization.

For example, when I led recruiting efforts, I managed partnerships with more than 20 professional associations and nontraditional networks, including veteran transition groups, women in STEM cohorts, coding bootcamp alumni, and organizations focused on people with disabilities. This approach consistently resulted in hires who not only brought technical acumen but also a wealth of creativity, resilience, and fresh viewpoints that sparked innovation across teams.

REMEMBER

Ultimately, the goal is to ensure your presence is both intentional and sustained, reflecting a true commitment to welcoming all types of talent, regardless of their background or the path they took to your door.

Early-career platforms and talent communities

The next generation of high performers, particularly Gen Z and Alphas, expects organizations to meet them where they are. Platforms like Handshake, LinkedIn communities, Indeed.com and online career forums have become go-to spaces for emerging talent. Engage authentically by highlighting your organization's culture, mentorship programs, benefits and perks, and innovation projects.

REMEMBER

High-performing teams benefit from intergenerational perspectives, so building a steady pipeline of younger talent ensures your team stays agile, tech-savvy, and future-ready.

Apprenticeships and earn-and-learn programs

Across the globe, modern apprenticeship programs are expanding beyond traditional sectors. Organizations in fields such as technology, healthcare, and finance are increasingly adopting "earn-and-learn" pathways, opening doors for candidates who may have pursued alternative routes to education and professional development.

By partnering with international, government-backed, or nonprofit apprenticeship initiatives, employers create mutually beneficial opportunities: Individuals gain access to meaningful careers, while organizations welcome highly motivated, adaptable talent who are equipped with the skills most relevant to their needs.

Strategic use of search firms and talent partners

Today, leveraging specialized search partners is essential for building a vibrant and multidimensional workforce. These firms possess deep knowledge of niche talent markets and maintain broad networks, enabling them to identify candidates who might otherwise remain off your radar. By engaging with search partners who understand both the industry landscape and your organization's unique needs, you tap into expertise that accelerates your ability to source, attract, and retain exceptional talent. Their involvement not only widens the candidate pool but also infuses your hiring process with fresh perspectives and best practices from across the sector, positioning your organization to stay agile and competitive.

TIP

If you engage external search partners, hold them accountable. Require them to present a broad slate of candidates and ensure they understand your organization's goals for cultivating a workforce rich in varied perspectives. Too often, organizations accept slates that look identical to their existing workforce. Set expectations upfront, and partner only with firms that can deliver the range of skills, experiences, and viewpoints you seek.

Go beyond transactional relationships with search firms by involving them in your ongoing efforts to foster a mosaic of backgrounds and talents. Share your company's mission, values, and success stories so they can represent your brand authentically in the marketplace. Conduct regular reviews of the candidate pools they present and provide constructive feedback to improve the breadth and quality of future searches. By fostering open communication and accountability, you ensure your search partners become genuine champions of your holistic talent strategy.

TIP

Request anonymized resumes during the early stages of search firm reviews. Removing personally identifying details helps minimize bias.

Employee referrals that break the mold

Referral programs can be powerful, but they can also reinforce sameness if employees only refer people from their own networks. Encourage referrals from staff across the organization, community engagement programs, and cross-industry partnerships. Reward employees for referring candidates who bring unique skills or backgrounds to the team.

To maximize the impact of referral programs, spotlight stories of successful hires who came from unconventional backgrounds or underrepresented groups. Host referral challenges focused on filling gaps that exist on the team and invite employees to participate in outreach events with employee networks or local organizations. When employees are inspired to look beyond their immediate circles, the referral pipeline becomes a dynamic force for innovation and inclusion, continually renewing the energy and perspective within your workforce.

Positive employer brand and visibility

Candidates will not just evaluate your job postings; they will evaluate your culture and reputation. They may reach out on LinkedIn to previous and current staff of your company for feedback, or they may tap into their social networks to ask others for information about the company. Make sure that you are fully aware of what your organization's reputation and brand are. Be sure that the company is visible where top talent gathers. This includes sponsoring local and national conferences, sharing employee success stories on social media platforms, and applying for awards that recognize workplace culture and inclusion.

TIP

Invest in multimedia campaigns that display your commitment to growth, mentorship, and diversity. Share authentic testimonials, behind-the-scenes videos, and interactive Q&A sessions with current employees on social media platforms frequented by your target talent pool. Participate in industry roundtables and thought leadership forums to highlight your organization's progressive practices. The more candidates see evidence of your values in action, the more likely they are to envision themselves thriving as part of your team.

REMEMBER

Transparency is key. Share your progress, tell authentic stories, and highlight how your teams succeed together. High-performing individuals want to join organizations where they see growth, mentorship, and long-term career paths.

Watching for Biases in Selection and Decision-Making

As human beings, we naturally attach certain beliefs to the work, talent, or performance ability of other individuals or groups. These assumptions and stereotypes (also referred to as biases or blind spots) are based on the messages that we were taught at a very young age and how they were reinforced over time through our family, communities, schools, places of worship, friends, experiences, and the media. When left unchecked, biases can undermine your organization's efforts to recruit, retain, and advance top talent (in particular, talent from underrepresented/minority groups such as women, people of color, people over 50, people with disabilities, those from lower socioeconomic groups, and so on).

Unconscious biases are our natural preferences. Biologically, we're hardwired to prefer people who look like us, sound like us, think the way we think, and share our interests. These hidden biases can impact us in a variety of ways, especially when it comes to interviewing and hiring. At times, interviewers make subtle assumptions about a candidate, and these subtleties may influence you, either positively or negatively, in your decisions. You may make some inappropriate or even bad choices. Research has shown that many hiring decisions are made within the first five to ten minutes of an interview. These decisions are not made based on whether the person is qualified or capable of performing the job. They're made on first impressions. We routinely and quickly sort people into groups, which is called social categorization. The problem with this is that the categories we use to sort people are not necessarily logical, modern, or legal.

In addition to these broad patterns, several specific biases frequently emerge throughout the sourcing and selection process. As you read each one of the biases in the following list, assess which of those you see the most in your organization. Also consider which of these biases may be yours:

>> **Name bias:** Judging candidates based on the perceived ethnicity, gender, or background suggested by their names, which can result in qualified individuals being overlooked.

>> **Affinity bias:** Favoring candidates who share similarities with the interviewer, such as upbringing, hobbies, or alma mater, which can unintentionally narrow the diversity of a team.

>> **Confirmation bias:** Seeking information that reaffirms initial impressions, while ignoring evidence that might challenge those assumptions.

>> **Recency bias:** Giving disproportionate weight to the most recent interactions or information about a candidate rather than considering their overall qualifications and experience.

>> **Halo/horn effect**: Allowing one very positive (halo) or negative (horn) trait to influence the overall assessment of a candidate, which can skew judgment.

>> **Age bias:** Making assumptions about someone's capabilities based on their age, rather than their actual skills or experience.

>> **Socioeconomic bias:** Letting perceptions about a candidate's education, neighborhood, or background influence decisions, rather than focusing on their merits.

Becoming aware of these biases is a critical step in creating fairer, more inclusive hiring processes. So, if you have these hidden biases, what can you do about it? The good news is that there are some processes you can put in place to counteract these biases.

As a first step, avoid an unstructured interview by planning in advance. Understand the role you're hiring for. Consider these questions:

>> What technical skills or academic credentials are desired in a candidate?

>> What qualities, skills, behaviors or experiences would the ideal candidate possess?

>> What type of candidate would fit in your workplace culture?

After answering these, develop interview questions that assess whether the candidate possesses these competencies.

Behavioral-based interviewing will help you avoid making selections based on assumptions, intuitions or solely on credentials. The foundation of behavioral-based interviewing is that one of the best predictors of a candidate's future job performance is their past job behavior. This can be explored by asking questions such as, "Describe a difficult work-related problem that required you to come up with a creative solution. Tell me the steps you took and why," or "Please give a specific example of when you collaborated with another individual." "How would you evaluate or describe the results from that effort?" By gaining insight into a candidate's past experiences, you'll develop a reliable indicator of how that individual most likely will perform in the future.

Once you've developed your questions, ask each of the candidates the same set of questions in the same way. Asking different questions may lead to skewed assessments of the candidates. Keep in mind that you should only ask questions that relate to the job the person is being considered for. You shouldn't ask any questions relating to age, family, marital status, pregnancy, gender, national origin, disability, and religion.

Here are some additional examples of how qualifications can reveal unconscious bias:

» Socioeconomic bias is often unintentionally at play in job descriptions that emphasize the need for advanced degrees from a set of high-profile universities or having studied a certain curriculum, neither of which may have been available to underrepresented talent.

» Gender bias is at play in programming jobs that require candidates to have spent time contributing to open-source software. If you know anything about open-source programming, you know that female-identified engineers have often experienced hostility in these spaces; so many simply don't engage. The reality is that, while having contributed to open-source development is a "nice-to-have," it's not a critical requirement for a role.

» Gender and racial bias is unintentionally at play in job postings that list seniority requirements. That's because female representation drops steadily as you move from entry-level positions up to the C-suite. So requiring past experience in seniority positions becomes a barrier to entry for qualified female candidates, especially women of color.

Reviewing Job Descriptions to Ensure Inclusive Language

Recruiting a broad talent pool is a top challenge and priority for most organizations. But many of them fail to take some basic steps to set themselves up to attract candidates with diverse backgrounds and experiences, especially when it comes to job descriptions. A job description outlines the responsibilities of the position and the desired knowledge, skills, experience, and abilities to perform a job effectively. It's worthwhile and strategic to first evaluate how any position being recruited for can advance the goals of an organization and how such expectations and responsibilities can be integrated into the job description.

A job description is often a candidate's first exposure to the job, but also to organizational culture and values. The way a position is written, the words that are used to describe the ideal candidate, and the information that is — and is not — included in a job description can speak volumes to candidates.

Job descriptions that are not inclusive may limit candidate interest and make it that much harder to attract diverse candidates, but when they're inclusive, it enables a variety of talent to more easily see themselves in a role and decide to apply. Writing inclusive job descriptions may require recruiters and hiring managers to reexamine what they should look and sound like, meaning, "What message are you sending to the candidate about your company culture?"

REMEMBER

It's important to not just list job requirements but focus on how candidates will contribute to the bigger picture. The better the job description, the more candidates (of all backgrounds) will want to apply. Be sure the job description absolutely matches the job you're hiring for. Nothing is more frustrating than a candidate finding out the job is different from the job description.

Job descriptions should also be free of company jargon and acronyms and not be filled with unnecessary requirements. They should provide key insights about your organizational culture and be free of language that may signal to underrepresented or minority talent that they won't feel welcomed, included, respected, or safe in your workplace.

The following sections elaborate on some tips for how to write more inclusive job descriptions.

Use gender-neutral language

Research reveals that women will typically only apply for a job if they meet 90 percent to 100 percent of the qualifications. To avoid unconscious gender bias that deters women from applying to your jobs, consider eliminating requirements that are not essential. If the position is one where training can easily be provided, don't ask for experience on software. Generalize areas where transferable skills are okay and clearly outline which qualifications are required and which are preferred.

Eliminate racial bias

Like gender bias, racial bias can be implicit. Oftentimes, it's unknowingly perpetuated by recruitment professionals. Some careful attention to words and phrases used can help eliminate implicit and explicit bias. Here are some suggestions:

>> When writing descriptions, be aware of the following:

- Never mention race or national origin.

- Phrases like, "strong English-language skills" may deter qualified nonnative English speakers from applying.

- A "clean-shaven" requirement can exclude candidates whose faith requires them to maintain facial hair. It also suggests the position is for men only.

» When reviewing candidates, keep the following things in mind:

- Avoid "cultural fit" and focus on "value alignment."

- Limit referral hiring and go beyond your network.

- Don't waiver from the qualifications for a select few.

- Ask everyone the same set of interview questions.

Minimizing bias against older workers

Workers ages 50 and older comprise roughly 35 percent of the workforce, according to a report from HR Executive. Some best practices for avoiding age discrimination include making sure your employer branding reflects a wide range of the age of workers at your company. Also, don't ask for grade point averages (GPAs) or SAT scores. Doing so implies that only recent graduates are being considered.

Additionally, avoid phrasing like

» Young and energetic

» Party atmosphere

» Work hard/play hard

» Digital native

» Calling all recent college grads!

» Athletic or athletically inclined

» No more than X years of experience

» Junior or Senior except as part of a job title

» Supplement your retirement income!

Be inclusive of disabled workers

Make sure your job postings are welcoming to workers of all abilities by advertising when there are accommodations like flexible hours or telework policies that would appeal to disabled workers.

Let applicants know your workplace welcomes and values all candidates with phrasing like, "Ability to complete tasks with or without reasonable accommodations." Instead of writing, "Access to you own vehicle isn't always necessary," try "Access to reliable transportation," which is more inclusive to people with disabilities.

Lay the groundwork for a more inclusive workplace

If your workforce is monocultural and lacking in diversity, your company is less likely to succeed. Writing more inclusive job descriptions can certainly help, but cultivating a more inclusive and diverse workplace requires awareness and efforts that may not be that obvious.

Building inclusivity starts well before the job posting goes live. You have to embed equitable values into your workplace culture, such as by offering regular training on unconscious bias, establishing mentorship programs for underrepresented groups, and ensuring your interview panels reflect a range of backgrounds and perspectives. By intentionally supporting and celebrating differences, you foster an environment where all employees feel welcome, respected, and empowered to contribute their talents.

In this section, I highlight several identity groups such as age, gender, race, and religion. These are areas where biased language often shows up in job descriptions, and I explain how addressing these blind spots strengthens the inclusive sourcing and selection practices you learned in this chapter and the previous one.

Age-specific descriptions

Specifying that your job is perfect for "new grads," "young adults," "retirees," or "older workers" is discouraging to candidates who don't fall neatly into those categories. Furthermore, the Age Discrimination in Employment Act (ADEA) explicitly forbids age discrimination against people who are age 40 or older.

With more baby boomers staying in the workforce longer, employers should keep ageism top of mind when writing job ads and during the prescreening, interviewing, and onboarding processes. It's also best to avoid phrases like "tech-savvy," "fresh," or "young and vibrant," which could dissuade older workers from applying.

Gender-specific terms

Certain traditional job titles imply a particular gender: waitress, salesman, cameraman, and foreman are examples. Using gender-neutral titles — wait staff, salesperson, camera operator, or supervisor, for example — will ensure the position appeals to a more diverse set of candidates. You may also consider using plural pronouns, "they" or "their" in lieu of "he," "him," "she," or "her," when talking about the ideal applicant.

TIP

Beyond more obvious language choices like those in the preceding paragraph, studies show that words with masculine undertones like *ambitious* and *competitive* may deter women from applying for a job.

TIP

In my book, *Diversity, Equity, and Inclusion For Dummies* (Wiley, 2022), I provide lists of words and phrases to avoid and how to be more inclusive in the selection and hiring process.

Mentions of race

Unless your business must abide by affirmative action requirements, never mention race in your job qualifications. If you're beholden to these requirements, you may disclose that you are an affirmative action program participant. Note that affirmative action also pertains to women, people with disabilities, and veterans.

Religious references

Avoid specifying preferences for candidates with certain religious beliefs, except if you qualify as a religious organization under Title VII. Further, the EEOC states that "questions about an applicant's religious affiliation or beliefs (unless the religion is a bona fide occupational qualification [BFOQ]) are generally viewed as non-job-related and problematic under federal law."

TIP

WRITING MORE INCLUSIVE JOB DESCRIPTIONS

Here are some suggestions for writing inclusive job descriptions:

- Check for gendered wording. Avoid relying on masculine language that can deter women from applying.

- Use plain speech rather than corporate jargon.

- Avoid phrases that imply a preference for young candidates, such as "fast-moving."

- Don't make level of schooling a requirement unless a candidate actually needs a degree to do the job, and don't put emphasis on GPAs.

- Avoid excessive and unnecessary requirements.

Chapter **11**

Orienting and Onboarding New Team Members

L eaders don't just manage tasks; they curate experiences. And when it comes to bringing new people onto a team, the difference between an employee who merely survives and one who thrives often begins with those first pivotal weeks.

With that in mind, this chapter offers a step-by-step deep dive into the art and science of orienting and onboarding new team members. High performance doesn't happen by accident; it's intentionally designed from day one.

Distinguishing between Orientation and Onboarding

Let me clear up a common misconception that I've encountered countless times in my career: Orientation and onboarding are not interchangeable. They serve distinct, critical purposes in assimilating new team members into your organization. If you're leading a team or managing talent, knowing the difference — and leveraging both intentionally — can transform your team's engagement, performance, and retention rates.

Orientation is your opening handshake, your "welcome to the family" moment. Think of it as the red carpet rollout — the company's way of saying, "We're glad you're here, and here's what you need to know right now." This typically covers the nuts-and-bolts essentials: company policies, compliance training, work-place safety, and a high-level overview of the organization's structure. In my experience, a well-executed orientation answers the immediate questions new hires have:

» Where do I park?

» Who do I call if I'm sick?

» What's the dress code?

Orientation is about removing uncertainty so people can breathe a little easier on day one.

Onboarding, on the other hand, is the journey from "new hire" to "high-performing, fully integrated team member." This is not a one-and-done session; it's a strategic, comprehensive process that can span weeks or even a full year, depending on your organization's complexity and culture. Onboarding is where you lay the groundwork for long-term success: clarifying expectations, nurturing relationships, building cultural fluency, and empowering growth.

Let me paint a picture: Imagine a new team member, eager but anxious, stepping into your organization for the first time. Orientation is the guide at the front desk, showing them the layout and handing them a welcome packet. Onboarding is the seasoned mentor who takes them under their wing, introduces them to the movers and shakers, helps them master the unwritten rules, and checks in regularly to ensure they're thriving.

The research is crystal clear here. According to a 2024 Deloitte Insights Report, organizations that treat orientation and onboarding as distinct, intentional processes see retention rates up to 50 percent higher among first-year employees. Why? Because people don't just want to be "processed"; they want to feel seen, supported, and set up for success. They want to know not just how to do their job, but also how to belong.

So, as you design your team's approach, ask yourself, "Are we rolling out the welcome mat and walking with our people down the hallway? Or are we leaving them at the door, hoping they'll find their own way?"

Creating a Memorable and Impactful Orientation Program

Now that we've established what orientation is, and isn't, let's talk about how to make it count. A memorable orientation isn't about bombarding new hires with PowerPoint slides and policy manuals. It's about creating a genuine sense of belonging from the very first interaction. The goal? For every new team member to walk away thinking, *I made the right choice. This is where I'm meant to be.*

In this section, I offer the steps you should take to give your new hires a meaningful orientation.

Rolling out the red carpet (literally and figuratively)

First impressions matter. Set the tone with a warm, inclusive welcome. This could mean a personalized welcome message from the CEO, a custom swag bag, or even a video montage introducing key team members. I've worked with organizations that assign a welcome ambassador or a peer coach whose sole job is to ensure every new hire feels celebrated on their first day. The impact is profound. Workers have reported higher morale, increased loyalty, and greater motivation to contribute.

Making orientation personal, not just procedural

Move beyond the checklist. Yes, compliance training and paperwork are important, but they shouldn't overshadow what makes your organization unique. Devote time to sharing company history, values, and the "why" behind your mission.

Bring in team members from different departments to share stories about their journey and growth. Consider adding interactive elements: icebreakers, team-building activities, and Q&A sessions that encourage honest dialogue. Let them hear from real employees — recently hired and long-tenured — to understand a day in the life.

Setting clear expectations and offer roadmaps

No one likes feeling lost. Create a detailed agenda for orientation day and share it in advance. Walk new hires through what to expect, not just in the first week, but in the first 90 days and beyond. Introduce them to resources like an organizational chart, key policies, a "who's who" contact sheet, and yes, even reveal the unwritten rules for how to succeed in the organization. Many times, these rules are not shared in the employee handbook, and this can be the difference between those who excel and those who don't.

Fostering belonging from day one

Inclusion and belonging aren't just buzzwords; they're business imperatives. Ensure that your orientation content reflects the diversity of your team and customers. Use inclusive language, share your organization's commitments to providing a fair, equitable, and respectful workplace, and create space for new hires to share their backgrounds, perspectives, and preferences.

TIP

Storytelling is powerful here: Highlight how different identities and experiences contribute to your team's success.

Gathering feedback and continuously improve

Orientation is not a set-it-and-forget-it proposition. Survey participants after every session by asking questions like these:

>> What resonated?

>> What felt rushed or confusing?

>> What wasn't covered that the employee wanted to know?

Use this data to refine your program. Celebrate what works and don't be afraid to experiment with new approaches.

TIP

Hybrid and remote teams need extra attention. Leverage technology to create engaging virtual orientations such as breakout rooms, live polls, and virtual meet-and-greets. Don't let distance become a barrier to belonging.

The Society for Human Resource Management (SHRM, 2023) found that organizations with structured, engaging orientation programs report 58 percent higher employee engagement scores within the first 90 days. The message is simple: When you invest in making people feel welcome, they invest back in your organization.

Clarifying Roles and Duties

Ambiguity is the enemy of engagement. One of the fastest ways to lose a new team member's enthusiasm is to hand them a job description and expect them to "figure it out." High-performing teams don't leave roles and responsibilities up to interpretation; they clarify, communicate, and revisit them as needs evolve.

REMEMBER

When you clarify roles and duties up front, you set the stage for autonomy, confidence, and high performance. You also reduce the risk of costly misunderstandings and turnover down the line.

In this section, I outline the steps you should take to clarify roles and duties to new hires.

Going beyond the job description

Job descriptions are a starting point rather than the finish line. While onboarding, sit down with each new hire and walk through their role in detail. Don't just discuss what they'll do; explain how their work connects to broader team and organizational goals. Use real-life examples and success stories to bring expectations to life.

Defining what success looks like

Set clear, measurable performance expectations. What does success look like at 30, 60, and 90 days? How will their contributions be measured?

Be specific. Vague goals breed confusion and frustration. Map out key milestones and provide resources to achieve them. In other words, shoot for SMART (specific, measurable, achievable, relevant, and time-bound) goals so that every team member is clear of "what, "how," and "when" success has been achieved.

Clarifying "how" as well as "what"

Culture is as much about *how* a group works as what they do. Outline preferred communication styles, norms around feedback, and collaboration expectations. If your team values transparency, explain what that looks like in practice. If innovation is prized, share examples of how team members have been recognized for creative solutions.

Encouraging dialogue and self-advocacy

Empower new hires to ask questions, seek clarity, and express concerns early on. This builds trust and psychological safety, which are essential for long-term engagement. Create regular check-ins during the first 90 days to revisit goals, address challenges, and recalibrate as needed.

Using tools for accountability and support

Leverage technology to document and track progress. Digital onboarding platforms, shared goal trackers, and feedback tools can help keep everyone aligned, even as teams scale or go remote.

Defining Your Team's Charter and What Success Looks Like

Every high-performing team has a North Star (a clear sense of purpose, direction, and shared values that guides every decision). This is also called your *team charter*. It's the "why" behind the work — the glue that binds people together, especially when challenges arise. Defining your team's charter isn't a one-time exercise; it's a living document that evolves as your team grows.

Follow these steps to create one for your team:

1. **Cocreate the charter with your team.**

   Ownership breeds commitment. Instead of dictating your team's charter, invite input from every member. Host a kickoff session during onboarding where everyone can contribute ideas, share experiences, and align on core values. Use vision boards, brainstorming sessions, or facilitated discussions to uncover what matters most.

2. **Articulate the team's purpose and impact.**

Go beyond tactical goals. Consider the following questions and anchor your charter in the answers:

- Why does your team exist?
- What unique value do you deliver to the organization and your stakeholders?
- How does your work make a difference?

3. **Define shared values and norms.**

What behaviors will your team celebrate and reward? How will you handle setbacks, disagreements, or failures? Codify expectations around collaboration, respect, and accountability. Make these visible. You can post them in shared spaces, reference them in meetings, and revisit them regularly.

4. **Set metrics for success.**

What does winning look like? Identify key performance indicators (KPIs) that align with your mission. These might include project completion rates, customer satisfaction scores, or employee engagement metrics. Make sure everyone understands how their work contributes to these outcomes.

5. **Celebrate milestones and success stories.**

Recognition fuels motivation. Celebrate wins (big and small) openly and often. Share stories of how team members embodied your charter, lived your values, overcame obstacles, or delivered exceptional results.

REMEMBER

A clear, cocreated charter transforms your team from a group of individuals into a unified, purpose-driven force. Defining what your team will be known for creates an identity. It empowers people to take ownership, innovate, and support each other because they know exactly what they're working toward and why it matters.

SAMPLE TEAM CHARTER

A consumer products client that I worked with several years ago created this charter. The name is fictional to maintain the client's confidentiality.

Our Purpose and Impact

We exist to uncover, interpret, and activate consumer insights that fuel innovation, elevate brand relevance, and drive market growth for Radiance Consumer Products.

(continued)

(continued)

Our Unique Value:

We serve as the voice of the customer, bridging data with empathy to anticipate needs, influence product development, and inspire marketing strategy.

Our Impact:

Translate consumer behavior into actionable insights

Launch consumer-first innovations that delight and disrupt

Strengthen brand loyalty and emotional connection with our diverse customer base

Our Shared Values and Team Norms

Our Values	How We Live Them
Collaboration	We brainstorm often, share credit, and support one another's work.
Curiosity	We ask why, dig deeper, and challenge assumptions.
Respect	We value every voice, listen actively, and practice empathy.
Accountability	We own our work, meet deadlines, and follow through.
Innovation	We embrace smart risks, test ideas, and learn from failure.

Our Behavioral Norms:

- We give and receive feedback respectfully and constructively.
- We honor diverse opinions and make space for quiet voices.
- We communicate transparently and proactively.
- We make decisions using data, insights, and inclusive dialogue.
- We hold each other, and ourselves, accountable for results and impact.

Reminder: We revisit these values quarterly to ensure they stay relevant and alive in our work.

Metrics for Success: How We Define "Winning":

Success Indicator	Measurement Tool
Project completion and on-time delivery	Agile sprint boards and project management dashboards

Success Indicator	Measurement Tool
Customer satisfaction with new products	Post-launch consumer surveys and focus group feedback
Insight-to-innovation activation rate	Ratio of insights adopted into product/ marketing pipelines
Internal stakeholder satisfaction	Quarterly partnership pulse surveys
Team engagement and retention	Annual engagement survey and quarterly check-ins

Celebrating Milestones & Success Stories

We commit to pausing and honoring our wins. Here's how we celebrate:

- **Monthly "spotlight moments":** Team members share stories of resilience, creativity, or lived values.

- **Quarterly shout-outs:** Team MVPs are nominated by peers for exemplifying the charter.

- **Innovation wall:** A visual showcase of product ideas and consumer feedback wins.

- **All-hands gratitude circles:** Five-minute rounds of gratitude at the end of major projects.

Celebration isn't extra, it's essential to building trust, morale, and momentum.

Sidestepping the Most Frequent Onboarding Pitfalls

Even the best-laid onboarding plans can go awry if you're not vigilant. Over the years, I've seen organizations fall into the same traps — often with costly consequences. Let's explore the most common onboarding pitfalls and, more importantly, how to avoid them.

> » **Treating onboarding as a one-time event:** If your onboarding ends after the first week, you're missing the mark. Research shows it takes months, sometimes up to a year, for new hires to reach full productivity. Extend your onboarding program to include ongoing check-ins, milestones, and opportunities for feedback and growth.

- **Overloading new hires with information:** It's tempting to "data dump" everything at once, but this approach overwhelms more than it enlightens. Stagger information delivery, prioritize what's truly essential for day one, and provide easy-to-access resources for ongoing learning.

- **Failing to assign a point person:** Every new team member needs a go-to contact (a mentor, buddy, or onboarding ambassador), who can answer questions, introduce them to other workers, show them around, share insights, and provide encouragement. This person should check in regularly, especially during the first 90 days.

- **Neglecting inclusion and belonging:** If new hires don't see themselves reflected in your culture or are made to feel excluded from team dynamics, engagement plummets. Make inclusion a central theme of your onboarding. Foster allyship and create space for people to share their perspectives and needs.

- **Skipping feedback and follow-up:** Onboarding is a two-way street. Solicit feedback from new hires regularly by asking them what's working, what's not working, and what would help them feel more supported. Use this feedback to iterate and improve your process. Celebrate your wins and address gaps proactively.

- **Inconsistent experience across teams or locations:** If each department or site does its own thing, new hires receive mixed messages about your organization's values and expectations. Standardize core onboarding elements while allowing room for customization based on team needs.

- **Ignoring remote and hybrid needs:** Don't assume what works in person translates virtually. Invest in robust technology platforms, schedule regular video check-ins, and foster virtual communities so remote team members feel just as connected.

- **Focusing solely on the work, not the person:** Every new hire is a whole person with hopes, dreams, anxieties, and aspirations. Take time to learn about their goals, strengths, and challenges. Show empathy, flexibility, and genuine care, people remember how you made them feel long after they've forgotten what you said.

Effective orientation and onboarding don't just "happen, they're intentionally designed, consistently delivered, and continuously improved. They're rooted in empathy, inclusion, and a commitment to helping every person thrive from day one. When you invest in these critical early experiences, you're not just building better teams, you're shaping a culture where everyone has a chance to belong, contribute, and excel.

So, as you reflect on your own team or organization, challenge yourself: How can you make your orientation more welcoming? How can your onboarding process foster deeper connections and faster growth? What stories will your new team members tell about their first days, and how will those stories shape the future of your workplace?

REMEMBER

Leadership is about the experiences we create for others. Make those first experiences count.

4

Creating and Sustaining a World-Class Culture Where Teams Can Thrive

Explore the key attributes of culture that shapes team performance, innovation, and engagement.

Address a toxic and disengaged team environment and rebuild culture after suffering major setbacks in the organization.

Promote positivity, resilience, and well-being so your team can stay energized and motivated.

Navigate conflict productively, break down silos, and develop techniques for having more impactful conversations.

Measure performance with meaningful metrics and keep your team at the top of its game.

Lead hybrid and remote teams with clarity, connection, and confidence while leveraging technology to enhance collaboration.

Operate as a savvy financial business leader by linking team goals to organizational priorities and applying financial acumen to decisions.

Chapter **12**

Understanding Company Culture and How It's Established

C*ulture* is a word that gets thrown around a lot when in discussions of team-work and performance. But what does it really mean? Is it just a "vibe" you get at a particular company? What makes a company culture healthy or toxic? What makes one company thrive and another one struggle? Does culture happen organically, or does it depend on careful planning and execution?

I find that the simplest definitions are usually the best, so I like to define *culture* as "the predictable beliefs and behaviors among any defined group of people." Culture can be national (for example, Japanese culture, Italian culture, or American culture), regional (the fast-paced culture of the Northeast United States versus the comparatively laid-back culture of the West Coast), or based on identity (for example, Millennial culture, Jewish culture, Deaf culture, male-dominated culture), or personality, industry, education, sector, and many other criteria.

As the title of this chapter indicates, organizations have cultures, too. You might work for a company that has been around for more than a century. If so, you probably work within a legacy culture that has passed down traits, practices, and legends from generation to generation. On the upside, if a company has been around that long, it's likely that the culture has served it well in many respects. On the downside, sometimes cultures need to change in response to external events (political shifts, world events, global pandemics, new technologies), and older cultures typically aren't as malleable as newer ones.

Within organizations, teams might have distinct subcultures. I notice this most when I work with clients in the advertising industry. Typically, ad firms hire both account professionals and creatives. While the account professionals are selling, managing rollouts, and meeting regularly with clients, the creatives are writing, drawing specs, casting actors and models, and managing the artistic side of the process. When I meet clients in this space, it's not uncommon for me to speak to a room where some people are dressed in business suits, and others are wearing T-shirts and jeans with cut outs in the legs. The conflicting beliefs (the need to represent the company well and the need to be comfortable at work) and behaviors (business suits, strict schedules, and order versus casual attire, a tendency to both arrive later and stay later than their colleagues, and spontaneity) are so stark it's almost comical. As you might expect, there is often conflict between the way the two sides of the business operate. And yet, from my outside perspective, it's easy to understand why these two teams function so differently because they have fundamentally different roles and needs. My goal in working with these clients is usually not to force them to assimilate but rather to guide each of them to a greater appreciation of the other because no advertising firm can survive without both.

Similarly, hospitals might often experience conflict between teams of nurses and teams of doctors (whose roles are more different than many patients appreciate), and restaurants might find friction between wait staff and kitchen staff, who perform very different functions.

As a team leader, it's your job to create a culture that aligns with the larger organization, works for every member of your team, and promotes a successful outcome (e.g., ad campaigns, successful client relationships, delicious food, courteous service, or excellent patient care).

In this chapter, I break down exactly how culture is created, how it shows up in your team's daily behaviors, and what you can do as a leader to intentionally build a culture that supports performance, belonging, and long-term success.

Describing the Key Components of Culture

Company cultures have four components: values, norms, behaviors, and attitudes. It's helpful to use these attributes to think about both the culture you have (current culture) and the culture you want (aspirational culture), which even in the best workplaces are never exactly the same.

Values

Every defined group of people holds specific values: principles that are important to them and help to guide behaviors, especially when facing a tough decision. What are the values of your team?

To discern this, one of the first jobs you have as a leader is to examine your own values. In fact, I often coach leaders not only to identify values but create a personal vision statement for themselves. These tools increase self-awareness and are a good starting place for seeing yourself the way your followers are likely to see you.

In addition, many organizations have core values that you'll find on their websites and other branding materials. Unfortunately, unless the organization's leaders have devised ways to operationalize their stated values or reward individuals and teams for embodying the core values of the organization, those values are often nothing more than words on a website.

TIP

Any stated core values of the organization are probably values that your individual team would do well to adopt as well. Even if they aren't well-known throughout the rank and file of your entire company, they probably weren't chosen randomly, and you can do your part as a team leader to instill them into your everyday work. Of course, if your team has a specialized role in your organization, you also may choose to instill some additional values in the working of your team.

If your organization doesn't have stated core values, then you have a bit more leeway when deciding on the values you'll try to impart to your team members. But first, you'd do well to diagnose the values of your current team (see Chapter 13 for more on diagnosing your current team culture).

Here's a sampling of some values that you, a team, or an entire organization might commit to:

☐ Abundance	☐ Daring	☐ Intelligence	☐ Preparedness
☐ Acceptance	☐ Decisiveness	☐ Intuition	☐ Proactivity
☐ Accountability	☐ Dedication	☐ Joy	☐ Professionalism
☐ Achievement	☐ Dependability	☐ Kindness	☐ Punctuality
☐ Advancement	☐ Diversity	☐ Knowledge	☐ Recognition
☐ Adventure	☐ Empathy	☐ Leadership	☐ Relationships
☐ Advocacy	☐ Encouragement	☐ Learning	☐ Reliability
☐ Ambition	☐ Enthusiasm	☐ Love	☐ Resilience
☐ Appreciation	☐ Ethics	☐ Loyalty	☐ Resourcefulness
☐ Attractiveness	☐ Excellence	☐ Making a Difference	☐ Respect
☐ Autonomy	☐ Fairness	☐ Mindfulness	☐ Responsibility
☐ Balance	☐ Family	☐ Motivation	☐ Security
☐ Being the Best	☐ Friendships	☐ Optimism	☐ Self-Control
☐ Boldness	☐ Flexibility	☐ Open-Mindedness	☐ Selflessness
☐ Brilliance	☐ Freedom	☐ Passion	☐ Simplicity
☐ Calm	☐ Fun	☐ Performance	☐ Stability
☐ Caring	☐ Generosity	☐ Personal Development	☐ Success
☐ Charity	☐ Grace	☐ Professionalism	☐ Teamwork
☐ Cheerfulness	☐ Gratitude	☐ Quality	☐ Thoughtfulness
☐ Cleverness	☐ Growth	☐ Recognition	☐ Traditionalism
☐ Community	☐ Happiness	☐ Risk Taking	☐ Trustworthiness
☐ Commitment	☐ Health	☐ Security	☐ Understanding
☐ Compassion	☐ Honesty	☐ Service	☐ Usefulness
☐ Cooperation	☐ Humility	☐ Spirituality	☐ Versatility
☐ Collaboration	☐ Humor	☐ Stability	☐ Vision
☐ Consistency	☐ Inclusiveness	☐ Peace	☐ Warmth
☐ Creativity	☐ Independence	☐ Perfection	☐ Wealth
☐ Credibility	☐ Innovation	☐ Popularity	☐ Well-Being
☐ Curiosity	☐ Inspiration	☐ Power	☐ Wisdom

In addition to thinking about what values you hold and the desired values for your team, think bigger. Consider the industry that your organization is a part of (for example, health care, retail, tech), how your organization differentiates itself in the marketplace (by having reasonable pricing, high quality, fast service), and the role that your specific team (marketing, HR, sales, IT) plays to contribute to your organization's success. Here are some questions to ask yourself:

>> **What values would best enable your team to succeed within your organization?** For instance, a team of nurses at a hospital might strive for compassion, or a sales team that relies upon repeat customers might aim for trustworthiness.

>> **What values will help your organization differentiate itself in the marketplace?** For instance, an organization with a higher price point

might choose to value quality, or a web-based service that markets itself as ahead of the technology curve might need to value innovation.

>> **What's important in the industry you're a part of?** For instance, a nonprofit organization might value making a difference, or a company in the hospitality sector might value cheerfulness.

In short, there's a lot to think about, including

>> Values you hold personally

>> Values you'd like to impart to your team

>> The stated core values of your organization, if they exist

>> Values that align with your team's purpose

>> Values that help your organization differentiate itself in the marketplace

>> Values that align with your industry

As you consider all of these, it's okay if there's some overlap, in fact, that's a really good sign.

Norms and behaviors

Norms are shared standards of acceptable behavior within a defined group, whereas *behaviors* are the actions people take in accordance with those norms. Norms can be informal, unwritten guidelines or codified into rules, policies, or even laws. Both formal and informal norms help to shape behaviors and guide interactions between people.

Anthropologists, who study culture, society, and human behavior, have broken down norms and behaviors into various categories, depending on severity of the possible collective response:

>> *Folkways* are everyday customs and social rules that, if broken, might result in mild disapproval. Greeting your colleagues with "Good morning!" might be an example of a team folkway if it's a behavior that occurs often on a team. Folkways generally create a feeling of harmony and goodwill on a team but aren't otherwise essential to a team's functioning.

>> *Mores* (pronounced mor-ays) are norms with stronger moral significance, and breaking them often leads to significant disapproval or even legal sanctions. Honesty might be an example of a more, resulting in punishment when an employee pads their timesheets or steals from the company. Mores can

and do change over time; in the 1940s, an openly gay man or a single woman who became pregnant would be unemployable in many corporate environments, but as the culture has shifted, so has the definition of acceptable family structures.

>> *Taboos* are deeply ingrained prohibitions that, if violated, are considered extremely offensive and elicit strong reactions. Harassment or hate speech are rightly taboo in most workplaces. Some taboos vary from workplace to workplace; for example, your organization might promote an unwritten taboo around political debates at work.

>> Finally, *policies and laws* are formal, codified norms enforced by authority structures such as HR or a police department. It's possible to see some overlap between mores, taboos, and policies within an organization (for example, stealing from the company, engaging in harassment).

As a leader in a team or organization environment, it's important not to codify all your desired norms into policy. After all, if employees are forced to greet each other with "Good morning!" every day, the gesture loses all its power to reinforce a genuine feeling of community at work. No one wants to be wished a good morning by a colleague who was forced to do so because of their employee handbook!

Of course, sometimes, it's important to create policies to create reasonable expectations around behavior and codify the appropriate consequences. For instance, using derogatory language to describe others isn't illegal; in the United States, this is actually protected speech under the First Amendment. However, the concept of "free speech" only means that the government cannot punish you for your opinions; it does not follow that employers need to tolerate speech that is harmful to others or makes it impossible for a team to work together. In that case, a policy around hate speech that includes the possibility of immediate dismissal might be an important addition to your organizational policies. And, of course, a team or organization should always follow the laws of the countries and regions they operate in.

It should be noted that just because something is written in a policy manual, it becomes a norm only if it's followed and enforced. For instance, if your policies state that employees must be at their desks at 9 a.m., but everyone routinely strolls in anywhere between 9 and 9:30 with no tangible consequences, then the norm of your office is that people arrive anywhere between 9 and 9:30. If your written dress code demands formal business attire, but your staff will occasionally be seen at the office in khakis, polos, and sundresses on days when they don't have client meetings, then more casual dress is the norm of your organization. It doesn't matter what the policies say. What ultimately matters is not the stated norm, but how people behave.

WARNING

If you notice that a stated policy has been overtaken by a consistent norm, tread carefully. When a behavior has been fully established for a significant period of time with no consequences, a leader should not suddenly begin enforcing a policy without warning. If this happens, team members will feel caught off guard, resentful, and less likely to trust you. If it's important to return to a policy that has been unenforced for some time, offer plenty of communication as well as the reasons for the change (and it is a change, even if the policy is remaining the same).

So how do norms influence behavior?

» **Social pressure:** Team members might unconsciously adopt a behavior if they notice that it's how everyone else is behaving.

» **Managing impressions:** If a team member wants to be seen as well-mannered, they will adopt relevant behaviors associated with politeness in that culture.

» **Social identity:** Sometimes, conforming to norms will signal membership in a particular group a person wants to belong to such as a work team, subculture, community organization, and so on.

» **Consequence avoidance:** Even if a person doesn't agree with a norm, they might follow through with the behavior just to avoid the hassle of any pushback.

Attitudes

Like values, attitudes are part of the belief system that an individual adopts when they align with a particular culture. Where values can be used as a "North Star" to help guide behavior during times of uncertainty, attitudes help an individual better understand their surroundings. While values are generally seen as positives, attitudes can be either positive or negative.

Of course, there are many overlaps between the areas of values, norms, behaviors, and attitudes. For instance, I've worked in very conservative offices where there was a strict taboo around emotional expression, especially tears, in the workplace. I've also worked in offices that were much more accepting of people showing emotion at work. In both places, I've witnessed people crying, either as a reaction to stress or a personal tragedy outside of work. The behaviors that result from seeing tears at work vary strongly, according to the culture. In some teams, the mere sight of tears will prompt everyone in the room to madly grab tissues and hand them to the crying individual. In others, people will generally focus their attention on the individual who is expressing their emotion and openly offer their support. Once, I witnessed a man who broke into tears at a team meeting after the death of his beloved wife, and the entire team continued their meeting as if nothing was happening!

With regard to emotional expression at work, the norms and behaviors may differ, but what's driving them are attitudes, ranging from "crying is unprofessional!" to "it happens" to "expressing your emotions is healthy."

Trying to figure out what drives culture: values, norms, behaviors, or attitudes, can be a bit like asking, "Which came first? The chicken or the egg." But closely examining all four can give you real insight into the culture that you have and help you plan for the culture you want (see Chapter 13 for more about culture change).

Detailing the Impact That Culture Plays on Performance and Business Success

A positive culture, one that satisfies the needs of your team members, helps your team do its best work, and aligns with the culture of the larger organization (see Chapter 13 for a look at the Culture Spectrum) can increase the performance of the individuals on your team and the team itself.

Improved employee performance

The experience of working in a vibrant and healthy culture leads to better individual performance in the following ways:

>> **Motivation and engagement:** Workers who are well-suited to their jobs and work in cultures that meet their needs and preferences feel happy at work, lucky to work for their team and their organization, and are motivated to perform better and help the organization succeed.

>> **Interpersonal relationships:** In a toxic culture, knowledge is a valuable commodity and likely to be hoarded. However, when a team values and rewards teamwork, the result is in better communication between team members, more productive collaboration, and information sharing, boosting efficiency and productivity.

>> **Reduced turnover and absenteeism:** While I generally encourage team leaders to allow staff to take "mental health days" as a form of self-care, if they need days off to escape the toxicity at work, you have a real problem. On the other hand, strong and positive cultures result in people feeling valued and supported at work, which discourages absenteeism and make it much less

likely that they'll leave, resulting in lower turnover. In this way, the knowledge and experience that you've fostered on your team stays with your team.

>> **Creativity and innovation:** If a culture promotes sharing ideas openly without risking one's place on the team (see Chapter 3 for more on psychological safety), this allows employees to take risks and be more creative, ultimately leading to better solutions coming from the team.

Enhanced business performance

A healthy culture also makes the team more productive, more profitable, and more flexible in the following ways:

>> **Increased profitability:** One of the benefits of reduced turnover is that replacing employees is expensive. Not only that but replacing someone with knowledge and direct experience with your team with a new person at the beginning of their learning curve (but earning the same salary) adds to your culture's price tag as well. Teams and organizations with healthy cultures save more money and therefore make more money.

>> **Stronger reputation:** A positive team culture enhances an organization's brand, attracting top talent. If your team is customer-facing, a positive culture also attracts better customers, adding to your bottom line.

>> **Customer satisfaction:** In addition to more customers, a customer-facing team with an excellent culture is more likely to deliver excellent customer service, turning new customers into repeat customers, and increasing financial stability through customer loyalty.

>> **Growth and adaptability:** When external changes force organizations and teams to adapt, a team with strong bonds can band together and weather those changes far more effectively than a team which is already fragile due to constant conflicts, poor communication, and little regard for colleagues. As a team leader, you never know when these external changes will necessitate these shifts, so it's best to always be prepared.

A thriving organizational culture makes employees happy to show up to work each day, valued by their leaders and colleagues, motivated to succeed, and empowered to do their best work, which all by itself is a win. The fact that these strengths also translate to increased productivity and profitability make a healthy culture not a luxury but a necessity.

Viewing Leaders as Thermostats: The Role of Leadership in Setting the Tone

It should come as no surprise that people tend to mimic their leaders. First of all, it makes perfect sense. If someone wants to succeed in a workplace, it follows that they would emulate those who have already succeeded, and the leader of their team is probably the "success story" they spend the most time with and are familiar with.

But research indicates that the tendency of human beings to imitate their leaders is hardwired into our brains. The "mirror system" is a network of neurons and neural pathways found in the most intelligent animals and human beings. It causes an unconscious drive to copy others, from their mannerisms and speech patterns to their emotional affect.

In humans, the mirror system is more relaxed when a person is feeling powerful — that is, when they have the ability to make things happen or change their environment in some way. However, when a person feels powerless or is aware that there are forces (including people) present that are more powerful than they are, the mirror system activates. Beyond ambition or the desire to succeed, this is an ancient survival mechanism.

The mirror system allows a person to quickly bond with their peers, finding safety in numbers when other sources of power are absent. When feeling especially powerless, peer groups can easily fall victim to groupthink, a mode of thinking that occurs when a group's desire for agreement overrides its motivation to analyze available alternatives. This is why it's important to allow team members to have some agency over the decisions they make.

The mirror system can also help people better understand their leaders, so that they can navigate power dynamics effectively and avoid displeasing those with power. Have you ever noticed that, when faced with a group decision, members often want to know which option their leader prefers before offering an opinion of their own? This is the mirror system in action, and it's a great opportunity for a leader to withhold their preferences at first to take advantage of their team's creativity.

In addition, the mirror system helps in skill transfer. When a person wants to acquire a new skill, they will automatically look to someone they believe has that skill, and they will begin to mimic. We can see evidence of this all around us but may not notice how it also applies to complex interpersonal skills such as negotiation, coaching, or mediation.

Mirror systems can explain why company cultures are so strong. When a team (or an entire organization) is led by a charismatic, easily recognizable leader, the urge to copy them in both form and style is incredibly strong. Therefore, behaviors quickly and easily become predictable across everyone who follows them. Not only that, but the beliefs that guide the behaviors are also soon adapted by everyone on the team (or in the company).

The words or actions of a leader are so much more impactful than a list of core values and their definitions posted in every work site. Therefore, when a leader endorses an organization's core values but acts in ways that work against those values, the values become about as valuable as the paper they're printed on. The more senior the leader, the more problematic this contradictory behavior can be, to the point where an organization's core values provoke more scorn than inspiration.

As proof of this, a well-known example is the Enron scandal. By the time the company declared bankruptcy, the aggressive and unethical leadership at the very top of the organization had filtered throughout the rank and file of the entire company to the point where overvaluing its assets was considered standard practice. During the Securities and Exchange Commission investigation of Enron in 2001, company executives were forced to admit that they'd been inflating its income for years. Even if a mismatch between your espoused values and observable actions doesn't result in scandal and bankruptcy, it will almost certainly erode trust, both inside your organization and with stakeholders and customers.

Matching your values and your actions may seem a little daunting. After all, no one, not even the best leader, is perfect. You, like everyone, have flaws. And just like your good qualities, those flaws will probably be emulated by those who follow you. The best way to navigate this is to

>> **Commit to ethical behavior at work.** Sure, you won't be perfect, but the knowledge that you're a living role model for everyone on your team should be enough to create some strong boundaries around your behavior, meaning there are some lines you simply won't cross.

>> **Commit to vulnerability, authenticity, and continuous learning.** When you do make a mistake, you can rectify the consequences by quickly owning up to it, apologizing, making amends if necessary, and observably learning from your mistake in the future. In such moments, leaders often feel like they're sacrificing their credibility among their followers. In fact, mistakes that are handled with integrity often create more trust among their teams, not less.

REMEMBER

Culture is not an initiative. It's not a campaign. And it's definitely not just an HR function. Culture is every single conversation, decision, meeting, reaction, and interaction. Whether you lead a team of five or an organization of five thousand, you have the power and the responsibility to shape culture every day. And keep in mind, the culture you create is the legacy you leave.

REMEMBER

You are always leading culture, whether intentionally or not. So why not be intentional?

Chapter **13**

Identifying and Addressing Work Culture Challenges

Every team has a culture, and aligning this culture with the team's members and functions can be a huge competitive advantage. The opposite is also true. Cultures can be unhelpful if they don't support what you're trying to accomplish. Some cultures are so bad, they're referred to as toxic.

Toxic cultures damage the people on your team and diminish their ability to do their best work. Rather than working together to solve problems, team members in a toxic culture often work at cross-purposes, motivated more by personal gain than team success.

This chapter covers how leaders can address challenges in their team cultures.

Diagnosing the Current State
of Your Team Culture

Obviously, before you can chart a path to your desired culture, you need to know what kind of culture currently exists. To do this, it's probably not helpful to read about your team's culture on your organization's website or a poster of your company's core values. These are artifacts of your *espoused* culture, and even the very best teams won't adhere to those attributes every minute of the day. Most teams experience some distance between their espoused culture and their actual culture. So how can you get a better sense of your team's culture?

REMEMBER

It's always important that you use your role as a leader to model the beliefs and behaviors you want others to emulate. At the same time, creating a team culture isn't just a matter of your personal actions. Culture is a shared phenomenon, and everyone on a team takes part in the creation of a culture. Even if you say and do all the right things but don't enforce your culture through rewards and consequences, it's not likely that your individual behavior will translate to team culture.

When diagnosing your team's actual culture, it's important to track what's visible and observable — in other words, the artifacts of your team's culture. Organization development scholar Edgar Schein identified five artifacts of a team's culture that you should examine: rituals and ceremonies, stories and myths, heroes, symbols, and language.

Rituals and ceremonies

The first of these is the rituals and ceremonies practiced by your team. While this probably sounds very formal and certainly includes formal structures, including the typical agendas of your team meetings, it also includes more informal practices, including when people generally get to the office, whether participation during team meetings is high, or the tendency for folks to gather in the break room at specific times during the day. In fact, the informal rituals might be a bit more helpful when diagnosing a culture because they tend to happen without as much thought.

Rituals and ceremonies serve to help team members socialize and form community. They can be a stabilizing force on a team. Through them, messages are conveyed to team members.

TIP

Ask yourself these questions:

>> What are some of the formal and informal rituals and ceremonies that happen on your team every day? Every week? Every month?

>> How can you translate these repeated collective behaviors into values and norms?

>> When celebrations occur, what is typically being celebrated? Who is invited, and who, if anyone, is excluded?

>> Do any rituals and ceremonies take place away from the physical workplace or outside of work hours (for example, a Friday happy hour before commuting home, annual holiday parties)? Are these well-attended or are only a few people invited? What are the advantages of participating?

Stories and myths

Most organizations and teams have stories embedded in their cultures. People will tell stories about the time when the team stayed up all night to finish a proposal or the time that someone tripped a fire alarm and the sprinklers soaked the entire team during a client presentation. Of course, stories tend to get a little embellished along the way.

Stories and myths are a great way to confer a sense of belonging on a team. Even if you weren't around when an oft-repeated story took place, knowing the stories and myths of your team makes you feel more a part of the team. In addition, they offer entertainment and a sense of fun. Often, they provide a kind of moral instruction for team members. For instance, the story about staying up all night to finish that proposal lets team members know how important it is to be dedicated. If the proposal ended up with a contract offer, the message is reinforced yet again.

TIP

Consider these things:

>> What kinds of stories and myths are told over and over again on your team?

>> Who are the stories about?

>> What characteristics — moral or otherwise — are being talked about in the stories?

>> What's the context for telling the story (for example, by a peer during a happy hour or from a leader during a formal team meeting)?

>> What values, norms, behaviors, and attitudes are present in the stories and myths you hear?

Heroes

When diagnosing any culture among a defined group of people, a particularly telling artifact are the heroes who are celebrated. For instance, when looking at American culture, two instantly recognizable heroes are George Washington and Abraham Lincoln, the first and sixteenth presidents of the United States. Washington was a general in the Revolutionary War and helped the new nation separate from the British monarchy, establishing a democratic government. Lincoln was a wartime president who resisted the South's attempt to secede from the Union over the issue of slavery. Despite extreme polarization, he kept the country together and signed the Emancipation Proclamation, ending the practice of slavery. Other heroes include Dr. Martin Luther King, Jr., and Rosa Parks, who led the fight for civil rights in the 1950s and 1960s. Through these heroes, we can infer a lot about American culture, most notably the values of freedom and individualism which frame the national character.

In organizational life as well as national history, heroes are an embodiment of the values of the people being discussed. If a person's words and deeds are still being celebrated years or even decades later, then diagnosing them will yield a lot of information about current culture.

TIP

Ask yourself these questions about your team's heroes:

>> In the stories and myths of a culture, who are the recurring characters?

>> What specific words and deeds are lauded and discussed?

>> What traits and values do the heroes show?

Symbols and artifacts

While language is often the best tool we have in understanding values and norms, we shouldn't ignore the visual data that's ascertained by looking around. This might be easier to do in a shared physical workspace, but if possible, take note of the symbols and artifacts you see, starting with the company or team logo (which is often invested in symbolism) to the things you see when you stroll around the office and through the hallways.

These objects capture cultural themes that language might miss. They often compress complicated issues into a single image and can serve as metaphors for a team's values.

TIP

Think about these things as you make your observations:

>> What does your organization's logo look like? Is there any symbology that speaks to the values of your team?

>> What objects are found consistently throughout the workspace?

>> Do people decorate their doors? If so, with what?

>> How have people decorated their offices? Is it all diplomas and awards, or are there personal artifacts like team and family photos or a recognition of hobbies or other personal activities?

>> On a virtual team, what's visible behind people when they're on camera during a team meeting? What virtual wallpaper do they choose to showcase on their profiles? What, if anything, is being conveyed by these choices?

Language

The things people say and write are often the best artifacts to use for diagnosing culture. The words that people choose (as well as the words people avoid) can tell you a lot about the values and norms of a team. Everything from catchphrases, acronyms, team or company jargon, team or company taglines, and email signatures can give a leader insight into their team culture.

Language sets the tone for the team. For instance, more formal language indicates a more rigid culture where doing things in a prescribed way is important, whereas informal language points to a culture that is laid-back and perhaps more creative. Language can convey comfort when necessary and often describes the culture through metaphor.

TIP

Consider these things when you examine the language used on your team:

>> What terms do you hear repeated on your team? What values or norms do the choices in language point to?

>> Are there organic pieces of jargon that are entirely unique to your team or organization?

>> What is the general tone of conversations on your team? Is it more formal or informal? Do people often communicate through stories, or do they tend to get right to the point?

Presenting the Culture Spectrum

Of course, what you're really interested in is whether your actual culture is a healthy one. To diagnose this, I've developed a useful tool called the Culture Spectrum.

Through a decade of research, I've identified six strengths of high-performing, inclusive cultures and six deficits in low-performing, toxic organizations. The Culture Spectrum model (Figure 13-1) helps leaders identify team/organizational strengths and weaknesses during culture change efforts. It guides the understanding of cultural dynamics within an organization, focusing on the contrast between Red Zone and Green Zone cultures shown in the figure and described in this section.

Culture Spectrum™
Moving from the Red Zone to the Green Zone

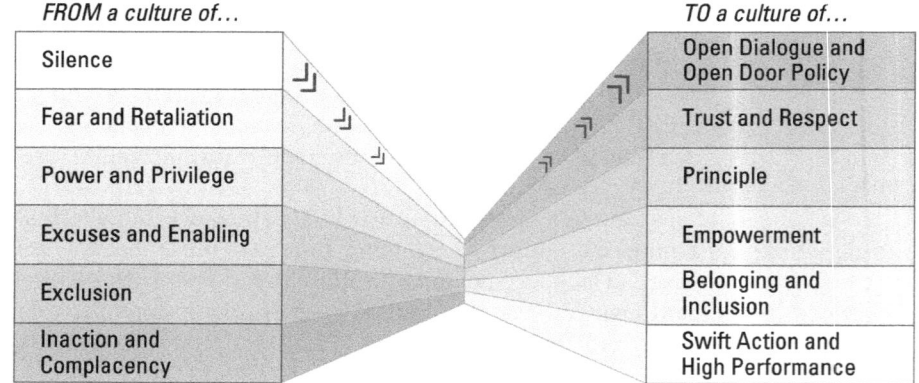

FIGURE 13-1: The Culture Spectrum.

Courtesy of Dr. Shirley Davis

The Red Zone

In the Red Zone (on the left in Figure 13-1), organizations show traits that can harm employee well-being and team performance. Here are six signs of a toxic and low-performing culture.

Silence

In safety-focused organizations, you often hear people say, "If you see something, say something." That's because the physical safety of everyone on a team is more important than anyone saving face or avoiding accountability for dangerous mistakes. In contrast, toxic workplaces often silence employees, so speaking up seems dangerous or pointless. Those who voice concerns may be ignored or face consequences for speaking up.

Fear and retaliation

The toxic traits of fear and retaliation can overlap. For instance, silence often occurs because people fear what will happen if they speak out or step "out of bounds," which can include doing one's work in an innovative way or reporting the unethical behavior of leaders or colleagues. In a culture of fear and retaliation, unethical actions thrive as individuals use them to advance without repercussions. Such environments are particularly hostile to marginalized groups, including people of color, women, LGBTQ+ individuals, those with disabilities, and any group that routinely faces harassment and discrimination.

Power and privilege

What does your C-suite look like? Is it predominantly white and male? Are there openly LGBTQ members or people with disabilities? How does it compare to mid-level managers and entry-level workers? If there is a lack of diversity, how do you explain it? If race, gender, sexual orientation, religion, gender identity, age, disability, or other identity markers are not true indicators of talent and work ethic, a lack of diversity suggests a culture of power and privilege. In such a culture, talented individuals from underrepresented groups may be denied advancement or leave before their careers can be stalled. If those resembling the organization's leaders are evaluated on perceived potential while others must justify their place, this is likely a cultural deficit that needs addressing.

Excuses and enabling

In an organization, when unethical behavior occurs, it's important to address and hold individuals accountable rather than making excuses. Statements such as, "He brings in a lot of money," or "She probably didn't mean it," contribute to a culture deficient in accountability and transparency. Justifying unethical behavior due to someone's ability to generate revenue or their valuable connections fosters a toxic environment. It often leads to the presence of double standards, where certain individuals are permitted to engage in inappropriate conduct while others are not.

Exclusion

When individuals are excluded from a group, neuroscientists can detect activity in the same regions of the brain usually associated with physical pain. Similar to the experience of physical pain, exclusion is encoded in the brain as negative and something to be avoided. For example, if you touch a hot stove and suffer burns, you're unlikely to repeat that action. Likewise, repeated exclusion from a group may lead to disengagement rather than persistence. Those with a healthy level of self-esteem might update their resume and seek out another workplace that's more inclusive. Alternatively, some may interpret this lack of inclusion as an indication that their ideas have little value and may choose to withdraw or "quit in place."

TIP

Consider these questions as you determine whether your culture is one of exclusion:

>> How engaged are your employees? Who's most engaged and who's least engaged, demographically speaking?

>> Does everyone feel they can have equal access to opportunities or get a seat at the decision-making table?

>> Which voices/ideas are heard loud and clear and which ones are drowned out or dismissed?

>> How much turnover do you experience, and how many dollars do you spend trying to fill the seats of people who have voluntarily separated from your organization? How do these numbers look demographically?

>> Are lively debates commonplace at your organization, or do most of your staff simply "go along to get along"?

>> What are you learning from conducting exit interviews when employees turn in their resignation?

>> Are there employees who have not formally resigned and who show up physically but contribute minimally because they no longer feel valued or included? This means they have "quit in place."

Inaction and complacency

How do people respond to discussions about inclusion in your organization? Is there a meaningful acknowledgment of the challenges and shortcomings, or is there a sense of resignation, hopelessness, or a belief that culture change is too difficult? While it is indeed hard, especially for longstanding companies, avoiding such efforts leads not only to difficulty in achieving inclusion but also to potential mediocrity and failure in business.

The Green Zone

Moving from the Red Zone to the Green Zone (on the right in Figure 13-1) involves prioritizing collaboration, inclusivity, and employee well-being. Green Zone organizations embrace creativity, fairness, open communication, and mutual respect. Leadership is distributed, encouraging idea exchange and shared responsibility.

TIP

The six strengths of a high-performing culture are the inverse of the six deficits in the Red Zone. As you read the following descriptions, assess your organization honestly. Don't be discouraged if your company isn't fully in the Green Zone. Many aren't, and even those that are can falter if they become complacent.

REMEMBER

Envision the potential strength and daily joy at work if this were a reality. Achieving this requires strategic effort and consistency.

Open dialogue and open door policy

Unlike the organizations that are shrouded in silence, this culture addresses issues affecting the organization and the world. Ideas come from all levels and are appreciated even if not acted upon, and bold thinking is rewarded. Leaders have an open-door policy, allowing staff to discuss project progress, career goals, or cultural challenges privately with their manager.

REMEMBER

Leaders may view frequent conversations about issues and challenges as weakness, but they actually signify strength. An open company culture allows employees to address these issues and create solutions, which is a valuable asset. Of course, lots of complaining without action is problematic, but it's generally a positive sign when people feel free to voice their concerns.

Trust and respect

Unlike teams rife with fear and retaliation, high-performing groups can handle tough conversations because they trust the organization to respond positively to difficult issues. These organizations respect and appreciate those who report unethical behavior, which is rare. In such a culture, ideas from all employees are valued and respected.

Principle

If your C-suite looks like the other levels in your organization, it indicates that your company may be closer to a true meritocracy than those affected by biases that prevent some people from succeeding. However, achieving this is not automatic and requires effort. In an open system, addressing the existing systems of power and privilege that exist everywhere in our society involves strategies such as equitable hiring practices, networking opportunities, training programs, mentoring initiatives, and other supportive measures.

Empowerment

The combination of open dialogue, trust, and a focus on people will encourage employees to make ethical choices. It will also empower them to take actions in this direction, including taking calculated risks to ensure proper conduct. In such organizations, mid-level employees are likely to address inappropriate behavior, regardless of whether it involves a high-paying client or senior leader.

Belonging and inclusion

Between 2012 and 2016, Google launched Project Aristotle, a study to identify the factors contributing to the success of high-performing teams within the company. The findings indicated that psychological safety, defined as the belief that one can express oneself freely without fear of negative consequences, was the most important attribute for a high-performing team. In any organization, individuals need to feel included and connected to their team to be productive. Even when tasks are repetitive or menial, a strong connection to team members leads to high-quality work and an environment conducive to mental health.

Swift action and high performance

High-performing cultures are marked by prompt action and results, unlike complacent organizations. Such culture develops when all the other Green Zone attributes are present: Employees voice concerns, trust in leaders and colleagues is strong, leaders respect staff, decisions are principled, and everyone is empowered to act responsibly. In these environments, swift change is achievable as all members perform and collaborate optimally.

Costs of a toxic work environment

Maintaining a healthy culture on your team isn't just a matter of everyone feeling good and enjoying their work. Toxic cultures come with very real costs. Research from Harvard University indicates that in a toxic work environment, 80 percent of employees report lost work time worrying about the bad behaviors of their colleagues. Seventy-eight percent said their commitment to the organization declined in the face of toxic behavior, and 66 percent reported a decline in their own performance. Toxic environments reduce innovation within teams, prompt higher levels of employee turnover (which can be both disruptive and expensive), and can lower a team's ability to produce high-quality work on time and under budget. Those who lead teams with toxic cultures spend more time on oversight and therefore less on strategy and the professional development of their staff.

Turning a Toxic Team Environment into a Positive and Inspiring One

If you've noticed areas of your culture that may need improvement, remember that it's common for teams to not be entirely in the Green Zone of the Culture Spectrum (which is discussed in the preceding section of this chapter). Even teams that usually operate in the Green Zone can occasionally fall into less effective practices if their culture is not actively maintained.

Obviously, no one is pleased when the team they lead is referred to as "toxic," but it's an effective descriptor if a leader can avoid taking it personally. It communicates a real sense of urgency to change things.

As I discuss in Chapter 12, I view leaders as thermostats for a team's culture. Team members are always observing their leaders to determine which behaviors they should emulate and what the rewards (or consequences) might be if norms are adopted (or ignored).

REMEMBER

However, it's important to remember that everyone on a team can have an impact on a team's culture. Oftentimes, a toxic work environment can be created when one or two bad actors on a team cause the beliefs and behaviors that unify the group to unravel.

I have two Maltipoos that I love and adore. Their names are Rilee and Chloe. I know from many experiences in my career and all the dogs that have been a part of my life that people are not dogs and vice versa. However, caring for my fur babies has taught me some important techniques that I've seen work well when dealing with human beings, so indulge me as I make this analogy. One of these lessons is the power of positive reinforcement. When you're training a dog, it does very little good to punish or scold them when they do the wrong thing. What works wonders is showering them with praise (and a treat) when they get something right. Unfortunately, many of our life experiences involving leaders (starting with our parents or other caregivers when we were young) put a much stronger focus on consequences than rewards.

TIP

That kind of negative emphasis can quickly create a team culture where punishment is a much more visible artifact than rewards. A positive culture should move in the opposite direction, beginning with recognizing and appreciating the contributions of others. While some managers only believe in rewarding work that far exceeds anyone's wildest expectations, I don't think there's anything wrong with saying "thank you" (especially in a public setting) when an employee does exactly what was asked of them. It costs nothing, and the impact on the culture is significant.

Likewise, when developing employees, many leaders tend to focus only on fixing their weak spots. It's often just as effective (and more fun for everyone) to deepen areas of strength. In either case, mentorship and coaching from a leader is a vital part of professional development.

TIP

Team cultures become much more positive and supportive when leaders take the time and make the effort to celebrate successes and work on team functioning. This could look like a day of team-building exercises or occasionally ordering some lunch (while mindful of dietary restrictions and preferences!) for everyone to enjoy together with no agenda other than to enjoy each other's company.

I've learned a few other steps about how to deal with behaviors that can be a significant disruption to the team. I've also gained skills for how to create an inspiring and positive work environment. Many lessons came from being a people leader and an HR professional. Others came from observing and working with other phenomenal leaders who were masterful at turning disruption into teachable moments. I describe them in the following sections.

Locate the source

One of the first steps in addressing a toxic or disengaged team is to discover the source of the problem. Consider the following things:

>> Is it widespread throughout the larger organization?

>> Is it a failure of team leadership?

>> Is it the result of one or a few people who are behaving outside the expected norms of the group?

From there, depending on your sphere of influence, you are ready to address the issue. If the culture of the entire organization is toxic, this may require building a broad coalition throughout the company to do the work. But if the source exists within the boundaries of a team, the leader can begin the process on their own.

Often, the source of the problem is a disruption that results in some of the toxicity we've discussed, making the workplace negative, secretive, and less productive. Disruptions can come from within the team or outside of it.

Examples of internal disruptions include

>> Poor communication, leading to misunderstandings, misaligned goals, safety issues, and conflict

>> Trust issues, leading to suspicion, animosity, and silence

>> Unresolved conflicts, including personal clashes, differing opinions, and lingering resentments

>> A lack of clarity on goals, roles, values, or vision

>> Micromanagement, which can make team members experience a lack of agency, thereby inhibiting creativity, innovation, and motivation

>> Lack of recognition, when people feel as if no one notices or appreciates their hard work

>> Negative behaviors from leaders or colleagues, including rude comments, gossip, exclusion, or harassment

>> Disengagement, when team members are dejected, sour, and can no longer be counted on to deliver high-quality work

Examples of external disruptions include the following:

>> Unforeseen events, including power outages, natural disasters, pandemics, or political violence

>> Reorganization and restructuring, especially when poor communication or sloppy implementation creates confusion, anxiety, and resistance among employees

>> Resource constraints, when a team doesn't have enough budget, staff, or supplies to effectively do their work

>> Technology issues, including outdated systems, software glitches, and long periods of downtime that cause delay and hinder workflow

Acknowledge and address the problem

When leading a toxic team, it does no good to try to fix the problem quietly while pretending everything is fine. Instead, leaders should openly acknowledge the toxic behaviors as well as the impact they've had on employee engagement, trust, and productivity. Chances are, your entire team is already aware of what's happening, and those who might be inclined to disengage from your team will appreciate knowing action is being taken.

TIP

Regardless of whether you, the leader, are entirely to blame for the toxicity within your team, it's important for you to take accountability for your role in the problem. Perhaps you made a mistake, and others felt free to repeat it. Perhaps you were too lenient when the bad behavior first surfaced. Perhaps you had no idea that the problem had been happening because people didn't feel safe letting you know. Whatever your contribution was to the issue, take ownership, apologize, make amends where possible, and commit to different behaviors going forward.

As you work to change harmful behaviors, you'll want to ensure that members of your team are willing to report whatever concerns they might have in the future, even if they didn't in the past. Therefore, it's crucial to create a safe and confidential way for them to do so. Make it clear that they will not be retaliated against — by leadership or their colleagues — for coming forward.

TIP

Individuals who willingly come forward are a great assistance during this kind of change effort, but you can't rely on that alone to give you the information you need. Anonymous surveys and focus groups can also be used to gather feedback and recommendations for improvement. These could include (but are not limited to) the following:

>> New policies that govern ethical behavior

>> Training on microaggressions, cyberbullying, or other forms of harassment

>> Reducing individual reward systems in favor of team-based rewards for excellent work

>> A defined process for conflict mediation

>> More or better channels of communication

>> More consistent enforcement of existing policies and norms

>> Opportunities to practice self-care or employee wellness

Whatever you decide is necessary, make sure you frame these activities in terms of goals that directly address the core issues and can be measured, so that you can know if and when you've succeeded.

Foster open communication and transparency

Once you have a path forward for your team, you can work on improving communication between yourself and your employees and among team members. Encourage open communication by adhering to a strict policy against retaliation. Role model effective dialogue and provide a model for having courageous conversations.

TIP

If you haven't already done this, implement regular feedback opportunities to allow employees to receive both positive and constructive feedback. While constructive feedback is best delivered in private, many teams benefit from beginning every team meeting with "kudos," where team members have the opportunity to highlight each other's great work and thank them for their contributions to team success. If you do this as a team leader, track who receives lots of kudos, but also who might be feeling a little left out and find a way to acknowledge those team members as well.

Finally, let your team know how instances of future toxic behaviors will be documented and/or reported. This will encourage consistency of practice and will prevent charges of overreacting if an employee is found to be behaving in a way that harms others.

Implement clear expectations

In any team change effort, a group cannot be reasonably expected to improve if they don't know what's expected of them. Don't assume that just because you've defined toxic behaviors, your employees will all discern what good behavior looks like on their own. Instead, make your expectations clear, in writing if possible. Everyone on a team should understand their role and what's expected of them. If the culture you aspire to is one where people are free to go above and beyond their job description, you can say that — but everyone should also know the minimum requirements of their position.

If necessary, new policies may need to be introduced regarding harassment, discrimination, and other inappropriate behaviors. Hopefully, these policies are organization wide. If your company doesn't have written policies that govern ethical and appropriate behavior, call HR for assistance. If your organization doesn't yet employ an HR professional, then it's probably small enough for you to speak directly to the CEO or de facto leader of the entire company to make this happen.

REMEMBER

Lastly, because this bears repeating, it's vital that leaders role model the behaviors they expect from others. These should include respectful interaction, empathy for others, positive communication, and working toward solutions that work for as many people as possible.

Provide ongoing mentoring and improvement

It's important to regularly track progress against the goals you've set, using both hard data and employee feedback to measure your success.

Even if you reach your goal within the expected time frame, don't call the change effort done and cease putting attention on it. Rather, view the process as ongoing. If feedback mechanisms have been constructed, continue to use them. If focus groups proved to be uniquely helpful, make them an annual event to collect feedback and make adjustments to create an even more positive and productive workplace.

Overcome workplace silos

In any team, a leader wants people to feel a strong sense of belonging and camaraderie. Doing so satisfies a fundamental human need that serves both physical and mental health, job satisfaction, and motivation to perform.

Sometimes, however, a group's culture can become so strong that it becomes exclusionary and cut off from the rest of the organization. *Organizational silos* are groups within an organization that are segregated from other segments due to limited information exchange, often due to the group actively not sharing information with others. This can show up in several ways:

>> **Departmental silo:** Your IT team is going to naturally function differently than your marketing team. This is to be expected, and it's for everyone's benefit. These structural separations are also the most common organizational silo.

>> **Rank or level silo:** Sometimes, the flow of information is impeded when those of a particular level within an organization withhold goals, strategies, important context, or other information to those either above or below them on the organizational chart.

>> **Location silo:** When organizations or teams are segmented by different office locations, information might not easily travel from one location to another. These silos are often created unintentionally, when information is shared informally in one office setting and people forget to share the information in a more official way during virtual team meetings.

>> **Schedule silo:** When team members work different shifts or hours, information silos can form, especially if the team is a 24-hour operation. New information might be shared by a leader during the day, and it never reaches those who work the evening and night shifts.

Strategies to address organizational silos depend on the root causes of the silo. Was the information blockage created intentionally or unintentionally? Are there physical barriers to information (as we often see in location silos or schedule silos), or are there technological impediments that hinder the flow of information?

TIP

Leaders can unintentionally create silos with negative judgments about other teams, leading to competition, miscommunication, and hostility. This can often be fixed by establishing clear, company-wide goals that provide leaders with knowledge of the organization's larger vision and how their particular team contributes to it. Focusing on a larger goal fosters cooperation among different teams and discourages unnecessary competition.

Leaders can also contribute to silos by sharing important information in an ad hoc way. This might look like sharing with people in your location or those on the day shift that you see regularly and simply forgetting everyone else on your team — out of sight, out of mind. To change this, remember that it's best when everyone receives important information they need to do their jobs at the same time, if possible. This might look like making the announcement in a team-wide email before saying anything to anyone or waiting (if possible) until a time when a team that operates in different locations have all logged into the same virtual meeting.

Sometimes, the structure of an organization simply does not allow for easy cross-team communication or collaboration. The solution here often points to new technology. If your organization doesn't utilize an effective work management platform, the result is a lack of a centralized system of record. Without that, there's no way for cross-functional teams to share information with others. Losing information across different platforms causes miscommunication, missed deadlines, lost documentation, and duplicative work.

TIP

Rarely, individual bad actors are intentionally holding on to information as leverage. In these cases, it's important to address the behavior promptly and directly. Confront the individual privately to discuss both the behavior and its impact and define transparent communication as an explicit expectation attached to their role. Document the conversation so that you have a record of your statements and any disciplinary actions taken.

IN THIS CHAPTER

» Understanding the current landscape of mental health in the workplace

» Recognizing how stigma affects productivity, innovation, and team relationships

» Detailing practices that foster team connection, trust, and mutual support

» Integrating flexible work–life approaches for hybrid and remote environments

» Evaluating the leader's mental health and the effect on team performance

Chapter **14**

Promoting Mental Health and Well-Being on the Team

I n today's hyperconnected, always-on world, the old paradigm of "leave your personal life at the door" is not just outdated but dangerous. We work with human beings who bring their complete selves to work every day, including their struggles, fears, hopes, and vulnerabilities. As such, promoting mental health and well-being on your team is the bedrock upon which all sustainable high performance is built. I have witnessed firsthand across more than 30 countries and countless organizations that teams who prioritize mental wellness not only perform better, but they innovate more boldly, retain top talent longer, and create cultures that become magnets for exceptional people.

The question isn't whether your team will face mental health challenges. The question is whether you, as a leader and a team member, will be prepared to respond with wisdom, compassion, and strategic thinking when they do. This chapter helps equip you with the knowledge, tools, and mindset to transform how your team approaches mental wellness, turning what many view as a liability into your greatest competitive advantage.

Describing the Current State of Global Mental Health

The statistics are staggering, and they demand our immediate attention. The World Health Organization reports that mental health conditions affect one in eight people globally, with depression and anxiety alone costing the global economy nearly $1 trillion annually in lost productivity. But numbers only tell part of the story. Behind every statistic is a human being who's struggling to show up as their best self while engaging in invisible battles.

According to the International Labour Organization's 2023 report, workplace stress is now one of the top drivers of absenteeism, presenteeism (being physically present but mentally unwell), and turnover worldwide. The U.S. Centers for Disease Control and Prevention estimates that nearly one in five adults lives with a mental illness, and the National Alliance on Mental Illness reports that more than 60 percent of employees say their mental health affects their job performance.

In this section, I shed some light on the hidden costs of ignoring team members' mental health and the ways mental health issues disproportionately affect certain groups.

The hidden costs of ignoring mental health

What many leaders fail to recognize is that mental health challenges don't disappear when employees clock in. They manifest in decreased decision-making ability, reduced creativity, impaired collaboration, and increased conflict. I've seen brilliant teams crumble not because they lacked talent or resources, but because they failed to address the mental health needs of their members.

In the U.K., the Mental Health Foundation found that 74 percent of adults have felt overwhelmed or unable to cope due to stress within the past year. These aren't just individual struggles; they're organizational challenges that require systematic solutions.

The disproportionate impact on vulnerable populations

Mental health challenges are not distributed evenly. Younger workers, women balancing multiple roles, and employees from marginalized communities often experience disproportionate levels of stress, anxiety, and burnout. As leaders, we must acknowledge these disparities and create targeted support systems that address the unique challenges different groups face.

Younger employees, particularly those entering the workforce during uncertain times, often struggle with imposter syndrome, career anxiety, and the pressure to constantly network and perform. Women, especially those juggling caregiving responsibilities, frequently experience the "double burden" that leads to chronic stress and burnout. Employees from marginalized communities may face additional stressors related to discrimination, microaggressions, and the exhausting work of code-switching between different cultural contexts.

TIP

Code-switching refers to the need to adjust one's language, tone, behavior, or identity to fit into the dominant culture in the workplace. The effort of adjusting can be mentally and emotionally draining over time.

Another mental health challenge impacting a disproportionate number of younger workers is workplace suicide. This remains a sobering concern, with the World Health Organization ranking it as the fourth leading cause of death among people aged 15 to 29. This reality should shake every leader to their core. People spend more waking hours with their team members than they do with their families. We have both an opportunity and a responsibility to create environments where people feel valued, supported, and hopeful about their futures.

REMEMBER

The reality is that ignoring the mental health crisis in your workplace isn't just harmful to individuals. It's a direct threat to your organization's performance, innovation capacity, and long-term sustainability.

Assessing How Stigma Influences Productivity, Innovation, and Team Dynamics

Despite increased awareness, stigma around mental health remains one of the most formidable barriers to workplace wellness. According to Deloitte's 2023 Mental Health at Work report, nearly 60 percent of employees globally said they would be uncomfortable disclosing a mental health challenge to their employer. This statistic represents a massive failure of leadership and organizational culture.

Stigma operates on multiple levels. There's personal stigma — the shame and self-blame individuals feel about their struggles. Social stigma is the judgments and discrimination team members fear from colleagues. And structural stigma is the organizational policies and cultures that inadvertently punish vulnerability and reward the appearance of invincibility.

I've worked with countless high-achieving executives who would rather suffer in silence than risk being perceived as weak or unstable. This toxic mindset harms more than the individuals themselves; it also robs organizations of the full potential of their talent.

REMEMBER

Creating a stigma-free environment requires intentional, sustained effort. The most successful leaders I've coached model vulnerability from the top. The most powerful stigma-reduction tool you have is your own authenticity. When leaders share their own struggles and how they've sought support, it gives permission for others to do the same. I worked with a CEO who openly discussed his anxiety disorder during a company meeting. Within weeks, three of his direct reports had reached out for mental health resources.

TIP

Successful leaders also normalize mental health conversations by weaving well-being check-ins into regular team meetings. But they don't make these superficial "how are you feeling" moments. Instead, they create structured opportunities for meaningful dialogue. They start meetings with intentional check-ins that go beyond surface-level responses and train their managers to ask follow-up questions and listen with genuine curiosity.

Language matters profoundly in stigma reduction. These leaders avoid harmful labels and language, replacing them with empathy and support. Words like *crazy*, *psycho*, or *mental* used casually can create environments where people feel unsafe sharing their struggles. They replace judgment with curiosity and criticism with compassion.

The most effective leaders share stories of resilience, showing that vulnerability is a strength. They create platforms for employees to share their journeys — not just their struggles but also how they've grown stronger through adversity. These stories become powerful medicine for others facing similar challenges.

Finally, they train managers and peers to recognize signs of distress and respond constructively. Mental Health First Aid training for leaders isn't optional; it's essential. Managers need to know how to recognize warning signs, have supportive conversations, and connect people with appropriate resources.

When you successfully reduce stigma, you create what Dr. Amy Edmondson calls "psychological safety" — the belief that one can speak up without risk of punishment or humiliation. Teams with high psychological safety are more innovative, make better decisions, and recover from setbacks more quickly. I share more about this in Chapter 3.

WARNING

Even small jokes, dismissive comments, or gossip about mental illness can reinforce stigma and prevent people from seeking support. Every interaction is an opportunity to build trust or erode it, so choose wisely.

When ignoring mental health backfires

WARNING

For those leaders who worry that focusing on mental health will make their teams "soft" or less driven, this thinking is not just wrong; it's dangerous. Poor mental health doesn't stay hidden. It shows up in the workplace. Gallup's State of the Global Workplace 2024 report reveals that employees who struggle with stress and anxiety are less engaged, less creative, and more likely to disengage from their roles.

WARNING

Global consulting firm Deloitte estimates that presenteeism costs employers more than absenteeism. I've seen this countless times where employees show up but can't focus, innovate, or collaborate effectively. They're occupying space but not contributing value. In some cases, their mental state becomes contagious, dragging down the entire team's energy and performance.

Teams bear the weight of this impact. Poor mental health reduces focus, diminishes collaboration, and weakens trust. When one team member is struggling mentally, it affects project timelines, meeting dynamics, decision-making processes, and overall team morale. The interconnected nature of modern work means that individual mental health challenges quickly become team performance issues.

The ROI of mental health investment

The business case for combatting mental health issues is undeniable: Research by *Harvard Business Review* highlights that companies that invest in mental health programs experience a return of $4 for every $1 spent, driven by higher engagement and productivity. A company's investment in mental health isn''t just good for people; it's good for business.

Organizations that prioritize mental health consistently outperform their competitors in key metrics. Employee engagement scores run 25 percent higher, turnover rates are 40 percent lower, innovation metrics improve by 30 percent, customer satisfaction scores increase significantly, and financial performance remains consistently stronger.

When employees feel supported, they're more energized, more creative, and more committed. The secret to sustainable high performance isn't pushing your people harder; it's creating conditions where they can thrive mentally, emotionally, and physically. When people feel psychologically safe, mentally healthy, and emotionally supported, they take more creative risks, collaborate more effectively, and recover from setbacks more quickly.

A high-performing team cannot thrive if its members are mentally exhausted, emotionally depleted, or silently suffering.

REMEMBER

Implementing Team Practices for Camaraderie, Trust, and Mutual Support

Creating a supportive team culture isn't about forced fun or superficial team-building exercises. Building camaraderie is about cultivating genuine trust and care. It's about creating an environment where people feel genuinely valued, understood, and supported through both victories and struggles.

The most successful teams I've worked with share a common characteristic: Their members genuinely care about each other as human beings, not just as work colleagues. This doesn't happen by accident; it requires intentional cultivation by leadership. Additionally, successful leaders encourage meaningful dialogue by beginning meetings with substantial personal check-ins. Instead of "How is everyone doing?" they say something like, "What's one thing that's energizing you right now and one thing that's challenging you?" These leaders give people permission to be real.

They celebrate both effort and achievement, recognizing achievements and effort equally. This is crucial for mental health because it acknowledges that value isn't just tied to outcomes but also tied to the human effort and courage it takes to try, fail, learn, and try again.

These leaders create connection rituals through shared lunches, virtual coffee chats, or wellness challenges that foster belonging. But they go deeper than surface-level activities, creating opportunities for people to share their stories, their struggles, their dreams. I've seen teams transformed by simple practices like "wisdom shares" where team members take turns sharing a life lesson they've learned.

TIP

Most importantly, they model empathy in action. When someone struggles, they offer patience, not pressure. This is where leadership is truly tested. When a high performer is going through a difficult time, the natural business instinct might be to push harder. The wise leader provides support and space for healing.

The strongest teams create informal support networks where members look out for each other. This happens when leaders create psychological safety where people feel safe being vulnerable and asking for help. They normalize struggle so everyone understands that challenges are part of the human experience. They provide resources so team members know where to find help and how to access it. They model healthy behaviors by demonstrating how to maintain boundaries and seek support. Finally, they celebrate resilience by recognizing and honoring those who face challenges with courage.

WARNING

Teams that ignore personal struggles or prioritize deadlines over people risk long-term disengagement and turnover. I've seen too many leaders make this critical mistake. In the short term, pushing through personal struggles might seem to maintain productivity. In the long term, it destroys trust, erodes engagement, and creates a culture where people hide their humanity.

REMEMBER

The way you respond to your team members' struggles defines your culture more than any mission statement or company value ever will.

Adopting Flexible Approaches to Work–Life Integration

The traditional concept of work–life balance is dead. In its place, you need work–life integration, a more fluid, flexible approach that recognizes that life and work aren't separate compartments but interconnected aspects of a whole person's experience.

The global shift toward hybrid work has permanently changed expectations. Employees now value autonomy and flexibility more than ever. PwC's 2023 Workforce Survey found that 64 percent of employees would prefer hybrid arrangements, citing better balance and reduced stress.

This isn't just about remote work preferences; it's about a fundamental shift in how people view the relationship between work and life. The pandemic forced everyone to integrate their work and personal lives in unprecedented ways, and there's no going back to the rigid boundaries of the past.

TIP

The most successful teams create flexible hours that work by allowing employees to manage personal responsibilities. But flexibility without clear expectations leads to chaos. These teams create "flex frameworks": clear guidelines about when collaboration is essential and when individual work can happen asynchronously.

They establish standards that protect everyone through clear boundaries around after-hours work. This requires leaders to model healthy boundaries themselves. If you're sending emails at 11:00 p.m., you're not demonstrating work-life integration; you're modeling work-life chaos.

These leaders also design hybrid schedules with purpose that prioritize collaboration while respecting autonomy. The key is intentionality. When your team comes together, make it count. Use in-person time for high-collaboration activities, relationship building, and creative problem-solving. Use remote time for focused individual work and smaller group collaborations.

They also implement technology policies that protect mental space by preventing digital overload. The always-on culture is a mental health killer. They create clear policies about response times, after-hours communication, and digital-free zones or times.

Salesforce is a model for integration. They introduced "Wellness Days" to give employees extra paid time off to recharge. They also implemented flexibility policies that improved retention, particularly among working parents. This approach recognizes that well-being isn't just about the hours you work but about the quality of rest and recovery you get between those hours.

REMEMBER

Flexibility is not a perk; it's a performance enabler. Employees who feel trusted to manage their time are more engaged and loyal. When people have control over how, when, and where they work, they bring more energy, creativity, and commitment to their roles. They consistently demonstrate higher levels of creative problem-solving, better stress management, stronger team relationships, lower burnout rates, higher employee retention, and better customer service because they aren't depleted.

Work-life integration isn't without its challenges. Some team members struggle with boundaries and work too much. Others have difficulty staying connected and engaged when they work remotely. The key is individualized approaches that recognize that different people need different types of support and structure.

TIP

True work-life integration happens when people feel empowered to bring their whole selves to work while maintaining healthy boundaries that protect their mental health and personal relationships.

Evaluating the Mental Health Needs of Leaders and Their Ripple Effects

WARNING

Leaders carry enormous responsibility. McKinsey's 2024 report found that 70 percent of executives report stress that negatively affects their effectiveness. If unaddressed, leader burnout spills over to the team as leaders model unhealthy behaviors and create environments of fear or instability. I've witnessed this phenomenon countless times. When leaders are mentally and emotionally depleted, they become reactive instead of responsive, critical instead of supportive, and closed off instead of connected.

The symptoms of leader mental health struggles show up in predictable ways: increased micromanagement and controlling behaviors, shorter tempers and more frequent conflicts, decreased empathy and understanding, poor decision-making and increased errors, withdrawal from team relationships, and modeling unhealthy work habits.

Much like airline preflight instructions to "put your oxygen mask on first, before helping others," leaders need to take a similar approach by managing their own well-being first. Doing so isn't selfish; it's strategic. You can't give what you don't have, and you can't lead others to a place you haven't been yourself.

TIP

Effective leaders practice setting boundaries to protect rest and family time. This means more than just blocking time on your calendar. It means having the courage to say no to requests that would compromise your well-being, and the wisdom to recognize that protecting your mental health protects your team's performance.

They prioritize physical health as the foundation of mental health through exercise, nutrition, and sleep. They understand that physical health directly impacts their mental and emotional capacity. Leaders who neglect their physical well-being inevitably struggle with stress management, decision-making clarity, and emotional regulation.

These leaders build peer support networks for encouragement and perspective. Leadership can be isolating, especially at senior levels. And having trusted peers who understand the unique challenges of leadership is essential for mental health. This might include executive coaching, peer mentorship groups, or professional leadership communities.

When needed, they seek professional mental health support. There's no shame in therapy, counseling, or psychiatric care. The most effective leaders I know have mental health professionals in their support network, just like they have financial advisors and business consultants.

THE LEADER'S SELF-CARE SETS THE TONE FOR THE CULTURE

A great example of the importance of leadership self-care comes from the story of Arianna Huffington, most known for cofounding *The Huffington Post*. After collapsing from burnout, Huffington founded Thrive Global to promote leader well-being. Her story demonstrates how leader health directly shapes organizational culture. Huffington's experience illustrates a crucial point: Leadership burnout isn't just personal; it's systemic. When leaders don't take care of themselves, entire organizations suffer.

You can learn more about Huffington's story here: www.youtube.com/watch?v= 2tCaXWDux38.

Finally, they practice mindfulness and emotional regulation through regular practices and reflection. Leadership requires enormous emotional intelligence and regulation. Regular mindfulness practices, reflection time, and emotional awareness are essential tools for maintaining mental health under pressure.

REMEMBER

Leaders who care for themselves demonstrate that well-being is integral to performance rather than optional. When you prioritize your own mental health, you give permission for others to do the same.

Another powerful step a leader can do for their team's mental health is to model vulnerability about their own mental health journey. This doesn't mean oversharing or making your team your therapist. It means being appropriately transparent about your humanity, your struggles, and the steps you take to maintain your well-being.

I've worked with leaders who transformed their team cultures simply by being honest about their therapy appointments, their meditation practices, their struggles with anxiety, or their need for mental health days. This kind of authentic leadership creates psychological safety faster than any policy or program.

REMEMBER

Your mental health isn't a luxury. It's the foundation upon which everything else you do as a leader is built.

Language and behaviors that heal versus harm

The words you use and the behaviors you model around mental health have profound impacts on your team culture. The path to a positive culture includes removing harmful habits. This section helps you identify and eliminate language and behaviors that perpetuate stigma while adopting approaches that promote healing and support.

First, here are a few common ways leaders unintentionally use language that minimizes the importance of balance and mental health:

>> Teams must avoid dismissing concerns with phrases like "just toughen up." Statements such as "just push through it," "everyone's stressed," or "that's just how business is," minimize real struggles and shut down opportunities for support and connection.

>> Comparing struggles with statements like "others have it worse" is equally damaging. Pain isn't a competition. When someone shares a struggle, responding with comparative statements like "at least you have a job" or "others are dealing with much worse" invalidates their experience and shuts down vulnerable communication.

>> Glorifying overwork as a badge of honor through language like "I haven't taken a vacation in three years" or "I work 80-hour weeks" doesn't demonstrate commitment. It models unhealthy behavior and creates pressure for others to sacrifice their well-being.

Leaders can create a healthier, more compassionate culture by choosing language that validates, encourages, and supports their team members' well-being:

>> Instead of using dismissive language, effective leaders respond with "That sounds really difficult. How can I support you?" or "Thank you for sharing that with me. What do you need right now?" or "I appreciate your honesty. Let's figure out how to help."

>> Instead of comparative suffering, they affirm with "Your feelings are valid, regardless of what others are experiencing" or "Everyone's struggles matter, including yours" or "I hear that you're having a hard time, and I want to help."

>> Instead of glorifying overwork, they model balance with "I'm committed to sustainable excellence, not unsustainable grinding" or "I believe in working smart, not just working hard" or "Taking care of yourself is part of taking care of our team."

>> One of the most healing things you can offer someone struggling with mental health challenges is simple validation. This doesn't mean agreeing with everything they say or solving all their problems. It means acknowledging their experience and affirming their worth as a human being.

WARNING

Careless comments about mental health can damage trust in ways that are difficult to repair.

REMEMBER

Confidentiality is one of the most important forms of respect you can offer when someone shares their mental health challenges. When a team member opens up, they're placing deep trust in you. Protecting that trust by keeping their disclosures private is essential. Breaking confidentiality, even with good intentions, can harm psychological safety, damage relationships, and discourage others from ever seeking support again. Honor their vulnerability by safeguarding their story.

Organizational systems and practices for mental health excellence

I've talked about what individual leaders can do to make a significant impact on their team's mental health, but sustainable change requires organizational systems and practices that support well-being at scale. Forward-thinking organizations embed mental health into their cultures in the following ways:

>> **Employee assistance programs** (EAPs) provide confidential counseling and crisis support. Organizations actively promote EAPs and normalize their use. They share success stories (with permission) and ensure that using mental health resources is seen as a sign of wisdom rather than weakness.

>> **Mental health paid time off** consists of designated wellness days for employees to recharge. This goes beyond traditional sick leave to specifically acknowledge that mental health maintenance is as important as physical health maintenance.

>> **Leadership training and development** means equipping managers with the tools to support team well-being. Every person in a leadership role should receive training in mental health awareness, supportive conversation techniques, and resource navigation. Doing this is essential.

>> **Peer support networks** create safe spaces for employees to share experiences. These might include employee resource groups focused on mental health, peer mentorship programs, or structured support circles.

>> **Technology-enabled support** includes mindfulness apps, resilience training, and stress management resources. But remember that technology is a tool, not a solution. The human connection and organizational culture remain primary.

One example of a company that embedded mental health into its culture is Unilever, which is one of the world's largest consumer goods companies. It offers a "Well-being Framework," that integrates physical, mental, emotional, and purposeful well-being. This holistic approach has become a model for global employers. The key insight here is that mental health doesn't exist in isolation. It's interconnected with physical health, emotional well-being, and sense of purpose.

Measuring and monitoring mental health

What gets measured gets managed. Organizations serious about mental health need to track employee engagement scores related to well-being, usage of mental health resources, manager training completion and effectiveness, team psychological safety assessments, stress and burnout indicators, and exit interview feedback about mental health support.

REMEMBER

Mental health initiatives fail when they're seen as HR programs rather than business imperatives. Success requires executive sponsorship and modeling, manager accountability for team well-being, integration into performance evaluations, regular assessment and adjustment of programs, and clear communication about expectations and resources.

Advanced strategies for mental health leadership

As you develop your capabilities as a leader who prioritizes mental health, there are advanced strategies that can exponentially increase your impact, such as ensuring psychological safety, employing trauma-informed leadership, building organizational resilience, and understanding intersectional mental health, which I describe in this section.

Psychological safety — which I cover in Chapter 3, is the belief that one can speak up without risk of punishment or humiliation — is the foundation of mentally healthy teams. Advanced leaders create this through systematic vulnerability by regularly sharing appropriate personal challenges and growth areas. They celebrate failure by treating failures as learning opportunities rather than performance problems. They encourage questions by rewarding people who ask difficult questions or bring up uncomfortable truths. They seek diverse perspectives by actively seeking and valuing viewpoints that challenge conventional thinking.

Many employees bring trauma from their personal lives, previous work experiences, or societal challenges. Cultural and historical trauma affects different groups in different ways. Trauma-informed leaders understand that people's reactions may be influenced by past experiences. Creating predictable, safe environments is essential. Control and choice help people heal, and healing happens in relationships, not isolation.

While crisis support is essential, advanced mental health leaders focus on building organizational resilience, the ability to adapt, recover, and grow stronger through challenges. This involves stress inoculation by gradually exposing teams to manageable challenges that build coping skills. They establish recovery rituals by building regular practices for mental and emotional restoration. They focus on meaning-making by helping people connect their work to larger purposes and values. They prioritize social connection by creating multiple opportunities for authentic relationship building. They cultivate growth mindset by framing challenges as opportunities for development rather than threats to avoid.

Mental health challenges don't affect everyone equally. Advanced leaders understand how factors like race, gender, sexuality, socioeconomic status, and other identities influence mental health experiences. This is called *intersectional mental health*. This awareness leads to targeted support programs for different groups, recognition of unique stressors faced by marginalized employees, inclusive mental health resources and messaging, and understanding of cultural differences in mental health expression and treatment.

TIP

The most effective mental health leaders do more than respond to problems. They proactively create conditions where mental wellness naturally thrives.

Reflecting on Organizational Practices That Build a Culture of Holistic Well-Being

Taking time for deep reflection is essential for developing your capacity as a mental health leader. Consider these four key areas:

>> **Personal reflection** involves examining how your team currently addresses conversations about mental health, what your own mental health practices are and how they influence your leadership, when you last shared an appropriate vulnerability with your team (and what the result was), and how you respond when team members share personal struggles.

>> **Team assessment** requires considering what stigma still exists in your workplace and how you can reduce it, which team members might be silently struggling and how you can create safe opportunities for them to seek support, what psychological safety looks like in your team meetings and daily interactions, and how your team handles failure, stress, and setbacks.

>> **Leadership development** means reflecting on the ways you as a leader are modeling healthy or unhealthy behaviors, what mental health training you need to better support your team, how you currently manage your own stress

and emotional reactions under pressure, and what boundaries you need to establish or strengthen to protect your mental health.

>> **Organizational systems thinking** involves considering how greater flexibility could improve your team's performance and well-being, what organizational practices you could advocate for to strengthen mental health support, how your organization currently measures and tracks mental health outcomes, and what resources are available to your team and how well they are promoted and utilized.

Building a Mentally Healthy Team

Future planning requires envisioning what your ideal mentally healthy team culture would look like in two years, what specific steps you will take in the next 30 days to improve your team's mental health support, how you will know if your mental health initiatives are successful, and who you can partner with to accelerate your progress in this area.

Given all that I shared in this chapter, the urgent need for action cannot be understated. The mental health crisis in our workplaces is not going away. If anything, the challenges are intensifying. The leaders who recognize this reality and respond with wisdom, compassion, and strategic thinking will create the workplaces of the future where every team member can thrive. In this section, I challenge you to take immediate and long-term actions because your team's health and wellness depend on it.

Use the following steps to formulate your plan for creating a mentally healthy environment for your team:

1. **Begin by assessing your current state through honest self-assessment of your own mental health practices, surveying your team about current mental health support and needs, and identifying existing organizational resources and gaps.**

   Start the conversation by scheduling individual check-ins with each team member focused on well-being, introducing mental health check-ins to team meetings, and sharing appropriate personal experiences to model vulnerability.

2. **Establish baseline practices by implementing clear boundaries around after-hours communication, creating team agreements about workload management and mutual support, and identifying and communicating available mental health resources.**

3. Over the next 90 days, invest in training and development by completing Mental Health First Aid training for yourself and key team members, attending workshops or seminars on psychological safety and trauma-informed leadership, and beginning work with a coach or therapist to enhance your own mental health leadership capabilities.

4. Build organizational support by partnering with HR to evaluate and enhance mental health benefits, advocating for organizational policy changes that support work–life integration, and connecting with other leaders to create peer support networks.

5. Implement systematic approaches by developing team practices for recognizing and responding to mental health challenges, creating structured approaches to stress management and resilience building, and establishing regular assessment and feedback mechanisms.

6. In the next 12 months, measure and refine by tracking key metrics related to team engagement, stress levels, and well-being, regularly assessing the effectiveness of mental health initiatives, and continuously refining approaches based on feedback and results.

7. Scale your impact by mentoring other leaders in mental health leadership approaches, sharing your experiences and lessons learned through speaking or writing, and contributing to organizational and industry-wide conversations about workplace mental health.

8. Sustain and evolve by embedding mental health considerations into all leadership decisions, continuing your own learning and development in this area, and adapting approaches as your team and organization evolve.

REMEMBER

The most powerful mental health interventions you can make as a leader are often the smallest, most human ones: the moment you really listen when someone shares a struggle, the time you adjust expectations because someone is going through a difficult period, the day you share your own vulnerability to help others feel less alone.

Chapter **15**

Navigating Team Conflict Effectively

When I speak to leaders about building high-performance teams, I often ask them to raise their hands if they believe conflict helps their team perform better. The response is always the same: very few hands go up. Most leaders view team conflict as something to be avoided, managed, or quickly resolved. But here's what decades of research and my own experience leading diverse teams has taught me: Teams that learn to navigate conflict effectively consistently outperform those that avoid it.

Today's highest performing teams bring together people with different backgrounds, experiences, perspectives, and approaches to work. This diversity creates tremendous advantages including better decision-making, increased innovation, and superior problem-solving capabilities. But these benefits only emerge when teams can effectively work through the inevitable conflicts that arise from different viewpoints, working styles, and priorities. The most successful teams I've observed don't avoid conflict; they harness it as fuel for breakthrough performance.

Addressing the Reasons for Avoiding Team Conflict

Team leaders avoid conflict for many understandable reasons. Early in my career, I dreaded team conflicts because I worried that they would damage relationships, create lasting divisions, or make me appear ineffective as a leader. I feared that addressing disagreements might escalate tensions or cause team members to lose respect for one another.

Many leaders avoid team conflict because they've been taught that harmony equals productivity. Organizations often reinforce this belief through policies that discourage "difficult conversations" or cultural norms that prize agreeableness above all else. In our social media age, leaders worry that mishandled team conflicts might become public relations disasters or legal liabilities.

But avoiding team conflict creates far greater risks. When teams suppress disagreements, several dangerous patterns emerge:

>> Surface-level harmony masks underlying resentment and frustration.

>> Important issues remain unresolved, leading to repeated problems.

>> Team members lose trust in leadership's ability to address real challenges.

>> Innovation suffers as people stop sharing controversial but valuable ideas.

>> Performance plateaus because teams never push through difficult growth phases.

The reality is that high-performance teams require psychological safety to engage in productive conflict. When team members feel safe to disagree, challenge assumptions, and work through differences, they unlock their collective potential.

Normalizing Conflict as a Tool for Higher Performance

Think about the highest-performing teams you've witnessed, whether in sports, business, or other endeavors. What made them exceptional wasn't the absence of conflict but their ability to channel disagreement into better outcomes. Championship sports teams argue about strategy, debate playing decisions, and challenge each other's performance because they share a commitment to winning.

The same principle applies to work teams. When team members come from different backgrounds, they bring diverse perspectives that naturally create friction. A marketing team with members from different generations will disagree with communication channels. A product development team with varying technical backgrounds will debate implementation approaches. A leadership team with different functional expertise will have competing priorities for resources.

REMEMBER

These conflicts aren't obstacles to performance; they're the raw material of breakthrough thinking. Research consistently shows that teams experiencing task-focused conflict generate more creative solutions, make better decisions, and achieve superior results compared to teams that maintain artificial harmony.

WARNING

However, not all conflict drives performance. Teams must learn to distinguish between productive conflict that focuses on ideas, processes, and outcomes versus destructive conflict that becomes personal, turns into a character attack, or undermines relationships. High-performance teams master this distinction and create norms that encourage vigorous debate while maintaining mutual respect.

The key is developing what I call "conflict competence" as a team capability. Just as teams must learn to collaborate, communicate, and coordinate their efforts, they must also learn to disagree constructively. This skill becomes even more critical as organizations become more diverse and teams span different cultures, generations, and ways of thinking.

Revealing the taboo topics we tend to avoid

What's a taboo topic? It's any conversation that you've been taught is off limits or out of bounds. It's anything personal and uncomfortable to talk about and specific to a person's unique difference. In my early days as an HR professional, it was either an explicit policy or an "unwritten" (but widely known and disseminated) rule not to broach certain topics at work. They included, but were not limited to

>> Race, ethnicity, national origin

>> Gender and sexuality

>> Religion/faith

>> Politics

>> Age

>> Disability

>> Dress

>> Body odor

>> Pay

>> Mental health

Making taboo topics even more difficult to discuss are many realities that are at play in our increasingly volatile, uncertain, complex, and ambiguous world. Gender inequities, racial/ethnic tensions, and other biases are embedded in human history and everyday interactions. In many ways, they determine the relative value of our multiple identities. These tensions and issues are amplified in current events, news coverage, political rhetoric, and on social media — and are therefore even more polarizing. Having empathy — a must whenever you're discussing a taboo topic — means taking the perspective of someone different from yourself, and that kind of openness and curiosity can feel very vulnerable. But the fear that we'll mess up or won't be able to find the perfect word can reinforce silence, and silence can often be perceived as complicity.

Other topics we tend to avoid within our teams

In my work with teams across various industries, I've identified several categories of conflict that teams typically avoid, even though addressing them could significantly improve performance:

>> **Process and workflow conflicts:** Teams often struggle to address inefficient processes, unclear roles, or workflow bottlenecks because these conversations can feel like criticism of established practices or individual performance.

>> **Performance and accountability issues:** Many teams avoid direct conversations about unequal contributions, missed deadlines, or quality standards because they worry about damaging relationships or appearing unsupportive.

>> **Communication style differences:** Teams that bring together people from different cultural backgrounds, generations, and professional training often experience friction around communication preferences. Some team members prefer direct, data-driven discussions while others value relationship-building and context. Rather than addressing how these differences impact effectiveness, teams often struggle silently with misunderstandings and frustration.

>> **Resource and priority conflicts:** Teams frequently compete for budget, time, and attention but avoid transparent discussions about resource allocation and competing priorities.

>> **Innovation and risk-taking tensions:** Teams often experience conflict between those who prefer proven approaches and those who advocate for experimental methods, but these debates rarely happen openly.

>> **Identity and inclusion challenges:** Teams may experience tension related to different backgrounds, perspectives, or treatment of team members, but these sensitive topics are often considered too risky to address directly.

>> **Decision-making and authority issues:** Teams struggle with unclear decision rights, competing leadership styles, or disagreements about who has final authority on specific issues.

While these topics can feel uncomfortable to address, avoiding them creates far more problems than confronting them constructively. Teams that learn to have productive conversations about these challenging areas consistently outperform those that sidestep difficult discussions.

The shift toward addressing these topics directly has accelerated in recent years as organizations recognize that diversity and inclusion require more than just assembling diverse teams. They require creating environments where different perspectives can clash, combine, and create something better than any individual viewpoint.

Seeing the Benefits of Engaging in Uncomfortable Conversations

Before diving into specific techniques for managing team conflict, consider these fundamental questions:

>> What kind of team do you want to lead?

>> What kind of team environment do you want to create?

If you envision leading a high-performance team characterized by innovation, trust, and exceptional results, then learning to navigate uncomfortable conversations isn't optional; it's essential. The benefits of developing this capability extend far beyond resolving immediate disputes to areas such as the following:

>> **Enhanced team performance:** Teams that can work through conflict effectively make better decisions, solve complex problems more creatively, and execute with greater precision. They don't waste energy avoiding issues or working around unresolved tensions.

>> **Increased innovation:** Breakthrough ideas emerge from the intersection of different perspectives. Teams that can engage in vigorous debate while maintaining psychological safety generate more innovative solutions than those that prioritize harmony over healthy disagreement.

>> **Stronger relationships:** Counterintuitively, teams that learn to disagree constructively often develop stronger relationships than those that avoid conflict. Working through difficult issues together builds trust and mutual respect.

>> **Improved team resilience:** Teams that regularly practice navigating conflict develop the skills and confidence to handle future challenges more effectively. They become antifragile, growing stronger through adversity.

>> **Better individual development:** Team members in conflict-competent teams develop better communication skills, emotional intelligence, and leadership capabilities through regular practice in challenging situations.

>> **Organizational reputation:** Teams known for their ability to have difficult conversations become magnets for top talent who want to work in environments where they can bring their authentic self and best ideas.

Interpreting Two Models for Managing Conflict

Understanding your team's conflict patterns requires frameworks for analyzing how team members typically respond to disagreement. The two models I cover in this section provide particularly useful insights for team leaders.

Thomas–Kilmann conflict modes

The first model of conflict management is the Thomas-Kilmann conflict modes. (See Figure 15-1.) This model differentiates between five different strategies of dealing with conflict. While most of us have a preferred strategy, don't think of these modes as a box that you're trapped in. Instead, they're a set of tools that you can choose from, depending on the issue, the personalities, and the problem at hand.

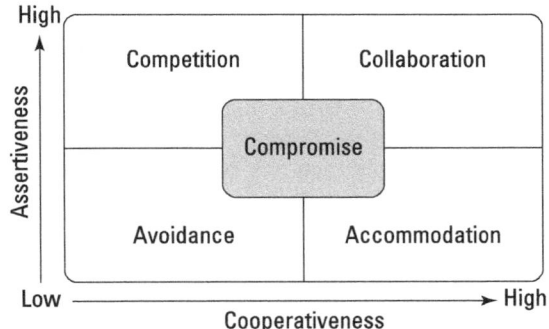

Avoidance

Most people don't like conflict, so it stands to reason that avoiding it altogether is a popular option for many. Avoidance is characterized by low assertiveness, but also by low cooperativeness. Many avoiders learned this tactic at home, where harmony was valued above all else. Unfortunately, if conflict is constantly roiling beneath the surface, the harmony that results is only an illusion. Think of unresolved conflict like a stick of dynamite that is stored away but never lit. Now imagine that every time conflict is avoided, another stick of unlit dynamite is stored in your mental cupboard. If you've soon got a warehouse full of dynamite stored away, it's not hard to imagine that a tiny little spark could lead to disastrous consequences. Therefore, if conflict avoidance is your preferred mode of dealing with conflict, you might be creating an environment that is just as toxic as one where everyone is fighting openly.

At the same time, it can be healthy to avoid some conflicts. For instance, if you have a team member who is constantly looking to you to manage all their conflicts for them, it might be the best idea not to get involved, lest you spend too much of your valuable time being a referee relating to squabbles that your team should be able to work out on their own. At other times, the stakes are so low that it's simply not worth having a conversation about it, and the best thing to model for your team is a healthy sense of priorities. However, if this is your constant rationale for avoiding conflict, I'd suggest reflecting on this tendency because it might be a flimsy excuse for not doing something simply because it makes you uncomfortable.

Accommodation

When in conflict with another person, the strategy of accommodation means you essentially let the other person have their way without any resistance to speak of. Unlike avoidance, this mode acknowledges the conflict and seeks to put an end to it and is therefore characterized by low assertiveness but high cooperativeness. Obviously, someone who relies too much on this strategy can be perceived as passive and unwilling to stand up for their principles.

However, there are situations that call for accommodation, particularly when the stakes are very low for you but higher for the other party. For instance, say you're planning an important all-hands meeting for your team. The dates available to you are in late September and late October. You prefer the September date because your favorite venue is available then, but before the decision is finalized, a member of your team reminds you that this presents a direct conflict with Rosh Hashanah, one of the most sacred dates on the Jewish calendar, meaning that any Jews on your team would either have to leave early or be late for services. Here, it's probably best to accommodate. Your reasons for preferring September (your favorite venue with the high ceilings and excellent pastry selection) are not as important as allowing your Jewish team members to practice their faith.

Competition

When a person engages in the mode of competition during a conflict, they are out to win. Characterized by high assertiveness and low cooperativeness, they believe they are right, the other person is wrong, and they are willing to take a stand to defend their position. Competition sounds very combative, and it can be — but it can also look like a leader pulling rank: "Because I'm in charge, that's why" is a classic way that conflicts can be managed through competition. Of course, no one is right all the time, but there are those in the workplace who have a difficult time admitting that they're wrong and will default to competition as a mode of managing conflict. These people are usually deeply unpopular, especially in industries or roles where people were hired because of their expertise and want their ideas to be considered.

TIP

There are times, however, when the competition mode is absolutely the right choice. Leaders might choose to pull rank if a decision needs to be made immediately. A good leader will not make a habit of this and will communicate clearly why there is no time to discuss further so that their team is not routinely disheartened. Another time to employ competition is when your values are at stake. If a member of your team is voicing comments that are openly bigoted and discriminatory, then a strong stance should be taken. If you are sure that you are right and the stakes are high enough, this can easily be your best option.

Collaboration

Defined by high assertiveness and high cooperativeness, the next mode of conflict management is collaboration. Of all the strategies we've discussed thus far, this is the best "default" mode for an inclusive leader to take. It involves a lot of listening to the opposing party, understanding not only what they want but why, and a willingness for both sides to search for a resolution that is a true win-win.

While it's wonderful when people are creative, collegial, and invested in each other's success enough to come up with a solution that is even better than the original stances, sometimes collaboration just isn't possible. Obviously, if one party is too eager to avoid, accommodate, or compete, it can be difficult to make true collaboration work. One reason why a person might be entrenched in another mode is that they simply don't trust the other person. Collaboration requires vulnerability, and a lack of trust can make that impossible. Also, collaboration takes time and energy, and most teams simply don't have the resources to make this their go-to strategy every time a conflict arises. But if it can work and the conflict is important enough to spend the time and energy, it can be the very best option available.

Compromise

The final mode of conflict management in the Thomas-Kilmann model is compromise. This mode requires each party to give up a little of what they want to reach a solution. When parties compromise, no one gets everything they asked for, but hopefully it's a resolution that makes everyone happy, if not ecstatic. Compromise is placed in the center of the model, but it requires participants to be both assertive and not, both cooperative and not. When engaging in compromise, it's important to know your why and be able to articulate what is important to you and what you'd be willing to sacrifice.

Ultimately, compromising isn't as satisfying as collaboration, but when there's a sense of urgency, it can be a solid option that, unlike competition, leaves all parties feeling heard and at least partially validated. When one party is entrenched in avoidance, accommodation, or competition, it might be easier to get them to engage in compromise rather than collaboration.

So which mode is best? Well, it depends on a variety of factors. Given unlimited time and resources, collaboration is usually a solid option, but can often be derailed by power dynamics, personality traits of all involved, the interpersonal relationships (and amount of trust) between the parties, or the nature of the problem itself.

REMEMBER

Leaders have an outsized influence on the culture of a team or organization. Therefore, your followers will have a strong tendency to mirror your preferred mode of conflict management, whichever it may be. However, if you can skillfully move between the five modes of conflict, depending on the context of each given situation, your followers will model that behavior, too.

TIP

When mediating conflict on the team, try to diagnose which mode of conflict the various parties are engaging in. Before discussing the unique concerns of each side, try to get everyone on the same page in terms of how you'd like to address the situation together.

Intercultural conflict styles

Another model of conflict management was created by Dr. Mitchell Hammer, and it describes a person's mindset as it relates to conflict. This model becomes important when you're engaging in or mediating culture across cultural difference, where learned mindsets might be misaligned. Often, if two people from the same cultural background are solving a problem together, they will hold the same mindsets and preferences. However, when people from two different cultural backgrounds are engaged in conflict, they would do well to understand the other's style before their different approaches cause further misunderstandings.

The model of intercultural conflict styles is depicted as a quadrant, with two axes. (See Figure 15-2.) The first measures a person's preference for either direct or indirect communication. Those who prefer it when people say exactly what they mean are typically aligned with direct communication. However, some cultures place a great deal of emphasis on "face-saving" or respect for elders and authority, making it very difficult to directly challenge someone else. In these cultures, a yes that isn't very enthusiastic can often be understood as a need to talk about the problem more. Obviously, when those who prefer direct communication and therefore take things literally hear a yes, no matter how tentative, they might predictably take people at their word, making any conflict worse.

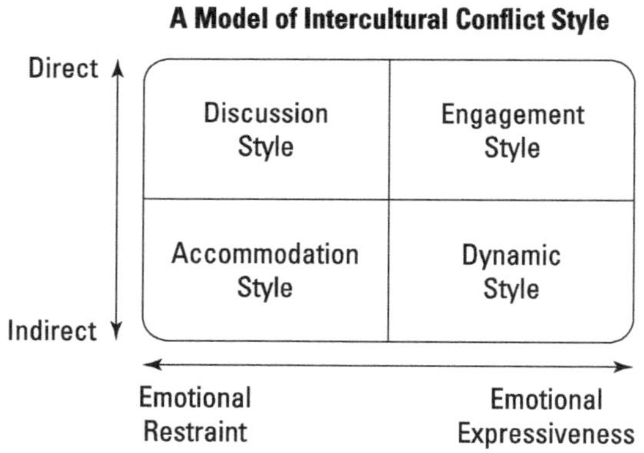

A Model of Intercultural Conflict Style

	Direct	
	Discussion Style	Engagement Style
	Accommodation Style	Dynamic Style
	Indirect	

Emotional Restraint ← → Emotional Expressiveness

FIGURE 15-2: Intercultural conflict styles.

Those who prefer indirect communication can easily perceive their literal rivals to be brusque and rude, while those who prefer direct communication might perceive indirect communicators to be impossible to understand, or even deceptive. It's important to remember that cultures are built around shared understanding, and in the context of many cultures, the less-than-enthusiastic "yes" is very clearly a "no," with no intent to deceive.

The second axis in Dr. Hammer's model measures a person's preference for either emotional restraint or emotional expressiveness. Those who prefer emotional restraint have often been taught by their home culture to value logic over emotion, or that too much emotion can cloud a person's "better" judgment. On the other side, those who value emotional expression are often taught that a cool, rational argument lacking in emotion is simply unconvincing. You can measure the importance of a topic by how much feeling accompanies any discussion of it. Those who exhibit emotional restraint can often view their expressive rivals as lacking in a logical basis for their arguments and attempting to win through emotional manipulation, while those who exhibit emotional expressiveness might believe that their more restrained rivals are either apathetic or hiding something and therefore unworthy of their trust.

REMEMBER

It bears repeating that none of these styles are "right" or "wrong," but simply different. It is common to believe that your preferred style is the "correct" one, but only because it's the one that makes you the most comfortable. Culturally competent leaders can switch styles when immersed in a culture that is not their own.

Discussion style (direct + emotionally restrained)

Team members with this style prefer straightforward, factual discussions that focus on issues rather than personalities. This approach, which is common in many Northern European and North American business cultures, values logical arguments and measured responses.

Discussion-style team members typically

>> State their positions clearly and directly

>> Focus on facts and data rather than emotions

>> Maintain composed demeanor during disagreements

>> Expect others to communicate their concerns explicitly

Engagement style (direct + emotionally expressive)

Team members using this style communicate their positions directly while openly expressing their feelings about issues. This approach is common in many Mediterranean, Eastern European, and African American cultural contexts.

Engagement-style team members often

>> Express their views passionately and directly

>> Use emotional expression to convey the importance of issues

>> Expect others to show similar investment in outcomes

>> View restrained responses as lack of commitment

Accommodation style (indirect + emotionally restrained)

Team members with this style prefer subtle communication that preserves relationships and group harmony. Common in many East Asian and some Latin American cultures, this approach prioritizes long-term relationships over immediate issue resolution.

Accommodation-style team members frequently

>> Communicate concerns indirectly through stories or examples

>> Avoid direct confrontation that might cause others to lose face

>> Work behind the scenes to resolve issues

>> Express disagreement through nonverbal cues or silence

Dynamic style (indirect + emotionally expressive)

Team members using this style express strong emotions about issues while communicating their positions indirectly. This approach appears in many Middle Eastern and some Latin American cultural contexts.

Dynamic-style team members may

>> Use metaphors and stories to make their points

>> Express passion while avoiding direct criticism

>> Build elaborate contexts before addressing core issues

>> Expect others to read between the lines of their communication

None of these styles is inherently superior; they're simply different approaches shaped by cultural learning. High-performance teams learn to recognize these differences and adapt their conflict resolution processes to accommodate various styles effectively.

Applying Best Practices to Real-World Scenarios

To practice applying these concepts, consider the following team conflict scenarios based on common situations that derail team performance:

» **Scenario 1:** Your cross-functional product development team is split on whether to launch a new feature immediately to beat competitors or delay launch to conduct additional user testing. Sarah, from engineering, insists the feature needs more testing to prevent customer complaints. Marcus, from sales, argues that waiting will cost market share and revenue. The team has been debating this for weeks without resolution, and stakeholders are pressuring for a decision.

» **Scenario 2:** During team meetings, you notice that Jennifer, an experienced team member, consistently interrupts and dismisses ideas from newer team members, particularly those from different cultural backgrounds. She justifies this behavior by saying she's "trying to save time" and "sharing her expertise." Several newer team members have started staying silent during discussions, and you're concerned you're losing valuable input.

» **Scenario 3:** Your team committed to equal workload distribution, but it's become clear that some members consistently deliver higher quality work while others meet only minimum standards. The high performers are becoming frustrated and starting to take on extra work to ensure team success. You're worried about burnout among your best contributors and lack of growth among underperformers.

Questions to consider for resolving team conflicts

For each scenario, work through these questions systematically:

» **Do you need to engage?**

While some conflicts resolve naturally, team performance issues typically require leadership intervention. Consider whether the conflict is affecting team results, relationships, or the ability to work together effectively. If team members could resolve the issue independently, you might coach them on conflict resolution skills rather than intervening directly.

>> **What is the source of the conflict? Where do you stand?**

Analyze the root causes without making assumptions about motives or character. Are these conflicts about different approaches to achieving shared goals, unclear roles and expectations, or competing values and priorities? Examine your own biases and preferences before engaging, as your perspective will influence how you facilitate resolution.

>> **How will you engage?**

Consider both your conflict style and those of your team members. Will you need to adapt your approach to match different cultural backgrounds or communication preferences? What conflict mode would be most appropriate given the stakes, time constraints, and relationships involved?

>> **What is the preferred outcome?**

Frame success in terms of team performance and culture rather than individual winners and losers. Focus on how resolving this conflict will help the team achieve better results, stronger relationships, or more effective processes.

>> **What barriers currently exist?**

Identify organizational policies, resource constraints, or team norms that might prevent effective resolution. Consider what you can influence directly versus what requires broader organizational support.

>> **What are the implications globally or among multiple stakeholders?**

Consider how your approach to this conflict will affect team norms going forward. What precedent are you setting for how the team handles future disagreements? How will other teams or stakeholders view your resolution approach?

Targeted responses for team conflict scenarios

Here's how to approach each scenario using the frameworks and principles outlined in this chapter. I detail how to analyze the scenario and provide a recommended approach with some cultural sensitivities to consider.

Scenario 1: Product launch decision conflict

Analysis: This represents a classic task conflict between competing valid priorities. Both Sarah and Marcus are advocating for legitimate business concerns: quality versus speed to market. The extended debate suggests the team lacks clear decision-making processes and criteria.

Recommended approach: Use collaboration mode to develop criteria-based decision-making. Facilitate a structured discussion where both parties articulate their underlying concerns and success metrics. Help the team identify what data would resolve the debate (customer impact tolerance, competitive timeline analysis, testing efficiency improvements). This builds team capability for future product decisions while addressing the immediate conflict.

Cultural considerations: If team members have different conflict styles, ensure both direct communicators and those who prefer indirect approaches can contribute. Sarah might prefer discussion style (data-focused, restrained), whereas Marcus might lean toward engagement style (passionate about market impact).

Scenario 2: Meeting dynamics and inclusion

Analysis: This scenario involves both relationship conflict (interpersonal dynamics) and process conflict (meeting management). Jennifer's behavior is suppressing diverse perspectives and creating an exclusive team environment that undermines performance potential.

Recommended approach: Begin with a private conversation with Jennifer using competition mode to address the behavior directly because team inclusion is a core value. Then facilitate team discussion about meeting norms and communication styles. Help the team develop agreements about how to ensure all voices are heard while maintaining efficiency.

Cultural considerations: Recognize that newer team members from different cultural backgrounds might prefer accommodation or dynamic styles that are being overwhelmed by Jennifer's approach. Create multiple channels for input (premeeting ideas submission, round-robin discussions, anonymous feedback).

Scenario 3: Performance and workload equity

Analysis: This represents both task conflict (work distribution) and relationship conflict (fairness and recognition). The situation threatens team sustainability and risks losing high performers while enabling underperformance.

Recommended approach: Use a combination of collaboration and competition modes. Collaborate on defining clear performance standards and workload measurement but compete when it comes to maintaining standards because team effectiveness is at stake. Address the systemic issue while coaching individual performance improvements.

Cultural considerations: Some team members might view direct performance discussions as face-threatening (accommodation style preference), whereas others expect direct feedback (discussion or engagement styles). Adapt your approach to help each team member understand and meet expectations.

Learning to navigate team conflict effectively requires practice, patience, and commitment to continuous improvement. Teams that master this capability unlock performance levels that harmonious but conflict-averse teams never achieve. The investment in building these skills pays dividends not just in immediate problem resolution, but in creating a team culture where diverse perspectives can collide and combine to produce extraordinary results.

Chapter **16**

Measuring and Maintaining High Performance

High-performing teams do not happen by accident. They happen by intention, design, and disciplined follow through. Measurement is the backbone of that discipline. When we define what matters, track it consistently, review it transparently, and respond to it quickly, teams get better, faster, and stronger. When we do not, energy drifts, standards slip, and excellence becomes an aspiration rather than a daily habit.

This chapter explores the full cycle of measuring and maintaining team performance by identifying the key performance metrics that provide a balanced view of success. It also describes key strategies for correcting low performance when metrics reveal dips or red flags and explains the critical role of demonstrating accountability, both as a leader and as a team.

Identifying Key Performance Metrics for Team Success

Accountability is the glue that holds high performance together. Without it, even the best metrics lose meaning. Leaders must model accountability through transparency, consistency, and follow-through, while also creating systems where every team member takes ownership for achieving performance goals. The art lies in selecting meaningful, actionable indicators and then transforming data into dialogue, using regular reviews not merely as compliance routines but as opportunities for honest reflection, swift adjustment, and shared ownership of progress. Only then can metrics become catalysts for excellence, guiding teams to focus on what drives performance and growth and equipping leaders to intervene before small issues become costly setbacks.

Globally, employee engagement remains far lower than most leaders think. Gallup's latest cross-country data shows only about one in five employees are engaged at work, and disengagement is costly and contagious. Gallup estimates the price tag of low engagement at about $8.9 trillion in lost productivity worldwide, which is roughly nine percent of global gross domestic product. Managers are the multiplier; Gallup finds that about 70 percent of the variance in team engagement links back to the manager's effectiveness. I'm not sharing these statistics as scare tactics; I'm giving them as invitations to lead with clarity and courage.

TIP

The quickest way to improve what a team delivers is to improve what a team discusses. Put performance, engagement, and learning on the agenda every single week, not just every quarter.

WARNING

Do not collect metrics you aren't willing to use. Data without decisions erodes trust.

Think of team performance like a portfolio. No single metric tells the whole story. You want a balanced set of indicators that reflect how people feel, how work flows, how problems get solved, how ideas move to impact, and how talent stays and grows. Use the five categories in the following sections to shape a practical "team scorecard" that fits your context.

Satisfaction and engagement

Engagement influences everything else. Highly engaged teams deliver stronger outcomes in productivity, quality, and retention. Two practical ways to track this are employee engagement scores and the employee net promoter score (eNPS), which asks how likely an employee is to recommend your workplace. Many organizations use a blend of pulse surveys and quarterly or biannual deep dives. Benchmarks vary by industry, yet global averages for engagement remain about 21 percent. eNPS benchmarks tend to cluster around the low teens across sectors, with wide variation by industry. Here are some ways to measure satisfaction and engagement:

>> Engagement index or pulse score, by team and by manager

>> eNPS, with open-text analysis for themes

>> Manager effectiveness items, such as clarity of expectations, quality of one-to-ones, and recognition frequency

>> Well-being indicators, such as perceived workload manageability and meeting quality

TIP

If you're new to this, start with five consistent pulse items every month and one open question. Tag comments by theme. Close the loop with what the team will start, stop, and continue based on the feedback.

For example, Microsoft's Viva Insights provides team-level and organization-level views into collaboration patterns, focus time, after-hours load, and meeting quality. Companies use these dashboards to spot overload, coach managers, and experiment with better meeting norms. Microsoft has documented how it uses Viva to improve productivity and well-being and publishes metric definitions leaders can understand.

WARNING

Engagement scores without manager coaching become vanity metrics. Use them to spark better conversations, not to label people.

Productivity, output, and quality

High performance is not about doing more; it's about delivering the right value with fewer friction points. Blend process efficiency measures with quality and customer impact. In project-based environments, visual progress tools such as dashboards or milestone trackers can help identify workflow bottlenecks, shifting priorities, and delays in delivery. Metrics for productivity and quality may include

>> On-time delivery rate across key milestones

>> Turnaround time for key deliverables or requests

>> Rework rate or defect escape rate; first-pass yield

>> Service level attainment and average time to resolution

>> Customer satisfaction or internal client CSAT

Pair every output key performance indicator (KPI) with a quality or customer KPI. Output without quality puts your reputation at risk.

Problem-solving

Exceptional teams treat problems as data, not drama. They define them precisely, find root causes, and fix systems. Measure the speed, depth, and durability of your problem-solving.

Here are some metrics to consider:

>> Average response and resolution time for significant issues or challenges

>> Root cause closure rate, not just incident closure

>> Recurrence rate within 30, 60, and 90 days

>> Cross-functional participation rate in retrospectives

>> Turnaround time for making decisions on key risks and escalations

TIP

Here's one practice that works: After every major setback or missed milestone, hold a learning review focused on identifying root causes and capturing lessons for next time. Track whether those fixes change the future incident curve.

REMEMBER

A "green" dashboard with recurring issues is not a success story. If the same problems repeat, your metric is vanity, not value.

Innovation and creativity

Innovation is not luck. It's a pipeline, a practice, and a set of behaviors you can measure. Google's well-known Project Aristotle found that psychological safety is a cornerstone of effective teams. In a psychologically safe environment, people take smart risks, share ideas earlier, and learn faster from experiments. Track the flow from ideas to impact.

Here are other methods to track:

>> Idea submissions per quarter and participation rate

>> Percentage of ideas that progress to pilot and to scale

>> Time to first test and time to decision on pilots

>> Revenue or cost impact from launches

>> Learning velocity, measured by experiment cadence and documented insights

TIP

Use a simple "innovation funnel" scorecard. For each quarter, show idea count, pilot count, launch count, and two lessons the team will apply in the next quarter.

Retention

People stay where they contribute, grow, and are treated fairly. Retention is a lagging indicator, so combine it with leading indicators like internal mobility, career development participation, and manager coaching quality. Workday, Visier, and other people analytics platforms provide packaged insights for trends, hotspots, and drivers of attrition.

Here are some other metrics you can capture:

>> Retention rate and voluntary turnover by team and by regrettable loss

>> Internal move rate and time in role before first move

>> First-year attrition and 90-day retention

>> Promotion of velocity by demographic cuts to ensure equity

>> Manager tenure and span of control versus engagement and exits

WARNING

Never weaponize retention metrics. Use them to learn and lead, not to shame managers or teams.

Correcting Low Performance

Every leader inevitably encounters periods of decreased performance. The key consideration is not the occurrence of these dips, but rather how promptly they're identified and systematically addressed. Adopting a structured "four-week fix" cycle enables leaders to diagnose issues, make informed decisions, and demonstrate measurable improvement.

Here are the steps:

1. **Detect and define.**

   Use your scorecard to spot gaps early. Define the problem clearly. What should be happening, what is happening, and where is the delta? Quantify the impact on customers, cost, quality, and morale.

TIP

Start with facts, then add feelings. People can handle the truth when it's delivered with respect.

2. **Diagnose root causes.**

Separate people issues, process issues, and priority issues. Use a simple fishbone, 5-whys, or a structured retrospective. Look for patterns in handoffs, decision rights, clarity of roles, and meeting load. Collaboration data from tools like Viva Insights can reveal where focus time disappears and which meetings drain energy.

REMEMBER

Most chronic performance problems are systems problems. Fix the system and people will look a whole lot better.

3. **Decide and act.**

Create a short action list with owners, due dates, and success measures. Examples include eliminating low-value meetings, redesigning a workflow, clarifying decision rights, pairing less experienced team members with mentors, or prioritizing one critical task that's delaying progress. Use visible tracking tools such as team dashboards or progress boards to keep plans transparent and maintain focus.

4. **Debrief, document, and reinforce.**

After four weeks, review results with transparency. What moved and why. What did not move and what is next. Document lessons in a shared playbook so the team institutionalizes learning.

WARNING

Do not substitute kindness for clarity. Clear expectations are an act of respect. Ambiguity is not compassion; it is avoidance.

Handling Persistent Underperformance at the Individual Level

Sometimes, despite coaching and systems changes, an individual's performance remains below standard. Address it with dignity and decisiveness using these steps:

1. **Clearly outline the performance standards with specific, measurable criteria.**

Define what successful performance entails, as well as what falling short looks like, and set a clear timeline for improvement.

2. **Offer real support.**

Provide targeted training, mentoring, and job aids. If your data shows skills gaps, point the person to specific learning paths. LinkedIn's Workplace Learning research continues to highlight the link between career development and retention, which means development is not a perk; it's a performance enabler.

3. **Use a time-bound improvement plan.**

Set milestones and feedback checkpoints. Track both output and behaviors. Be present, be specific, and be fair.

4. **Make a decision.**

If improvement happens, celebrate and stabilize. If it does not, choose reassignment or exit respectfully. High standards are not the opposite of empathy; they're the expression of it.

Demonstrating Accountability as a Leader and as a Team

Accountability is keeping promises to people and to performance. It's not a posture; it's a practice. Here is how great teams make it visible:

1. **Anchor accountability in purpose and values**

People take ownership when they see how the work connects to something that matters. Revisit your why every quarter. Measure whether your goals align with strategy and whether your daily work aligns with those goals.

2. **Make commitments public**

Use a shared dashboard where the team sees the same truth. Show green for on track, yellow for at risk, red for off track. For each red, show the recovery plan. Keep the story honest.

Dashboards are conversation starters, not scorecards for blame.

REMEMBER

3. **Coach managers like they're the product**

Managers are the amplifiers of culture. Gallup's research underscores that manager effectiveness heavily shapes engagement and performance. Invest in manager training, ongoing community of practice, and real-time coaching. Track the quality of manager one-to-ones and the frequency of meaningful recognition because these behaviors strongly predict team performance.

4. Inspect learning, not just results

Ask, "What did we learn this week? What will we try next week? What play will we retire?" Create a "kill list" of low-value reports and meetings so learning space increases.

WARNING

If every meeting is a status meeting, you will starve your team of strategy, creativity, and coaching.

Chapter **17**

Leading Hybrid and Remote Teams

R
emote work isn't new, but the COVID-19 pandemic fast-tracked its global adoption, creating a permanent shift in how, where, and when people work. Practically overnight, organizations had to pivot to virtual operations. What many thought would be a temporary adaptation has become the new normal, and there's no going back.

In today's workplace, hybrid and remote teams are not just common, they're expected. Even as the work landscape evolves, flexible work arrangements continue to grow in importance.

This evolution challenges you to expand your toolkit and shift from traditional, face-to-face leadership practices to more inclusive, human-centered, and digitally fluent strategies. Whether you're managing a fully remote team or a hybrid workforce, your role is to foster clarity, build connection, maintain accountability, and create a culture of belonging — no matter the zip code.

This chapter explores what it takes to lead with excellence in this new world of work.

Establishing Roles, Responsibilities, and Clear Expectations for Working Remotely

Working remotely brings freedom, flexibility, and autonomy, but it can also bring confusion, isolation, and blurred boundaries if the leadership isn't strong. Leaders must be intentional about setting the tone, defining success, and ensuring that each team member knows how they fit into the bigger picture.

When teams of people who have never worked remotely before dive in for the first time, it can feel a little scary. Perhaps team members see the benefits: more autonomy, the ability to quickly throw a load of laundry into the washing machine on a short break, less time spent in frustrating traffic jams to and from work, and even savings on wardrobe and dry cleaning bills. But there are downsides to think of as well: Remote work might be lonely and isolating, particularly for strong extroverts. The casual camaraderie of the employee break room that allows people to get to know their colleagues at a deeper level might hinder a sense of belonging on a team, and it's possible that people will get less credit for their work if the manager or supervisor isn't a witness to what's being done. Also, direction, coaching, and career guidance may be easier to come by when the manager's office is just down the hall.

These are valid concerns, but depending on the skill of a team leader, none of them are a certainty. Strong leadership from a leader who knows how to lead a remote worker can easily solve (or at least minimize) these issues so that the benefits of remote work shine through.

The following sections cover best practices that I used as a remote worker and as the leader of my remote team.

Implement frequent communication

When you can't walk from your desk to the printer without running into several members of your team, communication is easy. When spontaneous and informal meetings cease altogether, they need to be replaced by scheduled and formal meetings.

At first, a remote leader might feel as though they're overscheduling their team members with team meetings and check-ins, but there's far less of a cost to bringing everyone together and having a shorter meeting than expected than there is if you let days go by and important communications aren't shared, especially if the team is new to remote work. When implementing a schedule, try having shorter meetings more often, just to ensure that relationships are being built and information is routinely shared.

TIP

If it's your typical practice to meet with each of your direct reports one on one for a 30 minutes each week, try splitting that into 15-minute meetings twice a week. An hour-long team meeting that begins each week might be supplemented with a shorter all-hands "check-in" at the end of the week. Maintain a sense of flexibility and solicit feedback from your team members so that you can be sure you're meeting their needs.

Choosing your communication channels well

When working in an office, a team can generally rely on face-to-face meetings, both formal and informal, and email. When working remotely, it will probably be necessary to choose a platform for video meetings (such as Zoom, Google Meet, or Microsoft Teams) to facilitate virtual meetings, as well as a team-based social media tool (for example, Slack, Meta Workplace, or Blink) for more informal "chats" (including nonwork conversations that allow for relationship-building).

While it's important to have technological communication channels other than email, try to adopt only as many channels as your team needs. Aside from the channels I've already mentioned, your team might find it necessary to use a customer relationship management (CRM) platform such as Salesforce, HubSpot, or Zoho. However, too many separate platforms can overwhelm team members and allow important messages to slip through the cracks.

TIP

When using multiple platforms, be sure to provide clear direction on when each platform is to be used.

Establishing clear expectations

REMEMBER

Transparency builds trust. If team members don't know what their leadership is thinking and feeling, this creates a sense of unease (and a tendency to begin making up stories to fill the vacuum of information). When it comes to leadership transparency, nothing is more important than your team members knowing exactly what you expect of them and when.

When managing remote teams, set clear boundaries and expectations. For instance, tasks without deadlines result in missed opportunities and resentment on both sides. Unexpected on-camera virtual meetings can be uncomfortable for some employees (who may not be "camera-ready" at a moment's notice). Vague role descriptions can create situations where either important work is dropped or two members of a remote team each take responsibility for a task and then engage in a conflict about who is "stepping out of their lane."

When managing remotely, be clear about the following things:

>> Your values and norms that are important to you

>> The values and norms of your organization (its culture)

>> When employees and leaders are expected to be available

>> Conduct during virtual meetings (for example, camera use, hand raising, use of chat, and so on)

>> How calendars should be used to indicate availability

>> Guidelines specific to team members' work

>> Their roles and the roles of others on the team

>> Which communication platform to use for any given message

>> Expectations regarding workload and timelines

Reinforce these messages as often as possible, especially when someone new joins the team.

Documenting everything

Managing remote teams can quickly become complex. When transitioning project activities online, key tasks may be overlooked. For effective remote team management, document workflows, roles, and processes clearly and ensure they're accessible to all remote employees.

When conducting team meetings and regular employee check-ins, take notes (or use AI-generated notetaking programs) and store the notes where you can find them easily. Share the notes with the team and individual employees, and review them before the next team meeting or individual check-in.

Creating and Maintaining Connection, Community, and Engagement with a Distributed Workforce

High-performance teams are built on trust, connection, and community. That doesn't change just because the team is remote, but it does take more intentional effort. When Buffer asked survey respondents to report their biggest struggle with working remotely, 20 percent said that communication and collaboration was difficult, and another 20 percent reported feeling isolated and lonely. Some people (even self-described extroverts) thrive in a remote setting, enjoying the flexibility and autonomy that remote work provides. Others (even self-described introverts) can struggle when they spend most of their workday alone. In addition to the task-related aspects of leadership, those who lead remote teams also have to keep their team culture in mind.

In this section, I offer some ways you can build a sense of community among your remote and hybrid team members.

Prioritizing mental health

Out of sight should never mean out of mind. One of the biggest risks of remote leadership is overlooking your team's emotional health. Mental well-being must be a leadership priority.

WARNING

Neglecting to see team members as full, complex, and imperfect human beings — so they become more like cogs in a machine — is perhaps one of the biggest dangers of leading remotely. Over time, setting clear expectations and documenting both products and processes becomes easier. But what can be difficult is reading the subtle signs that indicate an employee is struggling. When leading in a colocated space, you might depend on your daily observations and intuitions to make these kinds of assessments. When leading remotely, you must be proactive in taking care of the humans who are following your lead.

In addition to the values-based reasons for doing so, investing in mental health and wellness also makes good business sense. According to the World Health Organization (WHO), anxiety and depression can be very costly to your organization. WHO also reports that for every dollar dedicated to protecting your workers' mental health, there's a return of four dollars in the form of greater productivity. (See Figure 17-1.)

FIGURE 17-1:
The ROI of
mental health
(according
to WHO).

$$\text{Mental Health ROI} = 1\,\textit{Investment} \rightarrow 4\text{ Return}$$
$$\text{(According to WHO)}$$

TIP

Therefore, begin most (if not all) of your regular check-ins with team members by asking how they are doing. If they admit to struggling with something, listen compassionately and without judgment. Normalize conversations about stress, burnout, and fatigue. Try not to leap to instant solutions but create a culture where this type of sharing is simply heard and respected. When it's appropriate to do so, ask your employees how you can best support them. Obviously, keep all conversations confidential if possible.

If your organization offers employee benefits related to mental health, ensure that everyone is aware of them (whether they report a struggle or not). When possible and appropriate, be transparent about the days when you're feeling less than your best to normalize these conversations among your team. After all, you might have an employee who would never make this kind of admission to a leader but might very well confide in a colleague and get the support they need if they felt the team culture would permit it.

TIP

Encourage all your employees to take breaks and share tips you find about self-care on your team's social media channel. When a team member is on vacation, make sure they know that they are not expected to check in when they should be relaxing or spending time with friends and family.

Making time for celebrations

When managing in a colocated space, small and spontaneous celebrations happen easily. Completion of just one milestone in a long, complicated project will likely result in a few high-fives and the random "Woo hoo!".

REMEMBER

As the leader of a remote team, it's your job to instigate team celebrations, both large and small. Large celebrations might look like having flowers or gift cards sent to the homes of team members or organizing a virtual party to celebrate a big win or a moment on the calendar (for example, a virtual gift exchange before the winter holidays or a costume contest on Halloween). A small celebration might simply entail a post on your team's social media congratulating the team for completing an important milestone, accompanied by a fun GIF of people tossing confetti.

Even if there's no specific moment to celebrate, promoting fun traditions like "Trivia Tuesday" or "Fun Fact Friday" when the leader posts a question at the end of a team meeting and the first employee who types the correct answer into chat wins a prize, even if it's only choosing the category for the next meeting's question can give everyone on the team a chance to laugh and enjoy each other.

These small moments of joy can add to an employee's sense of wellness, belonging, and fun, ensuring they feel valued, both for their work and for who they are as people.

Keeping professional development in mind

In addition to laughing together, *learning* together can bond team members to each other. While employees should be given access to individual professional development needs, it's also important to let them experience group learning. This could look like a three-hour virtual course led by a subject matter expert, or it could be a casual monthly "lunch and learn" facilitated by team members who are sharing the specifics of their work for the benefit of their colleagues.

Adapting Leadership Styles to Meet the Needs of a Distributed Workforce

As long as there have been teams and leaders, there have been scholars who observe the way human beings interact and write down what they've noticed to help leaders adopt behaviors that will make them and their teams more successful. Some of these leadership models complement each other more than others. But there's no "best way" to be a leader. Just as your team members are likely to have different needs and expectations of their leaders, leaders also have unique styles and personalities. My advice to anyone who wants to be a better leader is to look at all the models and find the combination that works the best for them (and for the people they lead).

In the following sections, I describe the different leadership styles.

Transactional leadership

Transactional leadership is a management style where leaders motivate others by offering rewards for meeting expectations and issuing penalties for noncompliance.

This model works best in an organizational culture that emphasizes hierarchy and strict adherence to rules and regulations, such as manufacturing, law enforcement, or fast food and doesn't rely too much on risk-taking, creativity, and innovation. Transactional leadership has obvious flaws, one of which is that it tends to ignore the complexity (and humanity) of team members and responds only to their output.

Honestly, it's not my favorite leadership model, although I do believe that in combination with other leadership models, there is some wisdom in its approach, especially for leaders of remote teams.

For instance, it can be very easy when working at a distance from your team members to avoid conflict or tough conversations. A conflict-averse leader might be generous with their praise when team members are successful but procrastinate when it comes to giving constructive feedback. Meanwhile, when the employee doesn't hear any response from their leader when subpar work is completed and submitted may believe that everything is fine.

REMEMBER

In this model, "consequences" doesn't have to mean punishment or something being taken away from an employee. It might simply mean a conversation that reviews an employee's work and explains exactly how expectations were not met. It probably doesn't feel good to hear such news, and it may not be much fun to deliver it, either. But constructive feedback, given at the earliest possibility, is the kindest thing you can do for an employee who's underperforming because it gives them an opportunity to turn things around before habits are formed, and it signals that their leader is paying attention.

REMEMBER

For the leader with the opposite problem — quick to criticize, but slow to praise — the transactional leadership model reminds us that rewards are just as important as consequences, if not more so. This model can remind a leader to offer a public acknowledgement when expectations are met and to really raise the roof when an employee goes well above and beyond what was requested.

Situational leadership

Situational leadership, a model by organizational theorist Ken Blanchard, involves adjusting your style to meet the particular needs and readiness of individuals or teams in different stages of their development.

The hallmark of this model is flexibility and adaptability, and it requires leaders to pay attention to the stage that each employee happens to occupy at any given time. The model is typically depicted as a quadrant (see Figure 17-2) that differentiates between high and low supportive behavior on one axis and high and low directive behavior on the other. In the following sections, I break down each of the stages.

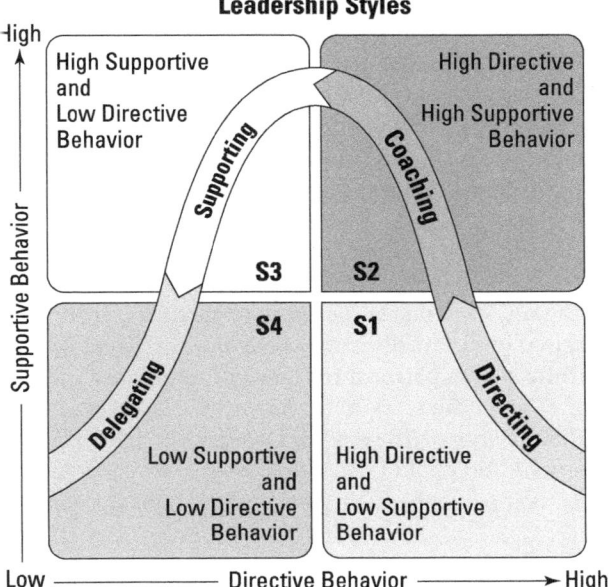

Leadership Styles

High Supportive and Low Directive Behavior

High Directive and High Supportive Behavior

Supporting

Coaching

S3

S2

S4

S1

Delegating

Directing

Low Supportive and Low Directive Behavior

High Directive and Low Supportive Behavior

Supportive Behavior

Low — Directive Behavior — High

FIGURE 17-2: Situational leadership.

Stage 1

Stage 1 of the model is called *directing*. It's especially useful when a team member is either new to the team or perhaps new to a particular task or skill set. At this stage, the most important thing a leader can do is impart knowledge. In this model, "low supportive" behavior doesn't mean a leader is intentionally unsupportive; it simply means they aren't prioritizing emotional support as part of their leadership approach. In fact, people who are very new to a task or team will feel the most supported when given a high degree of direction. For instance, it may not be enough to assign a task and be available for questions. You may need to walk through a process, step by step, to ensure that it is being done correctly. The directing stage can also be useful during an emergency when urgent action is required.

At this stage, the leader of a remote team might wish they could sit across the desk from their employee and feel frustrated that this is impossible. This is when a leader might make use of a virtual meeting platform with the option of screen sharing to ensure understanding.

Stage 2

Stage 2 of the model is *coaching* and is characterized by high directive and high supportive leadership behaviors. When your employee is still new to the team or task but ready to stretch their wings a bit, a leader can be less directive and spend more time checking in with the employee to make sure they're comfortable (high supportive) and being available for robust feedback (high directive) to ensure that the work is meeting expectations. Think of coaching like transitioning from a tricycle to a bicycle by using training wheels. At this stage, you want employees to learn by making occasional mistakes, but only if those mistakes are caught and corrected immediately and nonjudgmentally so that the employee can learn.

Stage 3

Stage 3 of the model is *supporting*. True to the label, high supportive behavior is key here, paired with low directive behavior. This style is useful when the team member is fully able to perform the task but might lack motivation or confidence in their ability to do the work independently. Leaders at this stage should spend almost all their energy on the emotional supports, which definitely include praise (both one on one and public) when processes are mastered. At this stage, leaders can delegate team members to give positive and constructive feedback when necessary.

Stage 4

Stage 4 is *delegating* and is especially useful when your team or an individual team member is highly skilled, confident, and self-motivated. Characterized by both low directive and low supportive behaviors, leaders at this stage can simply assign the work, communicate their expectations, and then give their employees the authority to complete the task however they want. Obviously, leaders should still be available for questions or notified of changing context and unexpected obstacles. "Low supportive" in this context simply means you're not coddling team members who have earned their autonomy.

REMEMBER

For a remote leader, this model can be a powerful reminder to ask their employees what they require from you. At a distance, it may not be as easy to discern how quickly skills have been mastered or how confident your team members are by simple observation. It's therefore important to have honest conversations about this, to ask your employees how they're feeling, and to model the kind of transparency you expect from them.

Transformational leadership

Transformational leadership (see Figure 17-3) is a model that emphasizes energy, enthusiasm, passion, and positive change. First introduced by leadership expert James McGregor Burns, the model contains four elements, sometimes referred to as the four I's:

>> **Intellectual stimulation:** This entails challenging the status quo and encouraging both creativity and constant learning. It not only leads teams to create new kinds of outputs but may also lead to changes in how routine work gets accomplished.

>> **Individualized consideration:** This means supporting each team member in a way that best suits the follower, not the leader, and being adaptable to changing circumstances. To provide this level of flexibility, leaders must communicate with each of their team members frequently and develop trust so that team members feel free to share ideas, ask questions, and contribute to the team's success.

>> **Inspirational motivation:** To provide inspirational motivation, leaders must first develop a compelling vision they're passionate about. Then they must articulate to their team in a way that ignites their passion as well. In daily practice, the leader should notice when the team is getting bogged down in the details and find ways to remind them of the larger purpose of their work.

>> **Idealized influence:** This element is all about role modeling the values, norms, behaviors, and attitudes that you want to see embodied in your team. It means setting a high bar for your own words and actions and being transparent about the moments when you fall short. See Chapter 12 for more about the importance of being a role model.

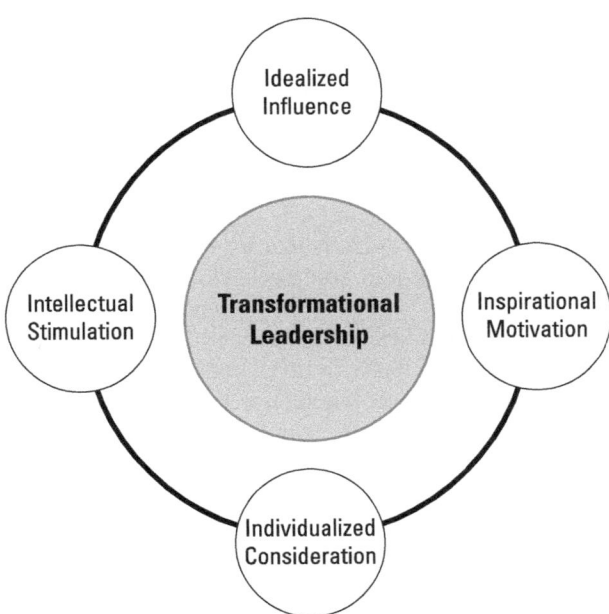

FIGURE 17-3:
Transformational leadership

The transformational leadership model can be challenging for a remote leader. So much of what it seeks to accomplish depends upon being emotionally intelligent and emotionally available for your team, which can be difficult when managing from a distance.

TIP

To do this well on a remote team, leaders must make communication a priority, to the point of feeling as though they are overcommunicating at times. They must take the risk to share both their passions and insecurities so that team members can do the same and work hard to establish trust by behaving with integrity and consistency. It's not an easy job, but those that can manage it will be rewarded with teams that are high performing and incredibly loyal.

Inclusive leadership

Inclusive leadership actively encourages valuing diverse perspectives and contributions and promoting a sense of belonging on a team. This style of leadership is characterized by empathic listening, self-awareness, and psychological safety.

TIP

Practice empathic listening by focusing fully on the speaker, reflecting back what you hear, and asking clarifying questions without judgment. Instead of preparing your response while someone is talking, pause and tune in to their words, tone and emotions. Simple phrases such as "What I'm hearing is" or "Help me understand" signal respect, create trust, and invite deeper dialogue.

To lead inclusively, leaders must be visibly committed to treating people well. At a time when words like diversity, equity, and inclusion are often misunderstood and weaponized, this can be more difficult than it sounds. But even if you don't use those specific words, an inclusive leader will ask a team if anyone has a different point of view (diversity), speak about the importance of meeting people where they are and treating them fairly (equity), will go out of their way to seek the input of those who are less likely to offer up suggestions, and will quickly shut down any behaviors that hinder group cohesion (inclusion).

Inclusive leaders are genuinely curious about other people. They don't focus solely on what they have in common with their team members but lean into the differences that are present on their team. Over time, their curiosity has resulted in a great deal of knowledge about how people of different backgrounds and with different identities experience the workplace. This, in turn, affords them the ability to be truly empathetic (able to see the world from another's perspective) in their day-to-day leadership.

Inclusive leaders are also self-aware. They know their own limitations, don't pretend to possess all the answers, are aware of the blind spots and biases they hold, and are constantly working to mitigate both in order to make better decisions based on their values.

For a remote leader, the challenges inherent in the inclusive leadership model are similar to those with transformational leadership. To achieve inclusive leadership with a remote team requires a great deal of communication but especially in the form of listening. As the member of a remote team, it might be easy to allow your leader to do most of the talking. The inclusive leader, therefore, must "flip the script" and encourage their team members to share openly.

TIP

Members of your team will be much more apt to share when you as their leader are accepting of what they say. Inclusive leaders must always remember that something can be true for one of their employees even if it isn't true for them, personally, especially when the employee is a part of a community that is often marginalized at work or in society. Simply believing people when they speak might be the single most important trait of an inclusive leader.

Agile leadership

Agile leadership is a model that adapts to change, accepts uncertainty, and empowers teams to make decisions in turbulent times with the assistance of a clear vision and guiding principles. This leadership style not only embraces change, but it actually drives and promotes change. In a world that is consistently more volatile and chaotic, this model is useful for many industries, not only those who are seeking to create new solutions that have never existed before.

Agile leaders embrace change and adapt quickly, valuing flexibility over rigid processes. They view uncertainty as part of progress, encourage experimentation, and see setbacks as learning opportunities. Their focus is on achieving results and delivering value efficiently.

Next, agile leaders empower their employees and foster collaboration. They provide autonomy and trust to their teams, enabling individuals to make decisions and take ownership of their work. They emphasize collaboration and welcome diverse perspectives, understanding that effective solutions can come from various sources. Agile leaders also focus on removing obstacles and fostering an environment where team members feel safe to take risks and learn from mistakes.

Agile leaders prioritize learning and lead by example, showing the behaviors and values they expect from their teams. They're dedicated to ongoing learning and personal development, encouraging their teams to do likewise. Agile leaders aim to develop leadership skills at all levels, acknowledging that everyone can contribute to a common goal.

Finally, agile leaders prioritize delivering value and achieving results, rather than following a rigid plan. They use evidence-based management (EBM) to focus on four key areas: current value, unrealized value, ability to innovate, and time to market. They track progress and adjust strategies based on real-time feedback and market conditions.

Agile teams don't wait for change; they adapt continuously. Building such a team remotely involves fostering continuous learning, focusing on the big picture, and encouraging autonomy to achieve goals effectively.

Overcoming Common Pitfalls in Leading Hybrid and Remote Teams

Of course, hybrid and remote teams come with their unique challenges, and certain difficulties are predictable, even when a team is managed well. If you lead a remote and hybrid team, you need to keep an eye out for these particular challenges:

>> Micromanagement

>> Proximity bias

>> Burnout

Micromanagement

You probably don't want to gain a reputation as a micromanager, but it can happen without you realizing it, especially if you're managing from a distance.

Micromanagement, or excessive control and scrutiny over employees' work, is almost always the result of a lack of trust and insecurity — except that the deficit is on the leader's side. You might be working hard to gain the trust of your team members, but you have to spend just as much energy in trusting them. Trust is earned (on both sides). Insecurity comes from one feeling inadequate in their own skills and in their own skin, and that can show up in many ways that range from undermining someone's ideas and talents to underappreciating their results or success.

To avoid being the kind of manager you'd personally hate to work for, consider the following strategies:

>> **Acknowledge the issue.** If you've ever been micromanaged, reflect on how stifling it felt. If you see yourself micromanaging, take stock of how stressful it feels for you. No one wins in this situation. Commit to trusting your team and doing better.

>> **Hold frequent check-ins.** This is a theme by now; there are many reasons to check in with your remote workers often, and this is just one of them. Keep in mind that check-ins shouldn't be 100 percent focused on tasks. They should also include checking in on a personal level. I'm not suggesting you be a therapist, but ask them how they feel about their work. Inquire about their work load. — Are they too busy or not busy enough? Do they have questions, and are they able to get the answers they need? Best of all, how can you best support them in their work?

>> **Reflect on how you assign tasks.** Are your assignments way too detailed? Are you tasking them with the "how" in addition to the "what"? If you're not sure, ask. Be transparent with your remote workers, by explicitly stating, "I don't want you to feel isolated, but I also don't want you to feel micromanaged. I'm trying to find the right balance. What works best for you?" Your workers will almost always be grateful to be considered in this way.

>> **Delegate.** Take note of how many tasks you're holding onto rather than trusting your team to handle them. Notice how it feels when you let go of a task and allow your employees to figure out the best way to complete their work. If that feels scary to you, that's a lack of trust. Start small, with low-stakes work, and let your skilled workers handle the details. If the work is returned on time with high quality, take that as a sign that you can trust them more.

>> **Track your feedback.** A recurring theme in this chapter is that some leaders of remote teams don't give enough feedback. Micromanagers tend to give way too much. Find the balance that works for you and your team, keeping in mind that some of your team members may require more attention than others (see "Situational leadership," earlier in this chapter).

Proximity bias

People tend to have a preference (often unconscious) for the people they see more often and work more closely with. This is an obvious problem for a hybrid team, where you might work in an office setting with a few people while a significant portion of your team works remotely. Recent research by Gartner finds that 64 percent of managers say onsite employees are higher performers than those who work remotely, and 75 percent say onsite employees are more likely to be promoted. Combined with confirmation bias (wherein people are drawn to data that confirms their preexisting beliefs but tend to ignore data that contradicts what they already believe), this can become a self-fulfilling prophecy. Meanwhile, research from the National Bureau of Economic Research says that the opposite is often true: Remote workers spend an average of an additional 48 minutes a day working than onsite workers — about four additional hours a week!

Proximity bias can also be a problem on a fully remote team (or any team for that matter) where some people are going to be in more meetings with you because of their roles or the projects they work on.

As with most biases, knowing that it exists and admitting that you're susceptible to it will go a long way to helping you mitigate it. Beyond that, I can suggest a few concrete steps you can take to limit proximity bias.

>> Ask remote workers to be on camera whenever they log into a meeting. This should be optional (many remote workers report camera fatigue, if they're on several virtual meetings a day) but strongly encouraged. Consider offering full transparency here; share with your team members what you've learned about proximity bias and let them know that this request is specifically to combat this.

>> If possible, ask all team members, even the ones colocated with you, to attend some or all team meetings from their laptop, using tools like chat and online polls to keep it interactive and maintain an even playing field.

>> When staffing projects or advocating for your team members, consider your remote team members first, and intentionally champion them.

>> Keep track of who has been rewarded, thanked publicly, or promoted on your team. If you notice that the numbers are skewed away from the employees you see less often, double-down on the tactics I've shared in this list and consider increasing the length of your one-on-one check-in meetings with those workers.

Burnout

Research by McKinsey finds that 49 percent of employees are experiencing burnout. The lack of boundaries when people work from home could make the problem even worse for them. When one's office is connected to one's home, the desire for a remote employee to prove their worth (perhaps as a result of observed proximity bias) might find them back upstairs after putting the kids to bed so they can do another hour of work as they neglect their own self-care.

Preventing burnout is all about enforcing healthy boundaries. Whether you're leading a hybrid or a remote team, make the boundaries around work equitable for everyone by doing the following things:

REMEMBER

» If an employee is taking a sick day, let them know that they aren't expected to log in to work just because their home office is just down the hall from their bedroom.

Remote workers are more likely to not take paid time off when they have a slight cold because they feel able to work and aren't contagious from their home office. This can be tolerated, but if an employee could benefit from taking a day and focusing on their physical health, they should do so.

» When on vacation, neither onsite nor remote employees should feel pressured to check in. Again, some might choose to peruse their emails if only to delete spam and prevent returning to an overwhelming inbox; that's their right. But you can make it very clear that you don't expect to hear from them while they should be resting or enjoying time with friends and family.

» Set start times and end times for your team. You might begin your day at 9:00 a.m. and end at 5:30 p.m., or you could tell employees that everyone is expected to be available during core team hours (for example, 10:30 a.m. to 4:30 p.m.) and either working the remainder of their eight-hour day earlier or later (or both) depending on their preference. (This is a good option when your team works across time zones.) Either way, every member of the team (including the leader) should avoid sending emails or posting work-related messages on the team's social media outside of business hours. If an employee chooses to do work at odd hours, encourage the use of the "schedule send" feature so it doesn't prompt everyone else on the team to adopt the habit of working off-hours.

» Encourage breaks and other methods of self-care. If you notice signs of burnout, talk to your team, and come up with a solution that works well for everyone.

» Be a role model. As with everything else, it's up to you to embody the behaviors you want your team to follow. Don't talk about boundaries while continuing to work through your own vacations and sick days or sending emails in the middle of the night. Your employees will hear what you say, but they're far more likely to do what you do.

Shifting from Remote to Return-to-Office Work

Remote work has a lot of benefits, but it's not for every person or every team. Some people find that they're far more effective when colocated with their colleagues, and some teams find that they can't properly function remotely due to the nature of their work.

If your team was once hybrid or remote but is due to return to a colocated space, it might be tempting to underestimate the transition. After all, you're just going back to the way things were, right? Well . . . maybe.

You can probably count on the fact that some of your team members prefer a remote work arrangement, and others on your team will be surprised by some aspects of remote work that they miss when they return to an office setting. Even those workers who dearly want everyone back in the office again will need to adjust to a change, especially if they were working remotely for a significant length of time.

Whether driven by strategy or necessity, this transition must be handled with care. To manage the transition effectively, keep the following best practices in mind:

>> **Communicate the "why."** To manage the resistance to change (see Chapter 8 for more on this), people need to understand why the status quo (in this case, remote work) wasn't working and have a compelling vision of how much better the change will be. Craft a compelling message around both of these ideas and repeat them as often as necessary.

>> **Consider a hybrid arrangement**. Offer team members the option of working from home one or two days a week. This is especially helpful for employees who dread returning to the office.

>> **Keep what worked well from your "remote" days.** Remember, you're not turning a dial and going back in time. The team that exists today is not the team that was colocated before. You've likely said hello to new team members and goodbye to others while working remotely, and even those who've worked onsite with you before will have been changed by the experience of remote work. You may have developed new habits, customs, and norms during your time away from the office, and many of them might be positive. Keep those, at least at first, even if they're "team building" activities that don't seem entirely necessary anymore.

» **Celebrate the move.** Even if not everyone feels like celebrating, make the move back as fun for your team as you can. Gift them with the office supplies they'll need to be productive, including a supply of each employee's favorite snack, if you know it. Hire someone to scoop ice cream in the break room on your first day back or schedule an in-person happy hour at 4:00 p.m. to cap off your first week back in the office.

» **Schedule breaks.** People who work remotely often learn when to stand up and move throughout the day but could forget to do so when they're back in the office. Encourage people to take breaks. If the weather is nice, announce that you're taking a stroll around the neighborhood during lunch and encourage others to join you, or consider leading your team in a few stretches to kick off your morning meetings.

» **Share best practices.** For a moment of team building, ask workers to share their best practices for commuting to the office. Some might offer podcasts or audiobooks as a productive and fun way to pass the time, or routes that help them avoid the worst traffic. It could be a way to take what is often the worst part of the office return and make it a fun and informative office activity. Later, consider asking via a social media post, "What's been the most challenging part of coming back to work?" and let team members respond. You might find that there are ways you can minimize these challenges as a leader or that team members can suggest ideas that can benefit one another.

REMEMBER

Wherever your team logs in from (whether home office, coworking space, or corporate headquarters) remember to be the kind of leader who connects, empowers, and inspires. Because great leadership isn't about proximity. It's about impact.

Chapter **18**

Operating as a Savvy Financial Business Leader

I n my many years of leading, training, and working with teams, I've seen a consistent pattern emerge. The highest-performing teams aren't just great at execution; the members fundamentally understand the business. They know exactly how their work connects to the bottom line. They speak the language of finance and strategy with confidence. And most importantly, they consistently think and act like owners, not just employees.

When I talk to leaders about building high-performance teams, this critical topic of business acumen often gets overlooked, which is tragic. Everyone wants to talk about psychological safety, communication, and collaboration, and those things absolutely matter. I literally wrote books and published LinkedIn Learning courses about these topics. But financial and business savvy? That's the secret sauce that separates average/good teams from truly exceptional ones.

Here are the challenges we face globally as detailed in the latest research studies. According to a 2023 PwC global study, only 33 percent of employees worldwide feel confident in their financial literacy skills. Furthermore, a 2024 TIAA Institute study revealed that while 69 percent of workers believe financial knowledge is important for their career advancement, fewer than half have received any financial training from their employers. This statistical disconnect represents a massive gap, one that's costing organizations billions in missed opportunities, poor decisions, and deeply disengaged team members.

The disconnect is further confirmed by the Organization for Economic Cooperation and Development (OECD), which found in a 2023 survey that only 38 percent of adults in surveyed countries could correctly answer basic questions about profit margins, revenue versus profit, and return on investment (ROI). Meanwhile, a 2024 Deloitte global workforce study found that 71 percent of nonmanagement employees reported never receiving training on how to read financial statements or make financially informed decisions, yet 89 percent of executives in the same study said they expected all employees to make "business-minded decisions." That gap is setting teams up for failure.

In this chapter, I outline step by step what leaders and every team member can do to upskill in their financial acumen to become more business savvy.

Understanding Why Financial Literacy Matters for High-Performing Teams

I want to start with the basics of what financial literacy means in the context of high-performing teams. I'm not suggesting everyone needs an MBA or the ability to build complex financial models. In this context, financial literacy means understanding the fundamental principles of how businesses operate, how they make money, and how they create value.

Financial literacy for your team includes a holistic understanding of how the organization generates revenue and manages costs. It involves knowing how to read and interpret basic financial statements. It requires recognizing specifically how individual and team decisions impact the organization's overall financial health. Teams must understand key business metrics and what drives them. Critically, it involves connecting daily work to broader business objectives and financial outcomes and making resource allocation decisions based on a clear understanding of ROI. I cover metrics in Chapter 16.

Don't focus only on doing your job well. Also understand how your work contributes to revenue, cost savings, or customer satisfaction. Ask regularly, "How does what I do affect the organization's financial health or strategic priorities?"

A comprehensive 2023 study by Ernst & Young, conducted across 45 countries, revealed powerful results. Organizations with financially literate workforces experienced 23 percent higher productivity, 19 percent better customer satisfaction scores, and 34 percent higher employee engagement compared to organizations where financial literacy was low. Think about those numbers for a moment. When people understand the business, they simply perform better. Period.

Financial literacy matters for high-performance teams. I tell every leader I coach, "Ignorance isn't bliss when it comes to business finances." When team members don't understand the financial realities of the organization, several negative issues and outcomes emerge, and none of them are good.

Negative outcomes of financial illiteracy

The first issue is that team members make decisions in a vacuum. I've observed brilliant teams pour time, effort, and resources into projects that had virtually no real business value because they lacked understanding of the strategic priorities or current market realities. Their intentions were good, but good intentions don't pay the bills.

Second, they can't prioritize effectively. If they don't understand which initiatives drive the most financial or strategic value, they lack the criteria needed to decide where to focus their time, energy, and resources. Teams end up treating everything as equally important, which inevitably results in nothing getting the focus and resources it truly deserves.

Third, they feel disconnected from the organization's success or failure. A significant 2024 McKinsey study found that employees who clearly understand their company's financial performance and know how their specific work contributes to it are an astonishing 4.3 times more likely to feel engaged and committed to organizational goals. When the quarterly results are released (whether good or bad), financially literate teams instantly understand what those numbers mean and, crucially, what role they played in generating them. That creates genuine ownership and critical accountability.

Fourth, they can't adapt to change. When market conditions shift unexpectedly, when the organization needs to pivot strategy, or when tough decisions must be made about resource constraints or priorities, teams that understand the business context can move quickly and intelligently. Those that don't tend to resist, question, and ultimately slow everything down, often becoming barriers to necessary change.

REMEMBER

Make financial conversations inclusive. Encourage open discussions about business performance during team meetings. Share key metrics in clear, relatable terms so that every team member, regardless of role, understands the "why" behind decisions. Financial transparency builds trust, alignment, and accountability across all levels.

Examples of closing the literacy gap

The good news is that forward-thinking organizations are actively closing this literacy gap, and they are seeing truly remarkable results. Here are some examples:

>> **Whole Foods Market** has been long recognized for its approach to financial transparency and education. Leaders utilize "open-book management," meaning team members at all levels have access to specific financial information regarding their stores and the company overall. More importantly, the company invests heavily in actively teaching team members how to interpret that raw information. Store teams regularly review profit-and-loss statements, understand their contribution margins, and use this real-time financial data to make operational decisions about everything from staffing levels to inventory management. The result is higher worker engagement, better localized decision-making, and stronger financial performance at the store level.

>> **The Ritz-Carlton** demonstrates a different, but equally powerful, approach. Every employee receives extensive training on the detailed economics of luxury hospitality. They're taught critical metrics such as revenue per available room (RevPAR) and, most importantly, guest lifetime value. When a front-desk associate is empowered to spend up to $2,000 to resolve a guest issue without needing management approval, they understand not just the immediate cost, but the massive potential lifetime value of retaining that customer. This is financial literacy directly driving exceptional customer experience.

>> **Patagonia** builds alignment between its mission and financial realities by making the financials transparent. Employees learn about the challenging cost structure associated with environmentally responsible manufacturing, the long-term ROI of sustainability investments, and precisely how mission-driven decisions impact profitability. This ensures teams aren't naive about the inevitable trade-offs; they understand them and are equipped to make informed choices.

>> **Microsoft** has implemented a globally comprehensive "Business Acumen" training program. According to a 2024 learning and development report, more than 85,000 employees have participated in modules covering financial statements, business strategy, competitive analysis, and value creation. Microsoft reported that teams completing this training showed a 27 percent improvement in strategic decision-making and 31 percent better alignment between project outcomes and organizational business objectives.

>> **Southwest Airlines** has a long-standing practice of sharing detailed financial information with all employees and teaching them how their specific roles impact the bottom line. Pilots understand the economics of fuel costs and scheduling efficiency, gate agents grasp turnaround time economics, and mechanics are trained on maintenance cost management. This widespread financial literacy is credited as one of the key factors behind Southwest's decades of sustained profitability in an industry notorious for chronic financial struggles.

These examples share a common core philosophy: transparency about financial realities, substantial investment in education, explicit connection between individual actions and broad business outcomes, and the underlying trust that employees will make significantly better decisions when they understand the complete business context.

Speaking the Language of Business with Confidence

Speaking the language of business is not about impressing others with needless jargon. It's about establishing a shared, clear vocabulary that enables accurate communication, and strategic thinking.

When training and consulting with teams, I pay close attention to how each team member talks about their work. Are they talking primarily about activities and tasks, or are they discussing outcomes and value? Are they focused merely on being busy, or are they focused on tangible impact? The language used reveals everything about their mindset.

TIP

Shift from activity to impact. High-performing professionals don't just describe what they do; they describe the difference it makes. Try reframing your language from, "I sent 20 reports this week," to "My reports helped leadership make faster decisions that improved project turnaround time."

High-performing teams must understand a foundational set of business concepts. This section is a glossary of essential business terms. As you peruse them, assess your own understanding and usage of the terms.

Revenue

Revenue is the total income generated from your products or services before any costs or expenses are deducted. This is frequently called your *top line*. When your team understands revenue, they grasp how the organization makes money and can ask crucial questions such as these:

>> What specific activities drive our revenue growth?

>> Which products or services contribute most significantly?

>> How do our team's activities directly support or accelerate revenue generation?

Profit (or net income)

Profit (net income) is what's left over after all expenses have been paid. This is your *bottom line*. Organizations don't survive on revenue alone; they survive — and invest — on profit. When teams clearly understand this distinction, they make significantly better decisions about spending, efficiency, and long-term value creation. I have seen teams dramatically reduce unnecessary expenses once they realize that every single dollar saved flows directly to that critical bottom line.

REMEMBER

Think like a business owner. Before committing resources, pause and ask, "Would I make this decision if I were spending my own money?" This mindset creates accountability and encourages smarter, more strategic financial choices at every level of the organization.

Margin

Margin tells you the percentage of revenue that successfully becomes profit. If you generate $100 in revenue but incur $95 to deliver that revenue, your margin is a tight 5 percent. If it costs $60 to deliver the $100, your margin is a healthy 40 percent. Understanding margins helps teams appreciate why some customers, products, or services are inherently more valuable than others. Not all revenue streams are created equal.

Return on investment

Return on investment (ROI) measures the gain or loss generated on an investment relative to the amount invested. The simple formula is this:

(Gain from Investment – Cost of Investment) / Cost of Investment

For example, if your team proposes spending $50,000 on a new system that will save $100,000 annually, that is an outstanding 100 percent annual ROI. If the same investment only saves $10,000 annually, the 20 percent ROI needs greater scrutiny. When teams consistently think in terms of ROI, they make smarter resource requests and prioritize high-impact initiatives.

Return on equity

Return on equity (ROE) measures how effectively an organization utilizes shareholder investments to generate profit. While this may seem distant from a frontline team, high-performing teams should understand it because it reflects overall organizational health and efficiency. A strong ROE signals that the organization is creating value effectively, which typically translates to greater resources being available for growth, innovation, and direct investment in teams.

Value proposition

Value proposition answers the fundamental business question, "Why should customers choose us?" It's the unique combination of products, services, benefits, and experiences that create value specifically for customers. When teams deeply understand the organization's value proposition, every decision, every project, and every customer interaction becomes aligned to strengthen it.

Key performance indicators

Key performance indicators (KPIs) are the specific, measurable metrics that indicate whether objectives are being achieved. The best KPIs connect directly to desired business outcomes. Teams must understand their specific, immediate KPIs and clearly know how those metrics ultimately connect to broader organizational goals.

Operating expenses and capital expenditures

Operating expenses (OpEx) are the regular costs required to run the business day to day — salaries, rent, utilities, supplies, and software subscriptions. When teams understand OpEx, they make more thoughtful decisions about resource usage. They might realize that a "small" software subscription, barely used, adds up significantly across the whole organization, or that energy-efficient practices genuinely impact the bottom line.

Capital expenditures (CapEx) are defined as investments in long-term assets, such as new equipment, technology infrastructure, or facilities. Understanding the distinction between OpEx and CapEx helps teams appreciate why some spending decisions require far more scrutiny and longer-term planning than others.

Cash flow

Cash flow is the movement of money both into and out of the organization. Here is a critical reality: Organizations can be profitable on paper but still fail due to severe cash flow problems. When teams understand cash flow, they understand why payment terms matter, why the timing of expenses is important, and why being efficient with resources is not just about saving money. It's fundamentally about organizational survival.

Customer lifetime value and customer acquisition cost

Customer lifetime value (CLV) is the total expected revenue generated from a customer throughout the entire relationship. This concept fundamentally transforms how teams view customer interactions. When you realize that acquiring a new customer might cost $500, but their lifetime value is potentially $50,000, the logic of going the extra mile for that customer becomes crystal clear.

Customer Acquisition Cost (CAC) is what it costs the organization to acquire one new customer. The relationship between CAC and CLV is crucial. If it costs $1,000 to acquire a customer who only generates $800 in lifetime value, the business has a serious, unsustainable problem. Teams that understand this relationship make far better decisions about marketing, sales, and service investments.

Earnings before interest, taxes, depreciation, and amortization

Earnings before interest, taxes, depreciation, and amortization, which is more commonly known as *EBITDA*, is a measure of operational profitability. It's often used to compare operational performance across different companies by removing the effects of financing, tax considerations, and accounting decisions like depreciation.

Other financial terms

Gross margin represents revenue minus the direct costs of producing goods or services, usually expressed as a percentage of revenue. It clearly indicates the organization's pricing power and production efficiency. *Net margin* is the net income as a percentage of revenue, showing overall profitability after *all* expenses have been accounted for.

When assessing short-term stability, teams should understand *working capital* (current assets minus current liabilities), which measures short-term financial health, and *liquidity*, which is the ability to quickly convert assets to cash to meet immediate obligations.

In terms of growth and risk, terms like *churn rate* (the percentage of customers who stop doing business with you over a period) and *debt-to-equity ratio* (indicating financial leverage and risk) are critical. *CAGR (compound annual growth rate)* helps you understand sustained growth trends over multiple years.

Opportunity cost is perhaps the most difficult concept psychologically. It's the cost of choosing one alternative over another. When a team invests time or resources in option A, they're giving up what they could have potentially gained from option B. Conversely, *sunk cost* refers to past expenses that cannot be recovered. Good business decision-making requires ignoring sunk costs and focusing purely on future potential, though this is often psychologically difficult for teams to do.

Scalability is key for high-performing teams because it's the ability of a process or model to grow without proportional increases in costs. When solving a problem, savvy teams look for scalable solutions.

I could continue to list important topics indefinitely, but the main point is clear. The idea isn't to memorize definitions; it's to have a deep understanding of the business concepts that are inextricably linked to driving performance and strategic decisions.

Understanding Operations and Managing the Business

Financial literacy would not be complete without a solid understanding of how businesses operate. The most effective teams don't just understand the numbers; they understand the operational realities behind those numbers. Operations management centers on efficiency, quality, and continuous improvement. It requires understanding how work flows through the organization, where bottlenecks occur, how quality is maintained, and how processes can be optimized to increase value creation and eliminate waste.

In this section, I've listed common operations management terms. Assess your level of knowledge and usage of these terms:

>> **Process efficiency** measures the value created relative to the resources consumed. Efficient processes minimize waste (of time, materials, and effort) while maximizing the quality of the output.

>> **Cycle time** is the total time it takes to complete a process from initiation to finish. Reducing cycle time often results in better customer experience and increased capacity.

>> **Throughput** is the rate at which work is completed (for example, units per hour, features deployed per sprint, issues resolved per day). Understanding throughput helps teams manage capacity and identify production constraints.

>> **Quality metrics** track defects, errors, rework, and customer satisfaction. The best teams recognize that preventing defects is always more cost-effective than fixing them later.

>> **Resource utilization** tracks how effectively resources (people, equipment) are being used. Utilization that is too low suggests inefficiency, whereas utilization that is too high risks burnout and errors. Finding the right balance requires business judgment.

>> **Value stream mapping** is a visual tool that allows teams to understand the flow of value from the initial request through to final delivery. Teams using this tool almost always discover surprising insights, such as non-value-add steps or hidden delays.

REMEMBER

Efficiency and quality aren't just management responsibilities; they belong to every team member. Encourage your team to make a habit of identifying one small improvement to streamline work or reduce waste.

Leading organizations embed these operational concepts into their culture. Toyota, for instance, built its legendary operational excellence by teaching every employee to think about efficiency and continuous improvement (*kaizen*). Similarly, Amazon has created a culture where operational metrics (delivery times, error rates, customer satisfaction scores) drive every decision, empowering teams to experiment and improve.

Navigating Economic Shifts and Marketplace Trends

The business environment your team operates in today will be fundamentally different five to ten years from now. The pace of change is accelerating, and volatility is increasing. The ability to anticipate and adapt to these constant shifts is no longer merely an advantage; it's a matter of survival.

A 2024 World Economic Forum study found that 83 percent of business leaders expect significant economic disruption within the next three years, yet only 34 percent feel their organizations are adequately prepared. This preparation gap represents both enormous risk and opportunity. Teams that develop the capability to understand and respond to these changes will inevitably thrive.

TIP

Stay informed about market dynamics and encourage regular discussions about trends affecting your industry. Instead of reacting to change, anticipate it. Ask your team, "If this trend continues, how will it impact our customers, operations, or revenue in the next year?"

This section covers some of the economic uncertainties your team should be prepared to navigate.

Economic volatility and recession risks

We are in an era of what economists term *permacrisis*, which is an ongoing instability driven by interconnected global shocks. A 2024 International Monetary Fund (IMF) analysis suggests the global economy faces an elevated risk of recession throughout the remainder of the 2020s.

High-performing teams must understand the fundamentals of how recessions impact their specific industry. Do customers cut spending immediately? Do your costs increase or decrease? Does demand shift?

You must incorporate resilience into planning by maintaining flexibility in resource allocation and having contingency plans. The teams that weather economic volatility best are those that can scale operations up or down quickly without fracturing. Most critically, teams must monitor *leading indicators* in the business (such as signals like declining customer inquiries, longer sales cycles, or price pressure). Savvy teams spot these trends early and adjust proactively rather than waiting for formal quarterly financial results.

Supply chain disruptions and resilience

The 2020 pandemic exposed global supply chain fragility, and this vulnerability remains a critical business issue. A 2024 McKinsey Global Institute study found that companies can expect supply chain disruptions lasting a month or longer every 3.7 years on average.

Every team, even those outside of logistics, must understand their supply chain dependencies. What inputs are required? Where do they originate? What alternatives exist if a key supplier fails or a critical component becomes scarce? Teams must build adaptability into their work, enabling them to pivot quickly if materials are constrained.

I saw this firsthand with a product development team during the 2021 to 2023 chip shortage. The teams that designed products with flexibility in component selection continued to launch products, whereas rigid teams were unable to deliver. Business literacy can save millions in lost revenue.

Climate change and sustainability imperatives

According to severe scenarios, climate-related risks could reduce global economic output by up to 13 percent by 2050. Consumer expectations are driving this reality, too: A 2024 Deloitte survey found that 69 percent of consumers now factor environmental sustainability into their purchasing decisions.

Teams must understand the carbon footprint of their operations and how extreme weather might disrupt supply chains. They must also understand evolving customer expectations. Teams that proactively address sustainability are managing risk and creating competitive advantage. For example, Unilever reported that their sustainable brands grew 69 percent faster than the rest of the business between 2018 and 2023, powerfully demonstrating the financial case for sustainability.

Technological advancement and digital transformation

We're experiencing the most rapid technological change in history, and the pace is only accelerating. Artificial intelligence (AI), automation, and advanced analytics are now current business realities.

PwC's global study released in 2024 confirmed that organizations investing in digital transformation achieved 31 percent higher profitability and 29 percent higher revenue growth compared to digital laggards. The key takeaway is clear: Technology alone isn't the advantage. It's teams that know *how* to use technology strategically to drive business results.

Every team member should understand how automation can streamline routine work, how AI can enhance decision-making and prediction, and how data analytics can drive better business choices. Technology doesn't replace the need for critical thinking, creativity, and judgment, but it dramatically increases the return on those uniquely human capabilities. Check out Chapter 6 for more information on the role of the leader in leveraging artificial intelligence.

Workforce transformation and changing talent models

The very nature of work is being transformed by hybrid models, the gig economy, skills-based hiring, and continuous learning imperatives. A 2024 Gartner study shows that 73 percent of organizations now use a blended workforce model, combining full-time employees, contractors, and gig workers. Furthermore, the half-life of professional skills has plummeted from 15 years in 1984 to less than 5 years today.

High-performing teams must embrace learning agility and continuously update skills. They need to understand how to collaborate effectively across different arrangements and locations. They must recognize that career paths are no longer linear and prioritize building portable skills. Teams that view skills as dynamic and embrace continuous learning adapt faster and create significantly more value.

Preparing your team for an uncertain future

How do you, as a leader, prepare your team for a continuous VUCA world (a world of volatility, uncertainty, complexity, and ambiguity)? In this section, I offer some best practices that I've observed in consulting with some of my more progressive clients:

>> They create regular space for environmental scanning. Build time into team meetings to discuss market trends, competitive signals, and external changes. Make this a regular habit, not just an annual exercise.

>> They develop scenario planning capabilities. Work through "what if" exercises: What if a key supplier failed? What if economic conditions triggered a 20 percent decline in demand? These exercises force teams to think through vulnerabilities and response options *before* a crisis hits.

>> They connect external trends explicitly to team decisions. When discussing a new project, they ask: Is this initiative resilient to supply chain disruption? Will it still be relevant if automation accelerates?

>> They build optionality and flexibility into plans. They avoid large, all-or-nothing commitments. They design projects with clear decision points where you reassess based on new information. This doesn't mean being tentative, it means being adaptive.

>> They celebrate and learn from adaptation. When they successfully navigate a disruption, they reflect on *what* enabled that success. When they miss a trend, they analyze why. They build the organizational muscle memory for adaptation.

Connecting organizational goals to team performance

I frequently observe a major failure within teams. Too many work incredibly hard on things that ultimately don't matter to the organization's overall success. The team is busy, they are productive, they are checking off tasks, but they're failing to move the needle on what the organization needs to achieve. I just finished coaching an executive on this very issue. His team was majoring on the minor projects that were taking up too much of their team's capacity. Instead of assessing their priorities and ensuring alignment with strategic objectives, they were requesting more resources to get the major projects done.

This disconnect happens when the clear line of sight between organizational strategy and team execution gets lost during translation. High-performing teams refuse to accept this ambiguity. They demand clarity about how their work drives organizational priorities, and they translate high-level strategy into measurable, meaningful goals that guide daily decisions.

Translating vision into financial and operating KPIs

The organization's high-level statements must be translated into measurable strategic objectives. For example, "Achieve profitable growth in core markets" might translate into specific objectives such as these:

>> Increase revenue by 15 percent year over year

>> Improve operating margin from 18 percent to 22 percent

>> Grow market share from 23 percent to 27 percent in the primary segment

As a team, you must not simply accept the targets handed down; you need to understand the business logic behind them. Why is 15 percent revenue growth the target? What are the market assumptions driving that goal? What constraints exist? When you understand this business context, you're empowered to make better decisions about how your team can contribute.

Once the business logic is clear, you translate those organizational KPIs into team-specific KPIs that are within your team's control and strong influence. Good team KPIs must clearly connect to organizational objectives, be measurable with reasonable accuracy, and drive the right behaviors and decisions. Crucially, they must balance multiple dimensions of performance, such as balancing speed with quality or cost with experience.

Last year, I worked with a financial services customer service team whose organizational objective was to improve customer retention (acquiring new customers cost five times more than retaining existing ones). We redesigned their KPIs to focus on retention drivers. Here are few examples:

>> Customer satisfaction score (CSAT) on service interactions meets a target of 4.3 out of 5.

>> Proactive outreach to at-risk customers based on early warning signals meets a target of making contact to 85 percent within 48 hours.

>> Customer effort score measures how easy it is for customers to get what they need — answers, support, order fulfillment, or problem resolution. The lower the effort required, the better the customer experience.

>> Issue escalation speed tracks how quickly complex problems are transferred to the right person or team when front-line staff can't resolve them.

The result was a transformation. The team realized they weren't just answering phones and closing tickets; they were actively protecting and growing millions in recurring revenue. This profound understanding of their business impact transformed their engagement and decision-making.

Thinking and Acting Like an Intrapreneur

Intrapreneurship is something I believe is the greatest demonstration of business acumen. I use this term because I believe the best team members blur the false distinction between risk-taking entrepreneurs and compliant employees.

An *intrapreneur* is different from the common term entrepreneur in that they treat the organization's resources, reputation, and success as if they were their own. They weigh risk and reward, proactively look for opportunities to create value, and take initiative without waiting for explicit permission. They're accountable for tangible outcomes — not merely for completing tasks.

This term has been studied in recent years by global research firms. A 2024 Gallup study found that organizations cultivating intrapreneurial mindsets see 21 percent higher profitability and 17 percent higher productivity. A 2023 *Harvard Business Review* analysis revealed that teams exhibiting high ownership behaviors generated 2.3 times more innovation.

Core behaviors of intrapreneurs

Intrapreneurs understand the full profit & loss (P&L) impact of their decisions. They think about total business impact, not just their siloed piece of the puzzle. For example, when I worked for a global credit card company, I remember a marketing manager that I worked with as her HR business partner that proposed a $200,000 campaign and built a detailed business case showing projected customer acquisition, estimated lifetime value ($800,000 total), customer acquisition cost ($160, below target), and time to break even (4.2 months). She was celebrated among her mostly male colleagues, and by the end of the year, she was promoted to chief marketing officer.

Intrapreneurs optimize for organizational success, not just team success. This means they ask, "What's best for the overall business?" even if it means their own team receives fewer resources. A previous client in the tech industry openly advocated giving engineering resources to another team because the data showed the other team's project would drive 3X more business value. I remember thinking how sacrificial and strategic it was to put the needs of the organization over her own team's needs.

Intrapreneurs manage risk like investors and are stewards of resources. They take calculated risks where the potential reward justifies the exposure. I witnessed a great example of this when a product manager I coached wanted to enter a new market segment with $50M revenue potential. Instead of proposing a massive upfront investment, she designed a phased approach: low-cost market research ($15K), then a minimum viable product test ($150K), with a full launch only if clear product-market fit was achieved. She had clear go/no-go criteria at each phase. This is how owners manage risk.

Intrapreneurs proactively identify and pursue opportunities. They do not wait for projects to be assigned.

REMEMBER

When I worked in banking as a customer service representative, I tracked the volume and nature of calls related to a confusing bank policy. I calculated the cost of handling them ($125,000 annually) and presented a policy clarification to my branch manager and the head of HR. Ultimately, it was implemented, and it reduced call volume on that topic by 73 percent. In this case, I saw a problem, took ownership, and offered a solution that saved the company thousands of dollars.

Developing intrapreneurial skills on your team

These critical ownership behaviors can be developed by actively creating the right organizational environment. In this section, I share a few considerations:

TIP

>> **Expect it.** Set the explicit expectation that everyone is expected to think and act like owners. Make intrapreneurship part of how roles are discussed and ensure it's clearly valued and rewarded.

>> **Provide the information and transparency.** You cannot expect people to make business-minded decisions if they don't have access to the business information. Share financial data, explain strategic context, and be transparent about constraints.

>> **Delegate decision authority.** Push decision-making down to the lowest appropriate level. Define clear guardrails and principles; then trust people to make calls within those boundaries.

>> **Make the business case a standard practice.** Require that all project proposals include a formal business case and teach people how to build them. Over time, evaluating decisions through an ROI lens will become automatic.

>> **Celebrate intelligent failures.** Intrapreneurship necessitates risk-taking, which means some ventures won't work out. If you only celebrate successes, people will play it safe. Value smart risks and learning from disappointments, even when outcomes fall short.

To structure this thinking, use the Intrapreneurship Decision Framework. When faced with any significant decision, an intrapreneur asks the following questions:

TIP

>> What's the business impact?

>> What are we optimizing for? (Short-term results versus long-term capability?)

>> What's the ROI?

>> What are the risks, and how can we manage them?

>> What's the opportunity cost?

>> How does this build capability for the future?

>> What would an owner do?

Making this framework a regular part of team discussions quickly transforms employee mindset into owner mindset.

Building Financial Literacy: Practical Exercises and Applications

This chapter is full of theory, statistics, strategies, and workplace examples. Now I'd like to give you the opportunity to apply it all to real business scenarios. Work through these practical exercises on your own and then have your team work through them together. Feel free to debate the answers and discuss the underlying business principles.

Exercise 1: Understanding profit and loss

Scenario: Your team runs a subscription software service with 10,000 customers paying $50 per month ($500,000 monthly revenue). Your monthly costs are

>> Software infrastructure and hosting: $125,000.

>> Customer support staff: $95,000.

>> Sales and marketing: $150,000.

>> Product development: $80,000.

>> General and administrative: $30,000.

Consider these questions:

1. What is your monthly profit (or loss)?

2. What is your profit margin?

3. If you reduced customer support costs by 20 percent, how would this affect profit and profit margin?

4. If you invested an additional $40,000 per month in sales and marketing and this generated 15 percent more customers, would this improve profitability? Show your calculations.

5. What is your break-even number of customers at current pricing and cost structure?

6. If a competitor dropped their price to $40 per month and you matched to avoid losing customers, what would happen to profitability?

The following are my recommended responses and key learnings to the preceding questions:

1. Monthly profit: Revenue ($500,000) minus total costs ($480,000) equals $20,000 profit.

2. Profit margin: $20,000 / $500,000 = 4% profit margin. This is quite thin, leaving very little room for error or future investment.

3. Reducing support costs: A 20 percent reduction saves $19,000 per month, increasing profit to $39,000 and margin to 7.8 percent. However, the team should immediately question whether cutting support costs might damage customer satisfaction and retention, potentially jeopardizing long-term revenue.

4. Additional marketing investment: New revenue would be $575,000 (15 percent growth). New costs would be $520,000 ($480,000 + $40,000). New profit equals $55,000. This significantly improves profitability if the 15 percent customer growth assumption is reliable.

5. Break-even customers: Total costs of $480,000 divided by $50 per customer requires 9,600 customers to break even. Currently at 10,000 customers, the business is only 400 customers above break-even, highlighting a high-risk scenario.

6. Price reduction: Revenue would fall to $400,000 ($40 × 10,000), while costs remain $480,000. This results in an $80,000 loss per month, which is unsustainable.

REMEMBER

The key learning is that profit margins show you maneuverability. Understanding break-even points reveals vulnerability. Growth is not inherently good if it is unprofitable growth.

Exercise 2: ROI decision-making

Scenario: Your team has been allocated $100,000 to invest in improvements, with three options:

>> **Option A:** Process automation (cost: $80,000; saves $30,000 per annum, plus $5,000 annual maintenance).

>> **Option B:** Customer experience enhancement (cost: $60,000; reduces annual churn from 15 percent to 12 percent for 5,000 customers, where average customer annual profit is $2,000).

>> **Option C:** Team training (cost: $45,000; avoids $120,000 in hiring and onboarding costs by delaying team expansion for one year).

Ask these questions:

1. Calculate the annual ROI for each option.

2. Calculate the payback period for each option.

3. Which option would you choose and why?

4. What factors beyond pure ROI might influence your decision?

Here are my recommended responses and key learnings:

1. ROI calculations:

   - *Option A:* Net benefit is $25,000 ($30k savings – $5k maintenance). ROI = 31% annually.

   - *Option B:* Churn reduction saves 150 customers (3% of 5,000). Value = $300,000 (150 × $2,000). ROI = $300,000 / $60,000 = 500% annually.

   - *Option C:* Net benefit is $120,000 in avoided costs. ROI = $120,000 / $45,000 = 267% annually.

2. Payback periods: Option B pays back in about 2.4 months. Option C pays back in about 4.5 months. Option A pays back in 3.2 years.

3. Recommended choice: Option B has extraordinary ROI and pays back almost immediately. However, the team must question the reliability of the churn reduction projection; if that projection is sound, B is the clear financial winner.

4. Other factors: Option C builds capability, providing value beyond the immediate cost savings. Option B carries significant risk if the churn projections are inaccurate.

REMEMBER

The key learning is that you should calculate ROI formally but always consider factors like risk, strategic long-term value, and capability building. Sometimes the highest calculated ROI isn't the correct choice if it carries disproportionate risk or fails to align with long-term strategic needs.

Exercise 3: Pricing and value proposition

Scenario: Your team developed a new service costing $200 per customer per year to deliver, which saves customers $1,500 annually in energy costs. Competitors charge $300 to $500, and your main competitor charges $450.

Ask these questions:

>> What pricing would you recommend? Explain your reasoning.

>> How would you communicate the value proposition to justify your pricing?

>> How would you structure pricing if some customers save much more than average (for example, $3,000+)?

Here are my recommended responses and key learnings:

1. Pricing recommendation: A price of $600 to $750 per year is recommended. Since the service saves $1,500, even at $750, the customer nets $750 in benefit. This is a premium price above competitors, justified only if you can demonstrate superior, guaranteed value.

2. Value communication: Focus the value proposition on the net benefit: "We guarantee minimum $1,500 annual savings — that's $900 in your pocket even after our fee."

3. Variable pricing: Consider a value-based pricing structure where you charge a percentage of the savings (for example, "40% of energy savings") rather than a flat fee. This aligns incentives with customer outcomes and captures more value from high-benefit customers.

REMEMBER

The key learning for this scenario is that price should be based on the value delivered, not just costs or competition. Customers will happily pay premium prices when the value proposition is clear and differentiated.

5

The Part of Tens

Chapter **19**

Ten Best Practices for Leading a Multigenerational Team

Today's workplace is one of the most generationally diverse in history. In offices, factories, retail spaces, hospitals, schools, and virtual environments around the globe, you can find early-career professionals, mid-career leaders, seasoned experts, and those approaching retirement all working together toward shared goals. This age diversity enriches the workplace by bringing a variety of perspectives, skill sets, and ways of thinking.

Yet it also introduces unique challenges. People at different life stages may have been shaped by very different social, cultural, and economic events. They may have learned to communicate in different ways, value different things about work, and have different expectations for leadership. These differences can lead to mis-understandings, friction, or even disengagement if not managed well.

When handled with intention and skill, however, a multigenerational team can become one of your greatest competitive advantages. In fact, the very differences that might create tension can also drive innovation, better decision-making, and stronger overall performance. The key is knowing how to bring out the best in each generation and create a high-performance environment where everyone can thrive.

REMEMBER

Multigenerational teams are not a problem to be managed; they're an opportunity to be maximized. When you lead with curiosity, respect, and adaptability, you can harness the collective strengths of every generation.

Stop asking, "Why do they work that way?" and start asking, "What can I learn from them?" High-performing teams are not built on sameness; they are built on synergy, where experience meets fresh ideas, tradition meets innovation, and leaders inspire everyone to succeed together.

Here are ten best practices that will help you create an environment where everyone thrives.

Know Your Generational Mix

Leading effectively starts with awareness. The more you understand your team's generational mix, the better equipped you are to engage, motivate, and manage them. This does not mean labeling people or making assumptions based solely on age. It means having a working understanding of the life stages, cultural influences, and formative experiences that may shape how each team member approaches work.

For example, some team members may value job security, formal processes, and clear hierarchies. Others may prioritize flexibility, purpose-driven work, and rapid growth. Still others may prefer to work independently with minimal oversight. Recognizing these patterns gives you insight into how to lead more inclusively.

TIP

Host a generational roundtable or "show and tell" session where each team member shares something that represents their view of work and leadership. This builds mutual respect and helps team members better understand one another.

Communicate with Agility

One of the most common pain points in multigenerational teams is communication. Different generations often prefer different methods, from face-to-face conversations to video calls, from emails to instant messaging, and from detailed reports to short, collaborative updates. There is no single right way to communicate with a multigenerational team, so your role as a leader is to be flexible and intentional.

Deliver important information using multiple channels, repeat key messages, and ensure that everyone has the opportunity to ask questions. Remember, effective communication is measured by what is heard and understood, not just by what is said.

Ask each team member how they prefer to receive information and feedback. Flex your style so that you can meet them where they are.

TIP

Encourage Cross-Generational Mentoring

Mutual learning is one of the most powerful tools you can leverage in a multigenerational team. Cross-generational mentoring allows more experienced team members to share wisdom, institutional knowledge, and lessons learned, while newer employees can offer fresh perspectives, digital fluency, and innovative approaches.

Reverse mentoring programs, where younger employees mentor senior colleagues on topics such as emerging technology or cultural trends, can break down stereotypes and create trust. The goal is not to replace one form of mentoring with another but to create a two-way exchange of value.

Pair team members from different generations for monthly "learning exchanges" with conversation prompts like, "What is one thing you wish people understood about your generation in the workplace?"

TIP

Align on Shared Values and Norms

Generational differences can sometimes lead to varying interpretations of professionalism, respect, and accountability. That's why it's critical to align your team on shared values, norms, and behaviors. A team charter can serve as your roadmap for how you work together, make decisions, and resolve conflicts.

When everyone has had a voice in defining these expectations, they're more likely to honor them. This creates a sense of belonging and reduces the potential for misunderstandings.

Work together to create a code of conduct with clear commitments such as, "We will communicate openly and respectfully" or "We will assume positive intent."

Personalize Your Management Approach

Different team members are motivated by different things. For some, it may be career advancement and recognition. For others, it may be meaningful work and a sense of purpose. Still others may be motivated by flexibility, skill-building, or financial security.

Leading a multigenerational team means avoiding a one-size-fits-all approach. Spend time in one-on-one conversations to learn what matters most to each person and tailor your management style accordingly.

When you're coaching team members, ask questions such as, "What inspires you right now?" or "What is the best way for me to recognize your contributions?"

Promote Psychological Safety for All

Psychological safety means that people feel comfortable speaking up, asking questions, and contributing ideas without fear of judgment or negative consequences. This is essential for high performance, yet it does not happen automatically, especially when there are generational differences in confidence, authority, or communication style.

Younger employees may fear being dismissed as inexperienced and overlooked because they're too junior. More seasoned employees may worry about being perceived as outdated or resistant to change. Leaders must actively invite contributions, affirm the value of diverse perspectives, and ensure that everyone's voice is heard.

During meetings, make it a point to call on different team members and acknowledge contributions from all generations.

Offer Flexible Career Development

Career development is not linear, and it means different things to different people. Some team members may be looking for advancement to leadership roles. Others may be seeking lateral moves, skill development, or opportunities to mentor and leave a legacy.

A great leader offers personalized development plans that align with each person's career stage, goals, and aspirations. Encourage learning in multiple forms, from classroom training to digital platforms, and stretch assignments.

TIP

Ask each team member to set one learning goal per quarter, and support them in achieving it through resources, coaching, and feedback.

Build in Flexibility and Autonomy

Flexibility is not just about working from home or adjusting hours. It's about trusting people to manage their time, energy, and resources in ways that help them perform at their best. People at all life stages value autonomy, although they may express it differently.

Rather than focusing solely on attendance or hours, define success by outcomes. Give your team the freedom to decide how they will achieve results, as long as they meet agreed-upon standards and deadlines.

TIP

Implement flexible work arrangements that prioritize accountability and performance over rigid schedules.

Celebrate Milestones and Life Moments

Recognition is a powerful engagement tool, and it's especially meaningful when it acknowledges personal as well as professional milestones. This could include work anniversaries, project completions, birthdays, promotions, or retirements.

Make recognition personal and inclusive. Some may prefer a public celebration, whereas others would appreciate a private thank-you. Take the time to learn each person's preferences.

TIP

Create a team celebration calendar where members can opt in to share the milestones they would like to be acknowledged.

Lead with Empathy and Emotional Intelligence

No matter how diverse your team is, the most effective leadership starts with empathy. This means seeing beyond job titles and roles to understand the human being, their experiences, and their needs. Emotional intelligence helps you recognize and manage your own emotions while navigating those of others.

When you lead with empathy, you build trust, strengthen relationships, and create a culture where people want to contribute their best. This is the foundation of high performance in a multigenerational team.

TIP

Begin meetings with a brief check-in, asking questions like, "What is one word that describes how you're feeling today?" This small act can set the tone for a supportive and connected environment.

» **Exploring practical team-building activities that strengthen team trust, collaboration, and communication**

» **Applying relationship-building strategies that boost connection and performance across colocated, hybrid, and remote teams**

Chapter **20**

Ten Team Activities That Build Trust, Collaboration, and Communication

Being a leader is hard work. When you accept a leadership role, you're being held accountable for your team's success. This often means getting projects done on time, under budget, and with high quality. It's a lot of responsibility. In addition to that, you're also answerable for your team's culture and for ensuring that anyone who reports to you feels like they belong, can succeed, and can communicate openly and honestly. Then, in your spare time (!!), you have your own work to accomplish.

With all that responsibility, it can be very easy to push aside anything that doesn't have a direct link to work getting done. But focusing only on the work can have cultural implications. Sometimes, activities that seem like fun for fun's sake can help a team function better when they get back to work. Not everyone who works together is going to become fast friends, but people who enjoy the company of their colleagues are more likely to cooperate, go the extra mile when they can, and ask for help when they need it.

In this chapter, I want to introduce you to ten ideas for team activities that allow team members to take a momentary break from their work but can improve the speed, resilience, and quality of your team's work in the long run. Most of these can be used with either colocated or remote teams, and I've tried to include activities that have the most direct impact on trust, collaboration, and communication. If you've participated in a team activity you loved but doesn't appear here, try it! There are lots of activities like this, and anything that allows colleagues to learn and laugh together is going to be a boon for your team in the long run.

"Teach Me" Presentations

This is one of my favorite team activities, and it works equally well for colocated, hybrid, and remote teams. What I particularly love about this activity is that it doesn't take much time and simultaneously can last all year if you want it to.

"Teach Me" presentations are led by individuals on your team about a special skill or hobby they enjoy, often from their personal lives. They usually take about 15 minutes and can be scheduled at the opening or closing of a team meeting, during "Lunch and Learn" sessions, or spaced evenly throughout a team retreat.

Topics can be as broad as the interests on your team, ranging from planting a vegetable garden to writing short stories to mixing the perfect martini or auditioning for a community theater to mastering a favorite video game. Sometimes, team members who are more private will feel more comfortable teaching others about a job-related skill, such as managing nerves when public speaking or using tools in your virtual meeting software to increase engagement.

When I'm doing this with a team I'm leading, I encourage people to use the opportunity to allow colleagues to experience a different side of them and not to worry if the topic seems a little frivolous. After all, the important thing is to enjoy the experience. I also encourage people to take the "Teach Me" to heart. If possible, allow participants to try what you're teaching them to do. This might not always be possible, but these presentations tend to be more valuable if all participants — not just the presenter — are actively engaged.

In addition to team bonding and getting to know each other, some side benefits of hosting "Teach Me" presentations include allowing each member of your team to teach and influence others, allowing them — even for a moment — to find their own leadership voice. People on teams are often surprised by the secret skills of their colleagues or the richness of their away-from-the-office lives. All of this eventually enriches their experience on a team.

Virtual Murder Mystery Party

Did you know this was a thing? Just Google "Virtual Murder Mystery Party Ideas," and you'll find tons of ways to host a murder mystery online. Solving a good murder mystery with your work colleagues generally takes about an hour.

Solving a virtual murder mystery is a good option if you have a lot of introverts on your team. When engaged in solving, people generally get wrapped up in the game (it's really fun!) and might chime in more often than they typically do on a work-related call, especially if they're a more junior team member. Longer activities like this are an investment, but they can also be valuable experiences of taking away the typical hierarchy of a team and noticing that good ideas often come from unexpected places, which is always a valuable lesson for teams to learn.

TIP

If your team is filled with amazing detectives and you solve the murder earlier than expected, you can fill the remaining time in a "post-mortem" of sorts (pun definitely intended!). I like to practice appreciative inquiry at moments like these; the questions don't focus on the moments where teams were challenged but rather point to what enabled the team to succeed. If someone brings up a challenge, a leader can quickly pivot by saying, "Yes, that was a frustrating moment. How did you overcome it?" These lessons can easily find their way back to work when a team is facing a similar challenge on a project.

Stop, Start, Continue

This is a simple activity — that works just as well for remote teams as for colocated ones — that could be work-focused if you want or simply a way to allow your team members to know each other better. It's a team discussion that answers three questions:

>> What aren't we doing that we should start doing?

>> What might be holding us back that we should stop doing?

>> What are we doing well that we should continue doing?

The activity can take as little as ten minutes on a small team. If the size of your team is manageable, I'd suggest facilitating the conversation in a "round-robin" format, where everyone on the team is called upon to give one answer to each question. On a larger team, I might send the team into breakout groups to discuss the questions and report back their responses to the full group at the end of the activity.

As I said, you can make this activity entirely work-focused, in which case the team members are giving the group feedback on what team behaviors, technologies, or processes could be started, stopped, or continued. Or, you might want to do a personal version, where people could share what personal behaviors or habits they'd like to individually start, stop, or continue. Either way, it's a good idea to let your team know this is an activity you'll be doing soon so that they can think a little about it and show up with responses that add value.

TIP

Depending on the personalities on your team, a few ground rules might be helpful here. For instance, focus on team behaviors rather than the behaviors of one or two people on the team and avoid passive-aggressive complaints about others, like "This year, I will stop covering for others when they miss deadlines." Those aren't really appropriate and should be brought to the leader outside of a team activity designed to promote collaboration. At the same time, it might be wise to advise everyone not to take anything personally, and this includes you, the leader. If you have a particular process you use to end your meetings, but it's not working for the team, this is their opportunity to say, "We should stop giving weekly prizes at the end of our team meetings." That might be your opportunity to show the team that you can accept feedback graciously.

Book Club

Are you a voracious reader? I love to read, but I'm also an incredibly social person, so when I've read something interesting, the first thing I want to do is discuss it with someone. Realizing that not everyone reads a book every month or more, when I bring this idea to an entire team, I usually provide everyone with a single chapter, or perhaps a short article that is germane to our work. Send it to everyone via email, give them plenty of time to read it, then find some time to discuss it as a group.

When I'm able to show slides (either via a projector or in a virtual meeting platform), I'll often pull the most interesting quotes from the chapter/article and place them on the screen to get responses.

REMEMBER

Like most of the activities in this chapter, this is an opportunity to let go of titles and hierarchy. Those with less experience and more junior job titles can use this as a time to speak up and be heard by the entire team. So coach your more senior members to cede the floor if a more junior team member has something to contribute. As a leader, notice who speaks often and who speaks hardly at all, and don't be afraid to invite participation in an open and friendly way — for example, "Sam, we haven't heard from you in a while. What's your take on this conversation?"

Film Festival

An idea that's similar to having a book club but may be better if your team isn't fond of reading is to do a film festival. Choose a video of reasonable length (less than 20 minutes, but between 5 and 10 minutes is best), send a link to your team with a request that they watch it in the next few days, and then meet to discuss what they liked, what they didn't, and if/how your team could incorporate whatever wisdom was shared.

Professional development videos are available for free online at YouTube or other video platforms. They might include tips on better collaboration, how to manage time, have a better brainstorm, how to combat procrastination, or ways to communicate more clearly. Some might even be tailored to your specific industry. I'm a big fan of TED Talks on any number of interesting topics!

Because the subject matter of the available videos is so wide and varied, this is something you can do regularly without it being boring or repetitive. In January, you might watch a video on how successful New Year's resolutions really are and how to make yours stick. (Then take a wider view and see if the insights could be applied to team goals!) In February, to celebrate Black History Month, you might highlight an African-American speaker at a TED Talk or even watch a short video about how racial bias impacts professionals in your industry. In the springtime, you might watch a video about how to construct a vegetable garden — and yes, you could absolutely ask the team if any of the pointers could be applied to life on your team — is overwatering your cucumbers the same as giving your colleagues too much feedback? The possibilities are endless!

Time Travel

Time Travel is a quick icebreaker that could be used to facilitate relationships by getting team members to answer noninvasive questions about their childhoods. This could be done round-robin style or conducted over a series of weeks or months by having a different person answer a question at the top of each meeting. Here are some example topics and questions:

>> Tell us about a childhood pet.

>> What was your favorite trip you took as a child?

>> What was your favorite meal growing up?

>> What was your favorite childhood memory?

>> What was a great piece of advice you received as a child?

Some people had very happy childhoods, whereas others had less happy, or even traumatic, ones. Most of us have enough happy memories to evoke a sense of nostalgia, even if we went through a rough patch here or there. Make sure your questions point solely to the positive to avoid any distressing memories that might not meet the needs of a quick, fun icebreaker. If you think it would be useful, provide a list of questions and allow your team members to select the one they will answer so they have ability to choose the story they'd like to tell and frame it appropriately.

If you're on a virtual meeting platform or working in a conference room with a projector, consider displaying a photo of the team member as a child (supplied by the team member beforehand) while they're speaking. For some reason, there's nothing adults love more than seeing photos of their colleagues when they were under the age of ten!

Copy-Paste

This is an activity that's entirely fun but actually leads to significant skill-building — specifically, more precise verbal communication and active listening skills.

Instruct your group to split into pairs (on a virtual meeting platform, you'll want to create breakout rooms for two people) and assign roles of Speaker and Artist. Furnish the Speaker with an image that they'll be describing to the Artist, who will be tasked with drawing the image based solely on the Speaker's instructions. At the end of the allotted time (a few minutes for a relatively simple image, up to 10 minutes if the images are more complex), bring the large group back together and ask the Artists to show their work. Then, one by one, ask the Speakers to reveal their images.

As you might expect, there's usually a lot of laughter when there's a mismatch. You might ask the Speaker or Artist to share what instructions were given and how they were perhaps misunderstood. If one of your pairs did exceptionally well, ask the Speaker if they had a strategy (for example, what the Artist should draw first, how certain parts of the image were described).

Repeating this activity, perhaps with more complex images as time goes on, will quickly reveal an increase in skill that is sure to please and delight your team and will likely improve communication when you get back to project work.

Theatersports

TIP

This activity and the next two are usually best when led by an outside vendor with real expertise. This costs money, obviously, but I've included them here because they can be extremely valuable. Of course, an additional benefit of a vendor-led activity is that the leader gets to be a full participant as well.

A team-building activity that requires a bit of courage on everyone's part but almost always results in laughter and fun is an experience doing improv, which is a form of theater with no prepared script. All of the words and actions on stage are improvised on the spot. To make improv work when more than one person is on stage, it's necessary to listen as well as act. While improv can be done in a dramatic context, it's almost always performed as comedy.

One of the cardinal rules of improv theater is known as "Yes, And." This means that when an idea is introduced by an actor, it must be embraced by all the other actors and incorporated into a scene. For instance, if one actor runs on stage and announces that Godzilla is attacking their city, this cannot be ignored, and another actor can't quickly find a way to dispose of Godzilla so that the troupe can return to the scene that they had planned. Obviously, this translates to team collaboration, where no one's ideas are dismissed out of hand.

Two teams compete by playing a series of defined games and then receive scores from a panel of judges. At the end of the performance, one of the teams has won!

Here are some of my favorite theatersports games, just to give you an idea:

>> **Actor's Nightmare:** Two players, one of whom has a script from an existing play or drama series (the more serious the script, the funnier the game, usually). The other player must play along with improvised lines but has to justify everything the scripted player says.

>> **Channel Surfing:** Four to six players receive a type of television show (for example, newscast, game show, reality show, and so on) that they must improvise. At a time of their choosing, one of the judges yells, "Switch!" The players must freeze in place while the judge announces what channel they are switching to with a different program (*Golden Girls*, *Law & Order*, *Jeopardy*). Players must begin depicting the new show mid-scene. After three or four switches, a judge ends the game.

>> **Dating Game:** One player leaves the stage, while the other three get suggestions from the audience about who they are (child genius, supervillain, femme fatale, and so on). The first player returns and asks three questions of the three "players," who must respond according to their character. At the end, the first player guesses who they're playing.

>> **Parallel Universe:** This is a difficult game, wherein the audience provides two different environments or locations. A single team splits into two groups to play both improvised scenes at the same time. Players do not acknowledge characters or events that do not happen in their scene. Both scenes must allow for silences so that others can have "scene time."

>> **Replay:** Two or three actors play a short, improvised scene, of no more than eight to ten lines total. Then they're asked to play the scene again, with various audience prompts. They might be asked for a specific emotion (anger, giggles) or set in a wildly different location (the jungle, while walking a tightrope). The most challenging adaption is to play the entire scene backward.

You might find that some members of your team are hesitant to "perform" for others, but it can help if the only "audience" are fellow performers. I can almost guarantee that you'll be amazed at just how funny some of your team members can be.

Indoor Ropes Course

You've probably heard of a "ropes course," an outdoor activity that involves climbing walls, grabbing onto ropes, and moving around obstacles. Some ropes courses are easier than others and depending on your team, might be a fun team-building activity. However, if your team includes people in various states of physical fitness or levels of physical ability, a fun alternative is an indoor ropes course, which is reminiscent of the outdoor version but usually focuses on mental challenges as much if not more so than physical ones.

Vendors who specialize in indoor ropes courses usually come to your workplace with a series of mats, small platforms, and yes, ropes, and use them to create games with specific rules for your team to follow. These games are usually not very physically taxing but are designed to improve communication and collaboration on a team. For instance, you might be asked to move from one side of the conference room to another without touching any of the ropes that facilitators have stretched across the room or any of the mats on the floor. What's more, you may be asked to do this while holding the hand of one of your colleagues. Perhaps your colleague is blindfolded, and you must do this silently!

These activities are designed to get people to think about creative problem solving, not physical agility. Typically, after each challenge, a facilitator will debrief the challenge, highlighting how different strategies worked, and sometimes asking, "How can we bring this technique back to work with us?"

WARNING

While the emphasis with an indoor ropes course is not on athleticism, there might be some people on your team who would rather not participate or who have disabilities that would prevent them from participating at the same level as everyone else. So be sure that the activities work for your team. Most indoor ropes course vendors have over sixty challenges in their repertoire and could certainly pick an entire slate to accommodate team members with a variety of disabilities. Indoor ropes courses are fun for most teams, but not the ideal activity for every team.

Personality Assessments

Finally, consider having a trained professional administer a psychometric instrument to all members of your team so that you can learn about each other's personality types. There are a number of assessments that you can bring to a team, including these:

>> **The Myers-Briggs Type Indicator** (MBTI), which measures personality on four scales: How a person receives energy, how a person prefers to take in information, how a person prefers to make decisions, and how a person prefers to approach the outside world. There are 16 Myers-Briggs Types in all, each with particular strengths.

>> **DISC**, which assigns individuals into four main types — dominance, influence, steadiness, and conscientiousness — in order to help individuals understand their behavioral tendencies and preferences in various situations, especially at work.

>> **The Predictive Index**, which measures four behavioral drives (dominance, extraversion, patience, and formality) to help individuals and teams understand their own drives and how to make decisions.

>> **CliftonStrengths** (formerly StrengthsFinder), which assigns each individual 5 top strengths (out of a possible 34). Many teams enjoy this assessment due to its sole focus on what each individual is good at, and how this focus can be used to allow each team member to reach their full potential.

REMEMBER

When conducting a personality assessment for your team, remind everyone that none of the options are bad but simply different from one another, and the best possible result is a team with many diverse types/strengths represented. These workshops (which can work well for remote teams as well as colocated ones) can teach everyone on your team a lot about each other but also much about themselves.

Chapter **21**

Ten Practices for Productive Team Meetings

M any workers in today's workforce view meetings as a necessary evil. They might recognize the importance of getting together (either virtually or in a conference room somewhere) to receive important updates, share information, or brainstorm new ideas with everyone's input. But still, many meetings are so poorly run that all meetings are presumed to be a waste of time and a drain on one's energy.

But it doesn't have to be that way. Meetings that are designed to be productive, efficient, meaningful, and useful can actually be something that people on your team look forward to and leave satisfied that it was time well spent.

Here are ten practices to keep in mind to create productive team meetings.

Make Your Meetings Consistent

One of the chief frustrations about meetings is spotty attendance. It's important, therefore, to do everything you can to encourage people to attend. Of course, there will be times when someone is sick, on vacation, or called away for an important reason. However, one way to allow people to build up a habit of attendance at regularly occurring team meetings is to hold them at a very specific time. If you need a weekly meeting, choose a day and a time that will work for the entire team (keeping time zones in mind if your team is geographically dispersed), and inform your team to keep that hour free.

TIP

If your team works Monday through Friday, consider an all-team meeting on Monday to kick off the week and another on Friday to reflect on the week and plan for the next. Rather than a two-hour team meeting, team members might enjoy two one-hour meetings instead.

Start and End on Time

Another frustration people have with meetings is when they do their best to be on time, only to sit there waiting for the meeting to start. A late-starting meeting is almost as frustrating as forcing people to miss either the end of the meeting or the beginning of their next appointment because meetings always run long.

When scheduling your meetings, ensure that you're blocking enough time to handle the business at hand. For regular meetings, if you sometimes need 90 minutes but other times need less than an hour, block off 90 (see the "Make Your Meetings Consistent" section earlier in this chapter) and give people the gift of time when possible. When you're getting close to the scheduled end of your meeting, gently interrupt the conversation and spend the remaining minutes strategizing how to handle the remaining agenda items and who should be involved. If at all possible, end the meeting at the scheduled time; this will result in your team members believing their time is of value.

REMEMBER

There is a cultural element to punctuality. If your team is global or culturally diverse, you may experience cultural differences with regard to being exactly on time. People from cultures that value punctuality could become frustrated with colleagues who are routinely "late," and those from cultures who value spontaneity and flexibility will soon resent those they experience as "rigid." In these cases, it's good to open a frank conversation about the cultural differences that exist on the team and encourage everyone to practice both cultural competence (an aware-ness of other cultural norms) and cultural humility (the belief that one's own culture should always be adhered to). You can also be creative in the ways that you create meeting agendas. Perhaps you could start most meetings at the top of the hour and schedule the first five minutes for optional socializing. As team leader, you should be on time and prepared to lead a conversation on a purely social topic (such as "What's everyone watching on TV these days?") before business begins and attendance is mandatory.

Create Your Meeting Agenda Collaboratively

First of all, well-run meetings have well-thought-out agendas. The agenda is the roadmap for your meeting and can prevent it from meandering aimlessly, which adds the perception that meetings are a waste of time.

Agendas should note topics or questions to be discussed, who will lead that por-tion of the meeting, what participants should be prepared to contribute, and how much time each portion should take. It's usually a good idea to err on the side of too much time for each agenda item because people would much rather a meeting end early than leave agenda items incomplete. Most importantly, note what will be accomplished regarding this topic or question during the meeting.

TIP

Share your agenda well in advance of the meeting. I prefer receiving agendas at least eight working hours before a meeting (that means sending agendas on Friday for a meeting that takes place on Monday!), so I have plenty of time to prepare or think about a topic or issue.

Set Clear Expectations and Group Norms

In addition to clear expectations about when meetings should start and end, it's important that people on your team have a strong sense of what's expected of them at each meeting.

First of all, team members should be prepared for the meeting. Sending out an agenda in advance (see the "Create Your Meeting Agenda Collaboratively" section) is helpful in this regard because it allows team members to see what will be under discussion and prepare if questions arise about their specific area(s) of responsibility.

Also, team members should have clear expectations around group norms. A list of behaviors should be drafted and, if possible, presented at each meeting (or simply listed at the top of each agenda, as a reminder). A list of ground rules could include, but should not be limited to, the following:

>> We will practice active listening (that is, listen to understand first, allow people to finish their thought before interrupting, ask clarifying questions if necessary).

>> We will disagree respectfully (practice curiosity; assume positive intent; take issue with the statement or position, not the person).

>> We will ensure that everyone who wishes to participate has space to do so.

>> We will welcome dissenting views.

>> We will stay on topic in order to respect each other's time.

>> We will respect each other's expertise.

Just as agendas can be created collaboratively, so can your group norms. If you don't have a list of meeting norms already, the next time your full team is meeting, make creating norms an agenda item. Encourage staff to list positive statements ("We will do this") as opposed to negative ones ("We will not do that").

TIP

For regularly occurring full team meetings, you could also collaboratively create a list of meeting roles (meeting facilitator, icebreaker lead, note-taker, and so on) and rotate roles to encourage everyone on the team to have the opportunity to demonstrate both leadership and support. Roles could be noted in each agenda.

Foster a Safe and Welcoming Environment

One way to ensure that staff dread coming to meetings is to send the message that they are there to listen rather than contribute. Therefore, it's important that you both encourage and reward their participation.

One subtle way to do this is to begin by facilitating a process that invites everyone to speak. If there are folks in the room that are new to the team, a quick round of introductions to make that person feel welcome should do the trick.

If everyone knows each other, another process can work. One nonprofit organization I worked with utilized a two-word check-in at the beginning of every meeting, where all participants would share two words to let everyone know how they were feeling or doing that day. The two-word check-in served a number of purposes:

>> It got everyone to speak.

>> It brought awareness to the room of how people were feeling. If a significant number of people noted they were "tired" or "overwhelmed," this was valuable data to the team leader.

>> It allowed for a moment of reflection on behalf of each participant. Noting out loud that you were "irritated" was a subtle invitation to set aside whatever external dynamics might be irking them and focus on the task at hand.

>> Allowing for two words allowed participants (if they chose) to express two things at once. Often, folks would say they were "frustrated" and "optimistic."

Beyond the initial icebreaker, leaders would do well to remember the four stages of psychological safety that I shared in Chapter 3, and apply them to their facilitation.

Inclusion safety

Inclusion safety occurs when people feel safe to be themselves, authentically. This means saying what's actually on your mind without feeling as though they must always agree with the majority. Sometimes, it also means calling attention to what makes you different than others in the room (for example, working remotely or in a different time zone) without fear of judgment. Leaders should invite these kinds of statements or other moments of authenticity, and — if possible — show appreciation to staff for sharing them.

Learner safety

Learner safety happens when people feel safe to learn on the job. This means having the ability to ask questions or admit that you don't know something. Especially when you work in an industry where knowledge is a form of status, it can be humbling, or even embarrassing, to admit that you don't know something. Leaders should invite questions or concerns and thank people for bringing knowledge gaps to their attention.

Contributor safety

Contributor safety is much like it sounds — feeling safe to contribute one's knowledge, ideas, and expertise in a room. Senior leaders generally do not hesitate to share the knowledge they've accrued, but junior staff often fear they will be perceived as cocky or arrogant if they share facts or suggestions for the rest of the group.

When contributions are solicited, team leaders should note who usually speaks up and who remains silent and encourage people who don't often add their views to do so. When a helpful note or idea comes from an unexpected source, thank them in the moment, and again in private. If necessary, institute a group norm (see the "Set Clear Expectations and Group Norms" section earlier in this chapter) to welcome new ways of thinking, even if they won't work in the moment.

Challenger safety

The final stage of psychological safety is challenger safety — or feeling safe to push back or disagree with either the leader or prevailing opinion of the group. This can be daunting for anyone on a team if either the leader or group seems firmly set on their way of doing things, but especially for new or more junior staff. Leaders should always invite dissent ("Does anyone see the situation differently?") and ensure that challengers are appreciated, even if their challenges aren't always successful.

Save Space for Appreciation and Positive Feedback

There's an old truism that positive feedback should be shared in public and negative feedback delivered in private. There are a few exceptions to this, but generally it's a good guideline to follow.

One way to build a culture of positive feedback and appreciation is to add an agenda item for every meeting for "Shout Outs" or "Kudos" — a chance for team members to thank their colleagues for good work and show their appreciation. Even if a team member has been privately thanked for a job well done, they'll appreciate the public recognition as well. On teams that do this regularly, team members not only want to be thanked but look for opportunities to deliver the kudos as well.

If you take up this process, keep track of who is often spotlighted and who receives kudos infrequently. In response, try to highlight the work of those who are less visible on the team. If possible, also note who often appreciates others and who is less likely to participate. For the former, this observation is good, positive feedback for a private meeting or even a performance appraisal; for the latter, this is something you might want to bring up in a one-on-one meeting, especially if there were obvious opportunities for the employee to highlight the good work of others.

Use a Virtual Meeting Platform

If your team is entirely colocated, meeting in a conference room is a great way to increase social bonds and make collaborative decisions.

However, if the team is working out of several different offices, or includes even one remote employee, causing some people to experience a meeting "live" and others to log in virtually and look at a wide shot of a conference table where it's difficult to make out faces or keep up with the flow of conversation, consider inviting everyone to log in from their desk and attend the meeting virtually. This will be greatly appreciated by remote or distanced staff because it allows them to see everyone's face and places the entire team on a level playing field. This change will make it much easier for the remote or distanced employees to engage with the meeting without feeling isolated from the team.

Encourage Varied Forms of Participation

Meeting virtually opens the door for participants to communicate in different ways. Most virtual meetings contain a chat window, which can allow people to submit contributions silently without interrupting a speaker. If you're using chat, consider a rotating role for a team member to keep an eye on the chat roll so that contributions don't get lost. Virtual meetings can also make use of breakout rooms, shared documents, anonymous polls, and other interesting ways to gather information in ways that are quick and introvert-friendly!

Even if the whole team is in the same space and you choose to meet physically, there are a range of communication methods at your disposal beyond verbal communication:

>> **A quick show of hands** to gauge opinion is a much more efficient way to take the pulse of a group without hearing from everyone.

>> **Secret ballots** can accomplish this if people in the room might be hesitant to be honest without anonymity.

>> **Round-robins** (where everyone at a table speaks in turn) ensures that you hear all voices in the room, not just those of the most outspoken or senior team members.

>> **Popcorn-style brainstorms** (where anyone can shout out an idea without first raising a hand) can be chaotic if overused, but they can also spur creativity and out-of-the-box thinking.

>> **Small group conversations** (usually followed by report-outs) allow more time to process thoughts before publishing them to the large group, ensuring that complex issues will be addressed responsibly and introverts will be more likely to contribute.

Varied forms of participation not only allow different kinds of contributors to engage but are also more interesting than meeting after meeting where everyone speaks in long paragraphs while other people must silently wait their turn.

End the Meeting with Accomplishments and Action Items

You don't want your team members to think of all the time they spend in meetings as "all talk and no action." Therefore, it's a good idea to end your meetings reminding people of what was actually accomplished during the time they spent there.

During the meeting, make a note of every decision that was made, and quickly list them off at the end of the meeting. This is not only a way to make people feel that their time was well used, but it also confirms the decisions made to everyone, both those who championed the decision and those who may have lobbied against it.

If a decision was not made but further action is still needed, make a separate list of action items. At the end of the meeting, reiterate what must be done, who is responsible for the task, and a date of completion, if you have it. This ensures that your commitment to action is felt by your team and also prompts team members to note what responsibilities they've agreed to, in case they failed to write it down.

Follow Up and Iterate

After the meeting, notes (including accomplishments and action items as described in the "End the Meeting with Accomplishments and Action Items" section) should be distributed in written form to all team members. If the meeting was virtual, make sure that those who could not attend also have access to a recording of the meeting. I wouldn't suggest making viewing the meeting mandatory, but it could be helpful if absent folks have any questions about what they see in the written notes.

Occasionally, it's also helpful to solicit feedback about the meeting(s), in case there are ways they could be improved that you, the leader, are unaware of. Of course, if feedback is given, it should be acted upon, even if that action is to decline the feedback with an explanation as to why.

IN THIS CHAPTER

» Examining how technology and workforce dynamics will reshape the way high-performing teams are structured

» Acknowledging the factors that will be the true markers of high performance

» Identifying how leaders must prepare now to cultivate the skills, mindsets, and environments that future teams will require

Chapter **22**

Ten Ways High-Performing Teams Will Evolve in Ten Years

t's often said that the only constant is change, and nowhere is that more evident than in today's workplace. Think about how much has shifted in just the last decade. Hybrid work went from being a rare perk to a mainstream expectation. Artificial intelligence (AI) is now writing emails, generating reports, and even helping us make decisions. New generations are entering the workforce every few years, bringing fresh values, demands, and work styles.

If so much has transformed in such a short period, what will teams look like ten years from now? What I know from decades of coaching leaders and studying workforce trends is that high-performing teams will not look the same as they do today. They will evolve in their structure, skills, expectations, and outcomes.

In this chapter, I share ten ways that high-performing teams will evolve in the future and why leaders need to start preparing for these shifts now. These insights are not predictions pulled from thin air. They're based on global workforce research, my experience working with organizations across industries, and the emerging signals we are already seeing.

Increased Collaboration between AI and Humans

By 2035, AI will be seamlessly interwoven into the very fabric of our workplace routines, like smartphones and cloud computing are today, but with even greater impact. High-performing teams will shift their mindset to see AI not as a rival, but as a strategic partner and multiplier of human potential. AI will handle repetitive tasks, conduct predictive analyses, and offer actionable insights in real time, freeing up team members to focus on what humans do best: innovation, critical thinking, and relationship-building.

Here's what that could look like in practice: Imagine a project team at a global retail company, collaborating on a new product launch. An AI-powered dashboard continuously scans customer feedback across five continents, highlighting emerging trends and even flagging supply chain risks before they escalate. While the AI synthesizes massive amounts of data, human team members interpret the nuances, asking the right questions, considering cultural differences, and making judgment calls that require empathy and ethical reasoning. Instead of drowning in information overload, the team is empowered to pivot quickly, align strategies, and make smarter decisions faster than ever before.

The most successful leaders will invest now in building AI literacy and digital confidence across their teams. That means offering ongoing training, not just for the IT department but for every employee, so that using AI responsibly, and understanding its limitations, becomes second nature. Leaders must also foster a culture where experimentation is encouraged and where team members feel safe to challenge the suggestions of an algorithm when something doesn't seem right. In the future, it won't be technology alone that sets high-performing teams apart, but their ability to harness the power of AI while fully leveraging the irreplaceable strengths of human ingenuity, heart, and diversity of thought.

More Globally Distributed Across Borders

In the coming decade, the influence of remote work will continue to dissolve the boundaries of geography, giving rise to agile, borderless teams. No longer will top talent be confined by city limits or country borders. Instead, teams will be assembled from a tapestry of individuals spanning continents, time zones, and cultures. This new paradigm will allow organizations to draw from a truly global talent pool, enriching teams with unique perspectives, specialized skills, and cultural nuance that would have been unimaginable in the old office-bound world.

Yet this transformation is more than just hiring internationally. High-performing teams will need to excel at cross-cultural communication, develop a strong sense of digital etiquette, and embrace flexibility in everything from meeting schedules to decision-making processes. Asynchronous collaboration where team members contribute on their own timelines will become the norm, making progress possible around the clock. To thrive, teams must establish shared rituals and clear protocols for handoffs, feedback, and accountability, ensuring that work flows smoothly even when people are oceans apart.

The advantages are immense: Borderless teams can respond more rapidly to global challenges, serve customers in any region, and innovate with a diversity of thought that sparks creativity. However, these benefits do not come without challenges. Cultural misunderstandings, time zone fatigue, and feelings of isolation can emerge if not proactively addressed.

WARNING

Don't assume that technology alone will create cohesion. While collaboration platforms and AI tools are essential, they cannot substitute for intentional trust-building and clear communication. Without a deliberate focus on inclusion and psychological safety, borderless teams risk becoming fragmented and disengaged.

By embracing both the opportunities and the responsibilities of global distribution, leaders can unlock the full potential of borderless teams, creating organizations that are not just more dynamic, but more human at their core.

Increased Diversity in Every Dimension

In the next decade, profound demographic shifts will continue to redefine the face of the global workforce. In many regions, including the United States, no single racial or ethnic group will constitute a majority, while younger generations worldwide bring with them heightened multicultural awareness, gender fluidity, and deeply held values around social responsibility. Teams will also become more inclusive of individuals with disabilities, neurodiverse talent, and professionals whose backgrounds diverge from traditional academic or career paths.

This evolution means the most innovative teams will not only mirror the world's diversity but harness it as a powerful engine for creativity and resilience. Diverse teams generate a broader range of ideas, anticipate the needs of wider markets, and challenge ingrained assumptions, often leading to groundbreaking products and services. For organizations to truly thrive, however, diversity must go beyond numbers. High-performing teams will focus on cultivating a culture of equity, belonging, and psychological safety, ensuring every voice is heard and valued. Genuine inclusion means designing meetings, workflows, and feedback systems that invite authentic contributions from all, regardless of background or communication style.

Consider how Johnson & Johnson, a global healthcare leader, intentionally constructs project teams that span continents, disciplines, and identities to maximize innovation and impact. For example, when developing new medical devices for international markets, Johnson & Johnson brings together engineers from Asia, clinicians from Europe, and marketers from North and South America, each contributing unique insights shaped by their cultural backgrounds and specialized expertise. These teams are often comprised of neurodivergent designers, multi-generational contributors, and professionals with varied educational histories, ensuring that each solution is informed by a rich tapestry of perspectives.

This collaborative approach has yielded breakthroughs in user-centric design, improved health outcomes for diverse patient populations, and enabled the company to anticipate regulatory requirements in different regions. Research within Johnson & Johnson has shown that when employees feel encouraged to share their authentic selves and challenge conventional thinking, engagement and innovation flourish. Their leadership credits this intentional cultivation of diversity, not just in visible traits but also in thought and experience as a cornerstone of the company's continued relevance and global success.

By 2035, the capacity to harness and empower the broadest spectrum of human experience will distinguish the world's top teams — transforming diversity from a well-meaning goal into a dynamic, strategic force that shapes the future.

Even Greater Prioritization of Well-Being

Burnout has already emerged as one of the greatest threats to workplace performance, and by 2035, forward-thinking teams will recognize that well-being is not a mere perk but a foundational requirement for sustainable success. Organizations will increasingly understand that supporting the mental, physical, and emotional health of employees is directly linked to creativity, productivity, and long-term engagement.

According to the 2024 "State of Workplace Mental Health" report by Mind Share Partners, 76 percent of U.S. workers reported experiencing at least one symptom of mental health conditions in the previous year, while nearly 60 percent said that workplace stress impacted their productivity. This underscores the urgent need for organizations to move beyond lip service and embed well-being into the core of team culture.

To address this, leaders must go beyond the basics to monitoring workloads and encouraging occasional wellness activities to actively redesign work itself for greater flexibility and balance. Expect to see an expansion of personalized well-being solutions, from virtual therapy sessions and meditation apps to AI-powered platforms that detect stress indicators and recommend timely interventions. Workspaces will be reimagined to support moments of respite, and schedules will be built to accommodate diverse life circumstances.

The cultural shift, however, will be just as crucial as technological advancement. High-performing teams will foster environments where open conversations about mental health are normalized, stigma is dismantled, and employees feel safe to voice their challenges without fear of judgment. Psychological safety will extend to the recognition that rest and recovery are not signs of weakness, but vital components of peak performance. For more on mental health refer to Chapter 14 and to Chapter 3 for more on psychological safety.

REMEMBER

Prioritizing well-being is not a one-time initiative but an ongoing commitment. Teams should regularly check in with one another, encourage honest dialogue, and ensure that policies translate into practical support. Consider scheduling dedicated well-being check-ins or sharing resources for stress management and resilience building.

More Multigenerational and Experience-Rich Teams

For the first time in history, six generations are working side by side. With advances in healthcare, improved quality of life, and the reality that many people need or want to work longer, older employees are staying in the workforce well beyond traditional retirement age. At the same time, younger employees are entering earlier through nontraditional pathways like apprenticeships, online platforms, gig work, and entrepreneurial ventures. To learn more about the changing workforce demographics, refer to Chapter 9.

This convergence will create both opportunities and challenges. On the one hand, organizations have access to an unprecedented depth of knowledge, wisdom, and life experience. On the other hand, they must also navigate differences in communication styles, work preferences, and values that are often shaped by each generation's unique cultural context.

High-performing teams will learn to harness the wisdom of experience from older generations alongside the fresh thinking, digital fluency, and risk-taking mindset of younger ones. Imagine the power of pairing a baby boomer with decades of client relationship expertise with a Gen Z team member who is highly skilled at leveraging AI tools and social media platforms to reach new audiences. Together, they can create solutions that neither would have achieved alone.

Leaders will need to act as translators across age groups, bridging generational divides and creating space where different perspectives are valued rather than dismissed. This means moving away from stereotypes like "millennials are entitled" or "baby boomers resist change" and instead focusing on individual strengths and contributions. It also means intentionally designing opportunities for cross-generational mentoring, reverse mentoring, and shared projects where mutual learning can occur.

By 2035, the most effective organizations will be those that do more than simply tolerate generational differences. They will intentionally cultivate multigenerational collaboration as a strategic advantage. They will invest in training leaders to understand generational motivators, communication styles, and career expectations. They will design flexible policies that meet the needs of both early-career professionals seeking rapid growth and seasoned employees seeking meaningful legacy work.

The richness that comes from six generations working together will be unmatched. When teams learn to embrace these diverse life stages, they will spark innovation, accelerate problem-solving, and create cultures of respect that attract and retain top talent. In short, organizations that embrace multigenerational synergy will not only perform better but will also become magnets for the best and brightest talent in the global marketplace.

Greater Mastery of Agility and Continuous Reinvention

The pace of disruption will only accelerate. Teams that cling to rigid processes will not survive. In the next decade, high-performing teams will embrace agility as a core competency. They will pivot quickly, learn rapidly from mistakes, and constantly reinvent how they work.

This means leaders will need to foster growth mindsets and psychological safety so that experimentation is encouraged and failures are reframed as learning. Teams will no longer wait for perfect conditions to act; they will launch, test, iterate, and improve in real time.

Think about it: Companies that failed to adapt to the digital age disappeared. The same will be true for teams that fail to adapt to the AI age, the climate age, or whatever disruptions emerge next. Agility will be the currency of survival and success.

Committed to Purpose and Values

The very definition of work will continue to shift. Employees will expect more than a paycheck or a promotion. They'll want their work to contribute to something meaningful. They'll want to feel proud of the company they work for, and they'll want to know that their skills and energy are being invested in causes that make a positive impact in the world. They'll want to know that their work matters and makes a difference.

High-performing teams of the future will be anchored in purpose. For some, that will mean solving climate challenges and innovating toward sustainability. For others, it may be advancing health equity, strengthening communities, or transforming education. Whatever the mission, it will serve as the North Star that aligns and energizes the team.

By 2035, the most high-performing teams will stand out because their purpose will be crystal clear, their values will be visible in their decisions and behaviors, and their people will know they're part of something bigger than themselves. Here's the best part: When employees believe in the purpose, performance follows. Purpose is not just a feel-good concept; it's a proven driver of engagement, productivity, and long-term organizational success.

We're already seeing signs of this shift today. Research by Deloitte has found that purpose-driven companies experience 30 percent higher levels of innovation and 40 percent higher levels of employee retention compared to their peers. Gallup's studies show that employees who feel connected to their organization's purpose are four times more engaged. In the next decade, these differences will be even more pronounced. Teams that connect their daily tasks to a higher mission will enjoy stronger motivation, deeper loyalty, and greater resilience when times get tough.

The best teams will not just ask, "What are we achieving?" They'll also ask, "Why does it matter?" They'll define success not only by revenue and growth but also by their alignment with core values such as integrity, equity, sustainability, and human dignity. In fact, future employees will hold organizations accountable for living out their stated values. Social media and increased transparency will mean that hypocrisy is quickly exposed.

Leaders will play a critical role here. It will no longer be enough to focus on performance metrics, cost savings, or quarterly targets. Leaders must become storytellers of purpose. They must help employees see the "why" behind the "what." That means weaving organizational values into team meetings, connecting projects to customer impact, and celebrating how the team's work is making a difference beyond the bottom line.

Radical Transparency and Trust

High-performing teams cannot thrive without trust, and in the next ten years, that trust will be built on radical transparency. Employees today already expect more openness from leaders, but the teams of tomorrow will require it as a non-negotiable. Transparency means more than sharing quarterly numbers or project updates. It's about creating an environment where information flows freely, decisions are explained clearly, and team members feel confident that what they see is what they get.

When teams operate with transparency, accountability increases, and silos decrease. Members know where the team stands, what progress is being made, and where the challenges lie. This shared knowledge fosters ownership, prevents misunderstandings, and builds confidence that everyone is pulling in the same direction. Real-time dashboards, open project boards, and collaborative tools will make visibility into performance standard practice.

Trust is the natural outcome of transparency. When leaders are candid about successes and setbacks, team members feel respected and valued. When team members know that their voices are heard and that mistakes will be treated as learning opportunities rather than punishments, they're more willing to take risks, share bold ideas, and support one another.

A Seamless Blend of Permanent, Gig, and AI Talent

The traditional model of full-time employees will give way to a more blended workforce. High-performing teams will integrate permanent staff, gig workers, contractors, and even AI bots into one ecosystem.

This flexibility will allow teams to scale up or down quickly, bring in niche expertise as needed, and stay competitive in rapidly shifting markets. But managing this blend will require new skills. Leaders will need to create inclusive cultures where all participants, whether permanent or temporary, human or digital, are recognized as equal contributors to the mission.

The most effective teams will not define membership by employment status but by shared goals and outcomes.

Measured of Impact, Not Activity

In the next decade, the metrics of success will shift dramatically. Gone will be the days of measuring productivity by hours worked or meetings attended. High-performing teams will be evaluated on their impact: the outcomes they achieve, the value they create, and the innovation they deliver.

Technology will help track this impact with precision. But equally important will be the mindset shift. Leaders will need to stop rewarding busyness and start celebrating breakthroughs. Teams will learn to ask, "What difference are we making?" rather than, "How many tasks did we complete?"

Impact, not activity, will be the new definition of high performance.

Index

G

Gen Alpha, 134, 156

gender bias, 161

gender diversity, 136–137

gender-neutral language, 162

generational cohorts, 134, 135

generational diversity, 134–135

Gen Z, 156

Gleicher, David, 124

globalization

acumen, 130

agility, 130

considerations for hiring, 131

definition, 130

in-country talent, 130

knowledge base, 130

knowledge management, 130

skillfulness, 130

goal misalignment, 40

Goleman, Daniel, 82

Google, 66, 107

grade point averages (GPAs), 163

gratitude, 57

gross margin, 279

growth mindset, 15

H

halo/horn effect, 160

Harris, Reuben T., 124

Harrison, Lee Hecht, 99

Harvard Business Review, 65, 109, 215

healthy conflict resolution, 54–55

hidden biases, 159

HubSpot, 66

I

imposter syndrome, 148

inclusion safety, 79, 315

inclusive job descriptions

age discrimination avoidance, 163

age-specific descriptions, 164

gender-neutral language, 162

gender-specific terms, 164–165

inclusive of disabled workers, 163–164

mentions of race, 165

racial bias elimination, 162–163

religious references, 165

suggestions, 165

inclusive leadership, 262–263

indoor ropes course, 308–309

informed decisions, 64–65

innovation, 61–62, 66, 100, 105, 111, 154, 189, 231, 246–247

stifled innovation, 105–106

inspirational motivation, 261

intact teams, 37

intercultural conflict styles

accommodation style (indirect + emotionally restrained), 238

direct/indirect communication, 236

discussion style (direct + emotionally restrained), 237

dynamic style (indirect + emotionally expressive), 238

emotional restraint/emotional expressiveness, 236–237

engagement style (direct + emotionally expressive), 237–238

overview, 236

schematic diagram of, 236

R

racial bias, 161
RACI model
  accountable, 52
  consulted, 52
  informed, 52
  responsible, 52
rank/level silo, 208
real-time data, 49
recency bias, 160
recession risks, 281
recognition, 62
Religious Equity, Diversity & Inclusion
  (REDI) Index, 141
remote/hybrid teams, 37–38
  advantages, 252
  common pitfalls
    burnout, 266–267
    micromanagement, 264–265
    proximity bias, 265–266
  communication channels, 253
  disadvantages, 252
  frequent communication
    implementation, 252–253
  leadership styles adaptation
    agile leadership, 263–264
    inclusive leadership, 262–263
    situational leadership, 258–260
    transactional leadership, 257–258
    transformational leadership, 260–262
  making time for celebrations, 256–257
  prioritizing mental health, 255–256
  processes documentation, 254
  professional development, 257

  roles documentation, 254
  shifting to return-to-office work, 268–269
  transparency, 253–254
  workflows documentation, 254
remote working, 132–133
reputation of business, 189
resilience, 13, 51, 111, 154, 281
resource utilization, 280
return on equity (ROE), 277
return on investment (ROI), 277
return-to-office work, 268–269
revenue, 276
reverse mentoring programs, 297
Richard Beckhard's GRPI model
  core components, 22, 23
  diagnosing team issues, 25–26
  goals, 23
  interpersonal relations, 24–25
  processes, 24
  roles, 23–24
Richard Hackman's five factor model
  common mission/specific direction, 27
  enabling structure, 27
  expert coaching, 27–28
  "real" team, 26–27
  schematic diagram, 26
  supportive context factor, 27
risk aversion
  consequences of
    cultural transformation, 108
    lower employee engagement, 107
    missed market opportunities, 107
    reduced agility, 106
    stifled innovation, 105–106

About the Author

Dr. Shirley Davis is an internationally recognized global workforce expert, culture transformation thought leader, three-time Hall of Fame professional, and President & CEO of SDS Global Enterprises, specializing in HR strategy, leadership development, and organizational transformation. With more than 30 years of business experience in Fortune 50 companies, global nonprofits, and government agencies, Dr. Davis has worked in more than 40 countries, served over 300 global organizations, and delivers over 100 presentations a year. She's been featured in nationally acclaimed publications including, but not limited to *Forbes*, *Fortune* Magazine, *CEO* Magazine, *Harvard Business Review*, and *Oprah Daily*. She was named one of the Top 50 Businesswomen of Tampa Bay for 2025 and inducted into the Prince George County Public School System's Hall of Fame for the global impact she has made in business, education, and personal development since graduating high school.

Dr. Davis is a popular author of five other books: *Living Beyond "What If?"* (Berrett-Koehler, 2021), *Diversity, Equity & Inclusion For Dummies* (Wiley, 2022), *Reinvent Yourself (2024), The Seat: How to Get Invited to the Table When You're Overperforming and Undervalued* (The Success Doctor, LLC, 2014), and *Inclusive Leadership For Dummies* (Wiley, 2024). She is a LinkedIn Learning author with 10 leadership courses, one of which was named among the Top 20 Most Popular Courses of 2024 ("Leadership Foundations"). Dr. Davis holds more than ten professional certifications and four earned degrees, including a Ph.D. in business and organizational leadership. She serves on the national board of the Make-A-Wish Foundation and is a member of the National Speakers Association's Million Dollar Speakers Group, Women Corporate Directors, and Tampa Bay Chamber of Commerce. Other accolades include being named Toastmasters International's Golden Gavel Award recipient (2022), induction into *Inclusion* Magazine's Hall of Fame (2021), induction into the state of Maryland Prince George's County Public Schools Hall of Fame (2025), and winning the national title of Ms. American United States (2000). Driven by a lifelong passion for philanthropy, she cofounded the Dr. Shirley Davis Foundation with her daughter, Gabrielle Victoria, to motivate, cultivate, and elevate aspiring leaders from underserved communities through coaching, support resources, and strategic development so that they can thrive in every area of their lives.

Dedication

This book is dedicated to every leader (whether you're a people leader or a team leader of a project or program) who has made the bold choice to build, grow, and sustain high performance on your team. It's for those who know that leading people is both a privilege and a responsibility, and who understand that great teams don't happen by chance. They're the result of being intentional and committed to excellence and demonstrating the behaviors that bring out the best in others.

This book represents more than only my voice; it reflects the collective wisdom of colleagues, clients, team members, and other business executives I've had the privilege to work with throughout my career. I thank you for sharing your knowledge, wisdom, and insights that helped shape this body of work.

For every leader holding this book, it shows your desire to be part of the solution in creating thriving, engaged, and future-ready teams. My hope is that you will use it as a roadmap and a tool to transform not only your teams but also your workplace culture and leadership legacy.

Author's Acknowledgment

A special thank you goes to two of my dear friends, HR colleagues, and leadership experts Todd Corley and Eric Peterson, MSOD. Your expertise and dedication to advancing leadership and organizational excellence shine throughout these pages. To both of you and to all who have supported me on this journey, I want to say thank you for making this book richer, deeper, and more impactful.

I can't thank the Wiley team enough, especially Tracy Boggier for seeking me out for this assignment. Thank you for assembling a great support team, including Charlotte Kughen, who guided me through the writing and editing process.

I thank God, my Creator, who has bestowed many gifts, opportunities, and blessings on me. I am so grateful that I wake up each day excited about living out my dreams, doing the work that I love, and leaving a significant legacy for the next generation of leaders.

Publisher's Acknowledgments

Senior Acquisitions Editor: Tracy Boggier
Managing Editor: Sofia Malik
Project Editor: Charlotte Kughen
Technical Editor: Todd Corley

Production Editor: Magesh Elangovan
Cover Image: © Ivan Smuk/Shutterstock